The Emmaus Mystery

The Emmaus Mystery

Discovering Evidence for the Risen Christ

Carsten Thiede

With an Introduction by Matthew d'Ancona

continuum
LONDON • NEW YORK

Continuum

The Tower Building	15 East 26th Street
11 York Road	New York
London SE1 7NX	NY 10010

www.continuumbooks.com

First published 2005

British Library Cataloguing-in-Publication Data
A catalogue record for this book is available from the British Library.

ISBN 0 8264 6797 0

Typeset by RefineCatch Limited, Bungay, Suffolk
Printed and bound in Great Britain by CPI Bath

In Memoriam

On 14 December 2004, Carsten Peter Thiede died suddenly at his home in Paderborn, Germany. This, his most important book, was also his last.

Two quotations came to me as I absorbed this terribly sad and shocking news. The first was Goethe's observation that 'a useless life is an early death'. Carsten was only 52 years old when he died. But – by Goethe's criterion, at least – his death was anything but 'early', drawing a veil, as it did, on a rich and joyous life, packed with scholarship, faith, service to others, and friendship. That is why he is mourned all over the world, not only as a man of awesome learning and an academic pioneer, but as an irreplaceable friend, colleague and enthusiast for life.

The second quotation was from St Paul's First Letter to the Corinthians: 'There are three things that last forever. Faith, hope, and love; but the greatest of them all is love.' Carsten had all three in abundance, but the way in which he lived his life showed that he agreed heartily with the Apostle. And it was his family – his wife, Franziska, and their three children, Miriam, Emily and Frederick – that he loved above all else.

As his friend and collaborator, I have no doubt that he would wish this book to be dedicated to them.

Matthew d'Ancona
December 2004

Contents

Matthew d'Ancona

Introduction

The image is haunting, mysterious, freighted with emotion. Jesus sits at the supper table, a still life of fruit, bread and wine: he looks down, his right arm raised in a dramatic gesture of revelation. He is flanked by two disciples, one standing, the other – an older, bearded man – flinging out his arms in astonishment. Light, and its absence, are of the essence: a strange luminosity shivers around the contours of the three subjects' faces, hinting at both the intimacy of the moment, and its spiritual intensity. Darkness lurks everywhere around them, as if kept at bay by this sudden illumination.

Caravaggio's *Supper at Emmaus* in the National Gallery, commissioned from the painter by the Roman aristocrat Ciriaco Mattei in 1601, is one of countless works of art that have been inspired over the centuries by a story that appears in Chapter 24 of St Luke's Gospel. Even by the standards of that loquacious Evangelist, it is a narrative rich in detail, rooted in the specific, and powerful in its drama.

Two followers of Jesus, we are told, are heading towards 'a village named Emmaus', about seven miles from Jerusalem. Confused and frightened, they discuss recent events which culminated in the hideous execution of their master. A third man joins them: they do not recognize him at first, but St Luke tells us that it is the resurrected Jesus. He asks them: 'What are these words that you are exchanging with one another as you are walking?' Cleopas – the other follower is not identified – replies: 'Are you the only one visiting Jerusalem and unaware of the things which have happened here in these days?' Jesus asks them what they are talking about and they speak of their hopes that the redeemer of Israel had come, of his death, and of the mystery of the empty tomb. Jesus – still unrecognized – sternly reminds them of 'the things concerning Himself in all the Scriptures'.

The trio arrive at Emmaus and Jesus is urged by his hospitable companions to stay. They sit down for supper. Jesus takes the bread and blesses it and – in the moment captured by Caravaggio – 'their eyes were opened and they recognized Him'. Jesus vanishes, and the astonished Cleopas and his companion recall: 'Were not our hearts burning within us while He was speaking to us on the road?' They return from Emmaus to Jerusalem, where they meet the eleven remaining disciples and share the news of the resurrection.

It is scarcely surprising that the dramatic episode at Emmaus has been so important to Christianity in the past 20 centuries, for it is one of the most vivid portraits of the resurrected Christ. There are others: in Paul's First Letter to the Corinthians, Matthew Chapter 28 and John Chapter 20. But the Emmaus story involves a collision of normality – the walk, the dinner, the conversation – with the miraculous that makes it unique. 'If Christ has not risen, then our preaching is in vain and your faith is in vain,' St Paul wrote to the Corinthians. St Clement of Alexandria, the second-century Greek theologian, declared that, by his resurrection, 'Christ has turned all our sunsets into dawns'. The Emmaus story is at the heart of this ancestral conviction.

Dürer, Titian and Rembrandt are only three of the other artists who have depicted the moment of stunning recognition when Jesus reveals himself over dinner at the village. In modern art, Tarkovsky's cinematic masterpiece *Stalker* is explicitly influenced by the Emmaus story. In literature, T.S. Eliot's question in *The Waste Land* – 'Who is the third who walks always beside you?' – is only the most famous reference to the road to Emmaus. There are Christian communities, projects, retreats, welfare services, publishing ventures and websites, all of which take their name from the ancient village. It pervades Christian culture and practice.

Malcolm Muggeridge captured the extraordinary appeal to the faithful of this story: 'I have never doubted that, wherever the walk and whoever the wayfarers, there is always . . . a third presence ready to emerge from the shadows and fall in step along the dusty, stony way.' For Christians, the message of the episode is one of consolation and of revelation. The two followers of Jesus are lonely, lost and dejected, and only see clearly when they break bread with him, and realize that he was with them all along. He is strict with them for neglecting the Scripture, but does not depart until he has filled them with the joy of his presence.

This, then, is the religious content of these 22 verses in Luke: enormously powerful for those who believe, of purely academic interest to those who do not. But is that the end of the matter? Carsten Thiede's book – his last and most remarkable – suggests otherwise. It tells the story of an extraordinary breakthrough in Christian archaeology: the reclaiming of a location which, for centuries, has existed only in the minds of Christian writers and the hearts of worshippers. No longer. Thiede's contribution to the story of Emmaus is a triumphant and conclusive one. He has found the long-lost village.

To understand the full significance of this breakthrough, one must understand its context. As Thiede explains in the early chapters of this book, Emmaus is unusual in that most scholars long ago gave up the search for the true site. Those that have been suggested are, for one reason or another, implausible. Debate has raged for two millennia about the location of, say, the tomb of Jesus, or the crucifixion site, or a thousand other places mentioned in the Gospels. In few cases have scholars more or less conceded defeat. But – remarkably and exceptionally – they have done so in the case of Emmaus. The vast majority of academics have accepted that the trail went cold long ago, and been content for the village to survive only in the prayers of the faithful.

This unusual scholarly surrender has only hardened the orthodox interpretation of the passage among theologians – that the verses are catechistic in character, and only look like narrative to uncomprehending modern eyes. According to this analysis, the story of Emmaus serves an exclusively liturgical function, and tells us about the practice of the early Church rather than about Jesus himself. On this basis, the passage is prescriptive: it explains, by example, how Christians were to encounter the Word and the Sacrament. It emphasizes the divine presence in the Sacrament (it is when Jesus breaks the bread that his followers recognize him). It is a model of how Christians should teach one another. All this is consistent with the tendency of contemporary scholars to see the Gospels primarily as handbooks for religious practice, in which stories were used to communicate theological truths and to prescribe liturgical practice.

I first encountered Thiede in 1994 as a journalist reporting one of his finds and I later co-authored two books with him. We tried to lay out the parameters of the 'new paradigm' which he and other scholars were seeking to establish in early Christian studies. The first book, *The Jesus Papyrus*

(1996), examined the evidence of the earliest surviving New Testament papyri and argued that these fragments – of St Mark and St Matthew – could be dated, using new forensic technology as well as more traditional analytical techniques, to the early sixties AD, and perhaps earlier. This was an ambitious claim, not least because it meant that the so-called 'tunnel' separating the life of Jesus from the work of Gospel writers was short – possibly years, rather than decades. It followed from Thiede's revolutionary analysis of these fragments that the recollections in such texts could not be *assumed* to be faulty or fictitious, and that the first readers of the Gospels could, quite conceivably, have heard the sermons recorded in them. To advance these suggestions was to fly in the face of a long-established orthodoxy: that the Gospels are late creations, that two or even three generations stood between them and the events they portrayed, that the texts were the joint records of second-century Christian communities rather than the work of individual authors, and that they have almost no claim to historical authenticity. The book became the centre of a remarkable international debate. It was described as a 'work of the greatest importance' and a book which 'every inquiring Christian – and open-minded sceptic – should read'. It was also attacked as an outrageous assault on respectable scholarship. It generated arguments all over the world in lecture halls and in broadcasts ranging from the BBC World Service to Brazilian television. It inspired a cover-story in *Time* magazine which predicted that 'the age-old battle over the truth of Scripture, far from being over, has just begun'.

Our second collaboration, *The Quest for the True Cross* (2000), explored the holy relics and sites of early Christianity, with particular reference to the Titulus, or crucifixion headboard, at the church of Santa Croce in Gerusalemme, Rome. This neglected artefact, allegedly discovered in the fourth century by Queen Helena, mother of the Emperor Constantine, was long ago dismissed as a risible forgery. In fact, as we tried to show, the more one analyses the Titulus, the less reason there is to suppose that it is the work of a fourth-century or medieval fraudster. Our broader purpose was to pay fresh attention to the symbols and sacred artefacts of the early Christian communities; to show the antiquity and profound significance of those symbols, and the care with which holy objects would have been safeguarded; and – above all – to demonstrate the critical importance in early Christianity of sacred locations and the preservation of their memory. Once again, the book was published all over the world: like its predecessor, it inspired a television documentary and a furious debate. When the newspaper for which I work, the *Sunday Telegraph*, serialized *The Quest for the True Cross*, one schoolmaster fulminated that our claims were based on 'pseudo-archaeology'. Another letter-writer implored me to go to Rome and 'take a hammer, and smash this "relic" to smithereens'. The Vatican appointed an inquiry to investigate the artefact.

This book brings to a triumphant conclusion Thiede's lifelong quest to give shape to his 'new paradigm'. In some respects, it is a corrective project, an attempt to restore balance to a field which has been rocked by anger, ill feeling and stubbornness. Although sometimes misrepresented as a mischief-maker, his true purpose was always to bring common sense, the lessons of ancient history and the most up-to-date forensic techniques to bear on an area of scholarship contaminated by fad and theory.

To grasp what has gone wrong with Gospel studies, one must retrace an intellectual path which stretches back three centuries. In the pre-modern West, the literal truth or 'verbal inerrancy' of the Gospels was taken for granted. One of the greatest legacies of the Enlightenment was to release the Word of God from the grip of the ecclesiastical authorities once and for all, and to apply the developing critical methods of scholarly investigation to the first Christian texts.

The Göttingen academic Johann David Michaelis (1717–91) pioneered the daring new campaign to explore the possibility that there might be contradictions in the Gospels. Hermann Samuel Reimarus (1694–1768), a professor at Hamburg, went so far as to question Christ's divinity – a suggestion so shocking that it was not published until after his death. In 1835, David Friedrich Strauss, a tutor at Tübingen University, declared in *The Life of Jesus* that the discrepancies between the Gospels showed that they could not have been written by eyewitnesses and that the miracle stories were the inventions of later writers. For this, Strauss was expelled from his post. In 1863, the French Catholic Ernest Renan drew a sharp distinction between the Jesus of history and the Christ of faith, denying that any evidence for miracles acceptable to a historian had ever been produced. Renan electrified – and scandalized – his readership by claiming that the Gospels told a purely human story. Meanwhile, the

English publication of the collection *Essays and Reviews* in 1860 provoked a petition of condemnation signed by 10,000 Anglican clergymen, but also marked the intellectual victory of those who argued that the inerrancy of the Bible as the product of divine inspiration could no longer be taken for granted.

This was one of the great victories in the history of Western ideas: scholars had at last claimed the right to analyse Scripture as texts, to explore their structure and to investigate the identity and intentions of their authors. In the twentieth century, however, this victory mutated into something rather different: an orthodoxy which, paradoxically, disguised the value of the Gospel texts as historical sources and relegated them unnecessarily to the status of myth and legend.

The most influential biblical scholar of modern times, Rudolf Bultmann (1884–1976), laid the groundwork of all that has followed. 'I am of the opinion,' he wrote, 'that we can know practically nothing about Jesus' life and personality, since the Christian sources had no interest in such matters.' This sentiment underpinned the school of 'form criticism', which argued that the Gospels are not historical records at all, but stylized collections of inherited 'forms'. Each Gospel, according to this analysis, was to be interpreted as an anthology which had evolved from the life, worship and oral traditions of the early Christian communities. These writings reflected the needs of the Church, rather than the reality of Jesus's life and death. In other words, they recorded a theological truth rather a historical reminiscence: the Gospels were to be understood as primitive ecclesiastical manuals rather than eyewitness accounts.

In the post-war period, Bultmann's orthodoxy has been widely criticized. The quest for the historical Jesus has continued in a variety of forms – the most popular being John Dominic Crossan's presentation of Christ as a teacher of subversive wisdom, whose message would have had profound implications for the social and political setting in which he lived, as well as for the souls of those to whom he preached. Nonetheless, Bultmann's influence has persisted in subtle and not so subtle ways.

In particular, the notion that the Gospels are the late creations of Christian communities has proved extremely robust. The proposition that these ancient sources might be early – before the destruction of the Temple in Jerusalem in AD 70 – and reasonably reliable remains essentially heretical. It is still assumed that a thick veil of tradition stood between the man who wandered through Galilee and the earliest worshippers of Christ. According to this analysis, the Gospels' purpose was not so much to record an astonishing series of events, as to express a religious tradition that had already developed over many decades before it was committed to papyrus. To suggest that the Evangelists meant what they said in anything like a literal sense is to court the charge of fundamentalism or uncritical conservatism. To suggest that the principal events in the Gospels probably took place in some shape or form is to ask for trouble.

In the USA the charge has been led by John Shelby Spong, who has said that Biblical literalism is 'mindless' and that it appeals to 'deeply insecure and fearful people'. Spong has gone so far as to call upon the righteous to rescue the Bible from the 'Babylonian captivity of the fundamentalists'. The sacred congregation of the contemporary liberal orthodoxy has been the 'Jesus Seminar', the loose-knit group of 100 scholars that first met at the Pacific School of Religion in Berkeley, California, to establish by a complex voting procedure which of the many sayings attributed to Christ reflect His authentic voice. The participants vote with a range of coloured balls to decide how trustworthy the Gospels are, and by their reckoning fewer than a quarter of the sayings recorded in the New Testament are worth taking seriously. The rest, apparently, is embellishment, hearsay and outright invention.

This, then, is the intellectual backdrop against which Thiede's 'new paradigm' must be seen: a setting in which the spirit of the Enlightenment has mutated into a sometimes pathological scepticism. As archaeologist, papyrologist and historian, Thiede tried to examine the Gospels as historical sources, and the world they describe not as a mythic Middle Earth of the Middle East, but as a historical reality which deserves even-handed scrutiny and exploration. Christianity is a belief-system which, more than any other, roots itself in the historical writings of identifiable authors, in events, in artefacts – and in places. Thiede's campaign was to examine these claims as an ancient historian rather than a theorist or polemicist. Although he was an ordained Anglican priest, it cannot be emphasized enough that his purpose in this work was scholarly rather than evangelical. Having known him for a decade, and travelled with him all over Europe and the Middle East, I can testify that his personal beliefs were not the well-spring of his intellectual project. This book is the work of a ground-breaking scholar, not a fundamentalist with an axe to grind. As his collaborator, I saw first-hand that Thiede was unwilling to advance a claim of which he was not absolutely sure: he was cautious by temperament and meticulous in his methods, as is essential for any scholarly pioneer who expects to be taken seriously.

The discovery of Emmaus is an absolutely sensational development both in the formation of this 'new paradigm' and in Christian archaeology generally. The site of the village described in Luke has been a mystery for more than one and a half millennia. Whereas Thiede's previous bestsellers explored artefacts which have been neglected – the St Matthew manuscript at Magdalen College, Oxford, and the Santa Croce Titulus – this book tells the remarkable story of a brand new excavation. The work it describes has hitherto been shrouded in secrecy.

Thiede has bridged the gap between pilgrimage and scholarship: believers who visit the Holy Land still travel along what they hope is the road to Emmaus, in most cases knowing that the precise location has long been lost. They perform, in other words, a ritual act of devotion, intellectually aware that they are not actually retracing the footsteps of Jesus and his followers as described in Luke Chapter 24. The story of Emmaus, therefore, is an excellent case study in the modern world's approach to Gospel sites: worshippers fulfil their pilgrimages as an act of faith, while scholars shrug their shoulders in scepticism. It has suited the prejudice of most contemporary academics that Emmaus has, literally, vanished from the face of the Earth: it matches their assumption that the story recounted by St Luke has nothing to do with the historical reality of first-century Judea.

In this book, Carsten Thiede challenges this assumption vigorously: not with rhetoric, but with an account of an extraordinary detective story – one which has consumed many years. He shows that the previous sites suggested for Emmaus can be dismissed out of hand, and then, meticulously, with a wealth of philological, historical and archaeological evidence, he builds up the case for the site of Moza, an ancient settlement which also served as a colony for 800 Roman veterans after AD 70/71. Aerial photography, sophisticated cartography, descriptions of Roman roads, close textual analysis of non-Christian sources: all are deployed in the pages that follow.

As he explains in his description of the long, sometimes frustrating but ultimately triumphant dig, the real Emmaus was 'a leafy suburb of Jerusalem', close enough to the Temple for its Jewish inhabitants to perform the necessary observances, but pleasantly close to fresh water and blessed with the fresh air of the Sorek Valley. Those who lived here – as the artefacts unearthed by Thiede's team show – were well-heeled and fond of creature comforts. They lived and ate well – as is suggested by the tantalizing discovery of the scales of imported Nile perch. As we follow the archaeologists' painstaking work, a rich portrait emerges of the place towards which Jesus, Cleopas and the unnamed third traveller made their way, and where they had supper together. This book breathes life into a story relegated for centuries to the status of legend, and reclaims its geographical setting. We do not know what happened on the day described by St Luke. But now we know where these events took place. We can imagine the sun setting on the three travellers, the lights of the settlement as the trio drew closer, the twilit hills, the warm April wind, the aroma of supper and freshly baked bread, and the bustle of villagers as they prepared for their evening meal. What happened over that meal – the moment of transcendental astonishment transformed into art by Caravaggio and so many others – is a matter of faith. But the place where that meal took place is now a matter of scholarly record. As Thiede puts it, St Luke's story is not 'a theological road movie'.

The great Benedictine geographer of the life of Jesus, Bargil Pixner, aptly named the landscape that he mapped 'the fifth Gospel'. Anyone who has visited these places in the Holy Land – the Holy Sepulchre, the Mount of Olives, Galilee – can attest to their resonance and power: one does not have to be a believer to experience this sense of wonder. General Charles Gordon, who wrote a famous (and fallible) account of Jerusalem's holy places in 1885, declared that 'these sites are in each of us'. What he meant was that the map of the Christian faith is an internal as well as a temporal one. Christian civilization has bequeathed to us – believer and non-believer alike – a collective memory of a particular place, at a particular time in its history. The secularization of the West has not snuffed out this memory: every child learns about Bethlehem, every adult recognizes the world of the Passion. Nazareth, Canaan, Galilee, Gethsemane, Golgotha: these names have meaning far beyond the pews of our churches. To live in the West – and many places besides – is still to be confronted by the culture of Christianity, to be presented with its questions: in this sense, we are all on the road to Emmaus.

The mysteries of that road – and of the revelation that lay at its end – are not the subject of this book. This is not a work of doctrine. It is, instead, an act of reclamation, of scholarly dedication; it is a historical settling of accounts. It will fascinate anyone who knows St Luke's story, who has wondered what it meant, who is intrigued by the stories of the resurrected Christ, and who, like Eliot, shivers to read of 'the third who walks always beside you'. But it will also compel those who find the science of archaeology and biblical scholarship intrinsically fascinating: only rarely, after so many centuries, is such an exciting discovery made. For so long, this village has been lost. But now, at last, after so many false hopes, dashed expectations and wrong turnings, the forgotten site of Emmaus is rising once more from the soil.

1

Trusting the Sources

The pilgrims' appetite, once awakened, was seemingly insatiable.
Peter Walker, Holy City, Holy Places?, *Oxford 1990, 17.*

As a child in a fairground might stick out her foot to prevent herself from
sliding down a ramp too fast and out of control, so many theologians have
refused to abandon themselves to the changes and chances of the historical
enterprise, and have either kept the brake firmly on or, in extreme cases,
simply refused to join in the fun at all. Or, to change the metaphor, they are
frightened of history as a walker is of a swamp: one might sink without
trace.
N.T. Wright, The New Testament and the People of God,
London 1992, 93.

One of the most dramatic and vivid episodes in the Gospels is the description by Luke of the encounter between two Jews and the risen Christ. It
took place on the road from Jerusalem to the village of Emmaus, in the late
afternoon of 9 April AD 30. Luke tells of their walk from Jerusalem, their
meeting with Jesus who has come back from the dead and whom they do
not recognize at first, and their journey with him to their home in
Emmaus. Luke writes as an educated historian, employing the methods of
the great Greek masters like Thucydides and Herodotus: but he also
knows that his story and its context are unique in the history of mankind.
Beyond the mere history, there is a message of suffering and salvation,
of death and resurrection, the likes of which no one, except his two predecessors Mark and Matthew, had ever dared to tell. And he is not just
writing for a nondescript readership. The man whom he addresses and to
whom both his Gospel and the second volume of his writings, Acts, are
dedicated, is a high-ranking civil servant, 'His Excellency' Theophilus.

To modern readers, this combination of factors – history, theology and
down-to-earth elements of Roman social structures – is not always easy to

disentangle. Many sceptics have been tempted to dismiss Luke's texts as subjective theology, with perhaps just a few credible historical snippets here or there. Professional historians, on the other hand, have learned to trust Luke as one of the outstanding virtuosos of classical historiography. The Emmaus story is a kind of litmus test: is it part of an early Christian resurrection myth, or is it first-century history, embedded in the real lives of real people, Jews, Greeks and Romans? Here is how Luke presents it in his Gospel, according to the 'Authorized Version' or 'King James Bible', using language that may sound opaque and archaic to modern readers, but which preserves the awe and mystique of an event which transcended everyday human experience even then:

> Luke 24. [13]And behold, two of them went that same day to a village called Emmaus, which was from Jerusalem about threescore furlongs.
>
> [14]And they talked together of all these things which had happened.
>
> [15]And it came to pass, that, while they communed together and reasoned, Jesus himself drew near, and went with them.
>
> [16]But their eyes were holden that they should not know him.
>
> [17]And he said unto them, What manner of communications are these that ye have come one to another, as ye walk, and are sad?
>
> [18]And the one of them, whose name was Cleopas, answering said unto him, Art thou only a stranger in Jerusalem, and hast not known the things which are come to pass there in these days?
>
> [19]And he said unto them, What things? And they said unto him, Concerning Jesus of Nazareth, which was a prophet mighty in deed and word before God and all the people;
>
> [20]And how the chief priests and our rulers delivered him up to be condemned to death, and have crucified him.

²¹But we trusted that it had been he which should have redeemed Israel: and beside all this, to day is the third day since these things were done.

²²Yea, and certain women also of our company made us astonished, which were early at the sepulchre;

²³And when they found not his body, they came, saying that they had also seen a vision of angels, which said that he was alive.

²⁴And certain of them which were with us went to the sepulchre, and found it even so as the women had said: but him they saw not.

²⁵Then he said unto them, O fools, and slow of heart, to believe all that the prophets have spoken:

²⁶Ought not Christ to have suffered these things, and to enter into his glory?

²⁷And beginning at Moses and all the prophets, he expounded unto them in all the Scriptures the things concerning himself.

²⁸And they drew nigh unto the village, whither they went: and he made as though he would have gone further.

²⁹But they constrained him, saying, Abide with us: for it is toward evening, and the day is far spent. And he went in to tarry with them.

³⁰And it came to pass, as he sat at meat with them, he took bread, and blessed it, and brake, and gave to them.

³¹And their eyes were opened, and they knew him; and he vanished out of their sight.

³²And they said one to another, Did not our heart burn within us, while he talked with us by the way, and while he opened to us the Scriptures?

³³And they rose up the same hour, and returned to Jerusalem, and found the eleven gathered together, and them that were with them,

³⁴Saying, The Lord has risen indeed, and has appeared to Simon.

³⁵And they told what things were done in the way, and how he was known of them in breaking of bread.

Anyone who tries to read this passage as a contemporary historical document, written in perfect Greek prose of the Hellenistic era rather than in seventeenth-century English, will see immediately that behind the holy language of Easter worship (this is, for example, the Gospel Reading according to the Book of Common Prayer for Easter Monday) there lurks an account which is brimming over with information. Readers of classical literature did not expect to find defined place names, distances, or times of day mentioned at every stage of a historical writing – in the texts of Greek and Roman historians, such details are the exception, not the rule. If and when they occur, the ancients knew that the author wanted to alert them to something special and noteworthy about the location and the circumstances. Luke is no exception. He insists on checkable data: or, to put it differently, he wants Theophilus (his dedicatee) and all other readers to understand that he is not making it up. 'That same day' – the third day after the crucifixion which he had reported in the previous chapter. 'A village called Emmaus' – not any Emmaus. The name, with different Greek or Hebrew spellings, was not uncommon and usually signified a settlement at a warm source of water (*Hammat* in Hebrew), and was well-known as a city some 32 kilometres west of Jerusalem. Luke means a village of the same name, 'about threescore furlongs' from Jerusalem, or, to quote the Greek text, 60 stadia (in modern terms, about 11.3 kilometres). Luke knows that there was more than one place called Emmaus, and so he makes sure that his readers do not confound them: his is a village, not a city, and the distance from Jerusalem is roughly 60 stadia, not the c.176 to the more famous city of the same name.

Some 60 years after Luke, in c.AD 120, the longer ending to Mark's Gospel, 16.9–20, which was probably composed by a presbyter called

Aristion, confirms Luke's account in one important detail: the author of this additional ending briefly refers to the Emmaus episode, and while he does not mention the name of the village, nor the distance, he notes that the two Jews who walked that road went 'into the countryside', or, in Greek, *eis agron*. In other words, by AD 120, the Christian community still knew that the story was not set near the famous city of Emmaus, but in the country near Jerusalem. Luke provides one further detail to make sure that his readers did not look for the wrong Emmaus: as soon as the two followers recognize Jesus, they leave their house and return to Jerusalem. By then, the sun had set, it was dark, the gates of Jerusalem were about to be closed, but they manage to reach Jerusalem in time and find the disciples and others awake and excited. This chain of events presupposes a comparatively short walking distance and again rules out the far-away city of Emmaus.

It all sounds pretty straightforward, but for centuries scholars have tried to work out where this Emmaus was: where, in other words, the risen Christ walked, ate and revealed himself. It is an absolutely crucial location on the map of Christian belief, and one of the great missing links of Christian archaeology, which has foxed excavators and biblical detectives for more than one and a half a millennia. Where is the true site of this astonishing event recorded by Luke?

Three sites have been favoured by different Christian churches and orders since the fourth century. First and foremost is the city of Emmaus, called Nicopolis, 'the city of victory', from AD 221. It was the place of Maccabean battles in the second century BCE (cf. 1 Macc. 3.40–57; 4.3–25), was chosen by the Byzantine Church in the second half of the fourth century AD, and remains the preferred site of most modern tourist guides, but is too far from Jerusalem to fit the story, and was a regional capital rather than the village described by Luke. Second, crusaders in the twelth century believed Emmaus-Abu Gosh near Qiryat Yearim (1 Sam. 6.21–7.2) to be the true site, but it was not called Emmaus in the first century AD and therefore must be ruled out. Third, El Qubeibe, halfway between Jerusalem and Ramalla, was favoured by the Franciscans after the fifteenth century but, again, was not called Emmaus in the first century AD.

In spite of its importance – this, after all, was a place where the risen Christ spoke and ate with his companions – the search for Emmaus had been given up by most scholars. In *Luke. An Introduction and Commentary* (1990), Leon Morris states categorically that 'the site cannot now be identified'. *The International Standard Bible Encyclopedia* (1982) says with no less confidence that 'the exact site of Emmaus is unknown'. The trail went cold long ago – or so it seemed. From time to time, scholars suggested alternative sites, obscure names like Beit Ulma, Beit Nekofa, Artas, Khirbet el-Keniseh and El-Hammam. None of them is even remotely plausible. Only one other place has been given credence by more than one scholar since the mid-nineteenth century: Qaloniyeh, near Moza. There is a good reason for this choice: in his *Jewish War*, written in c.AD 75, the Jewish-Roman historian Flavius Josephus mentions a Roman veterans' colony, established by Emperor Vespasian after the destruction of Jerusalem in AD 70, at a Jewish village called Emmaus, 30 stadia (c.5.7 kilometres) from Jerusalem.[1] The Latin word for colony, *colonia*, has survived in Hebrew and Arabic forms like Qalonye and Qaloniyeh to the present day. The site now comprises ruins and a few isolated houses, but a village, peacefully inhabited by Jews and Arabs, existed until the battles that followed Israel's Declaration of Independence in 1948. Since the distance Josephus records between the Roman colony and Jerusalem is only half of Luke's 60 stadia, most scholars ruled the site out straight-away; however, a few others considered this a minor problem for which a solution should be found, and tentatively identified Luke's Emmaus with that of Josephus.

Such a quest for a historical site is nothing unusual. Take the example of one of the most famous rivers of classical history, the Rubicon, which was crossed by Julius Caesar on 10 January 49 BCE. The devastating Roman civil war began when Caesar crossed it to march on Rome, exclaiming the proverbial *Alea iacta est*, 'the die is cast' (or some similar words, for the sources are far from precise). But where was the Rubicon? It marked the border between Gallia Cisalpina and Italia, but where exactly was that border? In the fifteenth century, the cities of Rimini and Cesena went to court, in an extended legal battle for the right to claim that the Rubicon was a river on their territory. Much later, when a milestone was found which gave a distance 'from Rubicon', scholars hesitatingly agreed that the Rubicon was the Fiumicino; and in 1932, under Mussolini, the Fiumicino was renamed 'Rubicone', and Mussolini's historians attached signs with the ancient name to all of the bridges over the river. Certainty, however, remains elusive to this day.

Similar questions have been asked about Old Testament sites. Only some ten per cent of places mentioned in the Old Testament have been excavated. Needless to say, this does not mean that they never existed; they merely have to be excavated, which is, to a large extent, a question of funding and having professional archaeologists and their teams of volunteers willing to invest time and detective work. Far from being a region where no square metre has remained without trenches dug by archaeologists, the Holy Land still is, amazing as this may sound, *terra incognita* in archaeological terms. The well-known sites of Megiddo, Hazor, Masada and Lachish, to name but a few, are the exceptions that prove the rule.

New Testament sites are much better documented: serious scholars agree that we know where Nazareth, Cana, Capernaum, Bethsaida, Caesarea Philippi, Herodian Jericho, Bethany, Betphage, the pool of Bethesda, Gethsemane, Golgotha and other places mentioned in the Gospels can be found. Moreover, there are hardly any 'rival' sites. The so-called Garden Tomb, for example, remains a favoured location for many Anglicans who follow General Gordon's lead and visit the location off the Nablus Road, which has a skull-shaped rockface and a tomb nearby that may just look like the description in the Gospels. It is a great place for quiet meditation, but since the tomb itself is Iron Age, it cannot be the new and previously unused tomb built by Joseph of Arimathea (John 19.40). Other archaeological considerations also rule out the general's choice: we now know that Golgotha and the tomb of Jesus are indeed covered by the spacious Church of the Holy Sepulchre; in AD 30, this area was just outside the walls of Jerusalem. Or take the disputed site of one of Jesus' miracles, the famous story of the Gadarene swine (Matthew 8.28–34 and parallels). Did it take place at Gadara, or at Gerasa, as some ancient manuscripts have it, or even at Gergesa? Recent investigations have shown that it was near the harbour of Gadara, on the southeastern shores of the Sea of Galilee. A third example: where was Jesus baptized, where was 'Bethany' (or Bethabara, as other manuscripts call it) beyond Jordan (Jn 1.28)? Again, recent excavations have shown that it was not west but east of the river Jordan, in the Wadi El-Charrar.

These are rare examples of more than one site claiming to be 'it'. Emmaus, on the other hand, really is an exception. Not one, but all in all nine sites have been suggested, three of them, as we have seen, from the fourth century to the late Middle Ages. In a sense, this shows how important to Christians the only appearance of the risen Christ – located at what appears to be a precisely named place with a distance from Jerusalem and even the time of day stated – has always been. And yet, is it really that difficult to solve the enigma?

In spite of the indications provided by Josephus and Luke for an Emmaus close to Jerusalem, nothing was done to follow these up in modern times: no archaeologist investigated the matter. Travellers found ruins near Qaloniyeh, even tombs, and before the modern road between Jerusalem and Tel Aviv was built, remnants of a Byzantine monastery could be seen. Today, they are lying under the A1 motorway, which was widened during the Yom Kippur War. Two leading Israeli archaeologists, Gabi Bakai in 1964/65 and Emanuel Eisenberg in 1972/73, saw these remains and recorded them;[2] Eisenberg found traces of Bronze Age settlements, walls of a Roman house with mosaics which apparently belonged to Vespasian's colony; one of the Emperor's coins, dated AD 71, was discovered at the site. Eisenberg realized he was on to something, but when he returned from the Yom Kippur War of 1973, his excavations had been covered by a new lane of the motorway, built to allow Israeli tanks better defensive manoeuvrability against the feared advance of Syrian and Jordanian tanks on Jerusalem. Not a single trace of a Jewish settlement that could be identified with the Emmaus of either Josephus or Luke had been discovered until then. Only one thing was certain in 1973: this had been an area of continuous settlements during the Iron Age, the Roman Empire, the Byzantine period, the Ottoman era, and the British Mandate, when the first asphalt road was constructed. Huge gaps remained, however: where exactly was the village of the late Second Temple Period which was called Emmaus until the Romans took over? What happened between the Byzantine centuries and the times of the Crusaders? Were the ruins of a Crusader watch tower, less than 100 metres west of Eisenberg's excavation, merely some impressive stone remains of an isolated building, or were they part of a larger establishment? Why was all knowledge of the real Emmaus lost after AD 70 – or was it? It is a mystery, and for almost 30 years, since Eisenberg stopped digging no one has investigated it. (Eisenberg left his earlier Roman discoveries in the subterranean collections of the John Rockefeller Museum in Jerusalem without publishing an extensive report.)

As Sherlock Holmes puts it in Arthur Conan Doyle's *The Sign of Four*: 'Eliminate all other factors, and the one which remains must be the truth.' Back in 2000, when I prepared a series of lectures on Gospel sites, it soon became apparent that not one of the locations commonly suggested for Emmaus could possibly qualify. It was, frankly, a disappointing result. If not even the Byzantine Christians of the fourth century, supported by the full might of the by-then christianized Roman emperors and their imperial archives, had managed to locate the true spot, something must have gone wrong somewhere. Only one site remained on the list: the Emmaus of Josephus. It had been noticed before but, as we have seen, no archaeological evidence for a Jewish village had been found. Was it worth trying all over again, trusting, as it were, the dictum of Sherlock Holmes?

Using ordnance survey maps, aerial photography, descriptions of Roman roads and other sources (more of these later), I concluded that the Emmaus of Josephus and Luke were one and the same village. It had to be just west of Vespasian's colony, the site of which had been established by Emanuel Eisenberg, and west of the ruins of the Crusaders' watchtower, not far from a well which was just about visible under shrubs, immediately adjacent to the A1 motorway. When I suggested as much to colleagues at the Israel Antiquities Authority, they smiled benignly. We have been driving past this place for years, they told me, there is nothing to be found. But as good friends, they agreed to do me a favour and joined me on a trip to the tiny area which I assumed to be the centre of ancient Emmaus. We climbed over the Crusader stones and the wild undergrowth, and when we reached the spot, we found the first roof tiles just centimetres under the surface. This came as a complete surprise, even to me. One doesn't expect ancient roof tiles underneath late twentieth century soil. It soon became obvious that people from the neighbourhood had shifted the earth – and the tiles – during work on an illegal building. We had arrived just in time. The appropriate authorities were informed immediately, the area was sealed off, and the following year, after a series

of proper surveys, it was established that we had discovered the site
of buildings which went back to pre-Roman times. Was this the village
mentioned by Josephus and Luke?

To my Israeli colleagues, a Christian site was of less importance than a
Jewish one. But then again, if this was Emmaus, it was a Jewish site even
from a Christian perspective: Jesus, Cleopas and the unnamed third person were Jews, and in AD 30, the village of Emmaus was of course a Jewish
village, not a Christian one. Christianity, the Gospels, and the collection of
the 27 writings of the New Testament came later. Thus, an excavation of
this site would satisfy a twofold curiosity. First, it would establish the
existence of a previously unknown Jewish village which existed until AD
70, very close to Jerusalem. It would provide information on the quality of
life, and the kind of people living in this part of the countryside, which
had always been privileged by its natural wealth: fertile soil, shady trees,
the water of the Nahal Sorek, an Iron Age source, and other amenities.
(Was this perhaps the archetypal 'leafy suburb'?) Second, readers of the
New Testament would gain valuable insights into the real existence of the
site of a resurrection appearance, or, to put it differently, of an event many
people still relegate to the realms of legend rather than history. If both
Josephus and Luke referred to the same village, two separate sources
could be brought into line – always a satisfactory result to classical historians. The first season of annual excavations took place in 2001, and the
results are presented in this book.

One of the first details we established during the initial surveys solved
the problem of the conflicting distances. Measuring the distance along the
reconstructable first-century road from the western gate of Jerusalem (not
to be confused with today's Jaffa Gate, since the so-called Second Wall,
which existed until AD 41, ran just east of the hillock of Golgotha) to our
location west of Vespasian's *colonia*, we established that the true distance
was c.46 stadia (8.5 kilometres). Josephus, with his 30 stadia (c.5.6 kilometres), underestimated the distance; Luke, with his 60 stadia (c.11.1
kilometres), overestimated it. A number of scholars suggested a subtle
solution to reconcile the difference: since Luke's two disciples returned to
Jerusalem, they argued, he may have doubled the distance, there and
back, and twice 30 makes 60. But this is too clever by half. Luke underlines
that he means a single journey when he gives the distance in 24.13. Obvi-

ously, neither Luke nor Josephus used ordnance survey maps and measuring tapes when they wrote their texts. They gave the rough distance, from memory or from the accounts of people who had travelled the route, taking about an hour and a half for the journey. To a slow walker, 30 stadia seemed feasible; a faster person, who knew the road well and travelled it frequently, could have covered twice the distance in the same time (interestingly, there is a modern translation of Luke 24.13 which omits the distance altogether and replaces it with 'two hours'[3]). And since there is no other first-century village called Emmaus between 30 and 60 stadia from Jerusalem, the conclusion is safe: both authors do indeed refer to the same place.

This book tells the story of the rediscovery of Emmaus: it returns to the ancient sources, unravels the mystery of knowledge lost and regained, and it shows, step by step, how ancient authors, 'even' a Gospel writer, can be taken seriously. At the same time, it investigates the rise and fall of Emmaus, its inhabitants and occupiers, from the first century BCE to the first Crusade. Emmaus, after all, is more than a rediscovered archaeological site: it opens a window onto some of the most controversial and cruel, as well as pioneering and crucial periods of ancient and medieval history. The risen Christ; the mysterious disciple Cleopas; Emperor Vespasian and his son Titus; the historian and Gospel author Luke; the pharisee, Jewish ex-general and Roman court historian Flavius Josephus; a Christian thinker and librarian like Julius Africanus; the Church Fathers Eusebius and Jerome; Knights Hospitallers like the Master Raymond du Puy – they all come to life in these pages as people who shaped and changed their worlds. Unlike the ever popular quest for the Holy Grail and the wayward fantasies about descendants of Jesus, this is the real stuff of true history, and it is no less fascinating for that. The road to Emmaus is a road which combines the ascertainable data of archaeology and historiography with the wonder of a new faith, the faith in the risen Son of God which began on that day, among a forlorn group of dejected disciples who had seen Jesus crucified by the Romans only two days before.

Often enough, people have tried to separate the Jesus of History from the Christ of Faith. The latter has been left to the doctrines of the churches, the shifting theories of theologians and the individual experiences of devout Christians. The former has been dismissed, not least by some leading New Testament scholars who have abandoned trust in the Gospels and see Jesus as a remote figure about whom little is known apart from his crucifixion on which (because it was mentioned by non-biblical authors) they base their assumption that he therefore must have existed in the first place. The rest is not quite silence. For there is a lack of understanding that history and faith are anything but mutually exclusive concepts. Hardly anyone will turn Christian because of an ancient inscription discovered among the ruins of a first-century village, and likewise no one will lose their faith if stories told in the Bible cannot be proven archaeologically. 'Proving' faith is a futile endeavour. Appreciating the intelligence and learning of the witnesses and writers of the first centuries, on the other hand, takes us closer to the roots of our civilization.

The Emmaus episode did not take place in an ahistorical vacuum. It happened at a site known to contemporaries during the Herodian period and the reign of Emperor Tiberius, when Pontius Pilate was Prefect of Judaea. The Temple, then still standing, was the focus of Jewish identity worldwide, and while Tiberius and his adoptive father Augustus were venerated as deities and Sons of God throughout the Empire (until AD 66, prayers were said daily in the Temple for the well-being of the Emperor, and Augustus had supplied funds for sacrifices to be offered on his behalf). It was a world challenged by the Jew Jesus, whom the representative of the Emperor had crucified and who appeared as one risen from the dead to sceptics like James and opponents like Paul. The consequences of these events are with us to this day, to believers and non-believers alike.

Emmaus represents the beginnings of a radical change, and more clearly than ever before we can see how it all happened, not in the imagination of deluded men and women, but in the very real world of a Roman province. From among the many accounts of resurrection appearances, Luke could have chosen one of several alternatives. He opted for Emmaus, and in this book it will become apparent why he did so. In one sense, the rediscovery of Emmaus is a case study. It should also be an encouragement: returning to our Judeo-Christian sources, we may find out more about ourselves. In the novel *Berlin Game*, Len Deighton has one of his characters say: 'Research and investigation are no damn use if they don't support those prejudiced judgements we've already worked so hard on.' This cynicism has been justified by much of New Testament research. But Emmaus shows that there are other ways of looking at our history.

Notes

1   *Jewish War* 7.217. We will return to Josephus and his evidence in a later chapter.
2   See A. Ovadiah and C.G. de Silva, 'Supplementum to the Corpus of the Byzantine Churches in the Holy Land', *Levant* 14 (1982), 157; E. Eisenman, 'Motza', *Revue Biblique* 82 (1975), 587.
3   The current revised German version of Luther's translation, published in 1984.

2

Looking for Emmaus: How the Traces were Lost and Rediscovered

Walking the line: Roads and travellers at the time of Jesus

Intrepid travellers in the Holy Land, pilgrims, tourists, or professional surveyors, may find stretches of ancient Roman roads here or there. Even in the Old City of Jerusalem, the original paving of Roman streets has survived in some places: in the former Herodian Quarter, for example, there are a few yards to be found oppposite the Austrian Hospice, and a few more near a red pillar box (a relic from British Mandate times). Descending into the Kidron Valley, visitors are shown stone steps that Jesus and his disciples might have used on their way to the Garden of Gethsemane. From Hadrian's times, the old east–west axis, the Cardo, was excavated in the Jewish Quarter; now as then, most of it is a shopping mall, where coins minted by Pontius Pilate, modern jewellery and junk can be bought at inflated prices. Roads heading across country connected the towns and cities, and occasionally Roman milestones and flagstones have survived, now safely tucked away in the underground vaults of the John Rockefeller Museum and the Israel Museum in Jerusalem, where the most valuable examples are on display.

One instance of the extent to which Roman roads still influence us today is reflected in an anecdote told by historians: the US standard railroad gauge (the distance between the rails) is 4 feet 8.5 inches. Why is that gauge employed? Because it was the standard in England, and English expatriates built the US railroads. Why did the English build railroads like that? Because the first rail lines were built by the same people who built the pre-railroad tramways, and that is the gauge they used. But why did they use that gauge? Because the people who built the tramways used the same jigs and tools that they had used for building road wagons, which used that wheel spacing. Why did the wagons have that particular wheel spacing? Well, if they tried to use any other spacing, the wagon wheels would break on some of the old, long distance roads in England, because that was the spacing of the wheel ruts. So who built those old rutted roads? Imperial Rome built the first long-distance roads in England for their legions. The roads have been used ever since. And the ruts in the roads? Roman war chariots formed the initial ruts, which all other vehicles had to match for fear of breaking their wagon wheels. And Imperial Roman war chariots were made just wide enough to accommodate the back ends of two war horses. In more recent times, the space shuttle had solid rocket boosters (SRBs) attached to its side. These SRBs had to be shipped by train from the factory to the launch site, and so had to fit through a railway tunnel, which was slightly wider than the railroad track. So, it can be said, a major design feature of what is arguably the world's most advanced transportation system was determined over 2000 years ago by the width of a Roman horse's backside.

This story has at least a kernel of historical and archaeological truth. In any case, the courses of these ancient roads have been reconstructed on special maps, and in Israel, those who want to follow Jesus and his group, using, for example, the Via Maris which passes through Galilee in linking Damascus with the Egyptian coast, can still do so. The Via Maris, literally the 'Road of the Sea', is one of the oldest roads of the Middle East, and was mentioned in the seventh century BCE by the Jewish prophet Isaiah (9.11). 'But there will be no gloom for those who were in anguish. In the former time He [God] brought into contempt the land of Zebulon and the land of Naphtali, but in the the latter time he will make glorious the way of the sea [in the Latin versions, *via maris*], the land beyond the Jordan, Galilee of the nations.'

For merchants, businessmen and marching legions, the Via Maris was at least as important as the more famous Via Appia in Italy, which had reached its longest extension at the time of Jesus, and linked Rome with the southeastern port of Brindsium (Brindisi), making it the most important route across Italy to and from Greece. Others, keen to reach Rome more directly by sea, would have landed at Ostia, Rome's own harbour town, or at Puteoli (Pozzoli) on the southwest coast, and then have travelled by land to the junction of the Via Appia, although this meant a longer and more dangerous sea journey. Like many others, the apostle Paul was shipwrecked on his journey from Crete to Rome (Acts 28.14–44), and historians acknowledge Paul's shipwreck account to be the most dramatic and knowledgable report by an eyewitness from antiquity.

Marine archaeologists often find the remains of such ships and their mer-
chandise at the bottom of the Mediterranean. Other dangers threatened
travellers everywhere on sea and land. There were pirates and highway
robbers. In Israel, revolutionary cells attacked Roman rear parties and
often enough singled out fellow Jews as particularly easy prey, whenever
they refused to join the brigands or support them. The story told by Jesus
in Luke (10.30–37) about a man who had been robbed and beaten half to
death on his way from Jerusalem to Jericho has the literary form of a
parable, but contemporary readers who read and heard it knew that such
things did happen, and that Good Samaritans were few and far between.
Emperor Augustus, during whose reign Jesus was born in 7 BCE, did
his best to 'clean up' the roads, and he was so proud of his success in
eliminating piracy that he mentioned it as his major achievement.[1]

The so-called 'Inn of the Good Samaritan' on the road to Jericho and the
Dead Sea is a fairly recent building, and merely serves the purposes of
modern daylight robbery, relieving guileless tourists who are willing to
pay for drinks and postcards and a visit to the Bedouins' tent of their
money. But in the real world of the first century, 'service areas' played an
important role. Experienced walkers had worked out the maximum distance a traveller would be able to walk on a normal day from one town to
the next, and if there were no towns, villages or hospitable farmsteads en
route, *karawansereis* or inns would be built for the purpose of providing
refreshment and shelter. Jeremiah mentions such a guesthouse on the way
from Bethlehem to Egypt in the seventh century BCE; and one assumes
that Mary, Joseph and Jesus would have stayed there during their flight to
Egypt (Jer. 41.17; Matt. 2.13–15).[2] Centuries later, when the group with the
apostle Paul approached Rome, they stayed at two such inns, at Forum
Appii and Tres Tabernae, and Christians from Rome came to these places
and greeted them there (Acts 28.15). The distances from Rome are known,
(although only Tres Tabernae has been partly excavated), and these give
us a rough idea of average walking distances: Forum Appii, the 'Market-
place of Appius', was at the forty-third milestone (63.5 kilometres) from
Rome. For someone in a hurry, it could be done in two days, but the
seasoned traveller would have taken three. Tres Tabernae, 'The Three
Taverns', an established overnight stop, was 48 kilometres from Rome.
Luke mentions the Forum Appii, as it was here that the Decemnovius

Canal ended and the people who had crossed the Pomptine Marshes in boats had to start walking. Horace, the Roman poet, hated the place, and describes how he caught an infection there from drinking water (*Satires* 1.5 3–6). Tres Tabernae was decidedly more civilized; the name itself promised a choice of guesthouses. Christians from Rome showed Paul how important he was to them when they met him at these two stations, still quite a distance from Rome. On their way back to the city, a place called Aricia would have been their final stop. Infected water or not, the system was in place and no one was forced to sleep under the starry sky on their way to Rome.

The guesthouses fulfilled an important social and economic function. One could never rely on peasants or other land folk to invite unknown travellers into their homes; they could turn out to be thieves, after all. Jesus once referred to such experiences in one of his parables (Matt. 25.43–46). Travelling and sleeping rough was of course an alternative for those who could not or did not want to afford the inns, or who preferred the loneliness of the countryside anyway. Jesus once referred to this obliquely: 'As they were going along the road, someone said to him, "I will follow you wherever you go." And Jesus said to him, "Foxes have holes, and birds of the air have nests, but the Son of Man has nowhere to lay his head" ' (Lk. 9.58). Sometimes, travellers had no choice: if the inn or *karawanserei* was fully booked, they had to make do with less comfortable solutions. When Mary and Joseph went from Nazareth to Bethlehem, it would have taken them six days, assuming that Mary, heavily pregnant, did not walk but rode on a donkey. Five nights in inns lay behind them before they reached Bethlehem – or perhaps four, if they had stayed with her relative Elizabeth, her husband Zacharias and their baby son John (the Baptist-to-be) in the village which tradition has identified as Ein Karem, just a few kilometres west of Jerusalem.[3] After a customary stopover at the Temple in Jerusalem, they would have walked the remaining ten kilometres to Bethlehem. A second-century tradition, told in the so-called Proto-Gospel of James, identifies a well and a resting place half way, the *Katisma*, where Mary, exhausted as she was from the long journey, had to stop once more to rest and drink water. The Byzantine Christians located the site and built a church, remnants of which were found a few years ago.

In Bethlehem, a tiny village, the only inn had no vacancies. The expect-
ant woman and her husband would not have been the only arrivals to be
turned away; it was the time of a Herodian census, carried out under the
authority of Emperor Augustus, and everyone who owned property in or
near Bethlehem had to be registered for taxation at their ancestral home,
as Luke accurately reports (Lk. 2.1–7).[4] It was December, a time of the year
when it was (and is still) possible to stay outside in this area well into the
night (cf. Lk. 2.8), but a woman who was about to give birth would want
some 'creature comfort', and this is quite literally what she got – a place
next to the animals in the stables on the ground floor of the guest house,
where it was warm and where the newborn baby could be laid in a cosy,
comfortable crib. [Photo]

Those who travelled took precautions and were often armed. Immediately before Jesus and his disciples went down from the southwestern hill
of Jerusalem (today's Mount Zion) to the Kidron Valley and the Garden of
Gethsemane, he predicted his suffering by quoting a passage from Isaiah
(53.12): 'He was counted among the evil-doers'. The disciples told him
that they were ready to defend him: 'Look, Lord, here are two swords'. He
knew that there was no point in raising swords at this stage, and replied,
'It is enough' – but it was obvious that they had these swords with them
anyway and were simply reminding him that they were armed as usual
(Lk. 22.38). Not much later, Peter did use one of the swords and cut off
the High Priest's servant's right ear – a deliberate act which demanded
a skill which should be taken for granted in a well-travelled fishing
entrepreneur like Peter.[5] In today's Israel, you may encounter groups of
Israeli school children visiting biblical sites and excavations, and it is the
law that they must be accompanied by at least one adult with a machine
gun on all such outings, to defend them against potential terrorist attacks.
Even university students are not spared these precautions. When I led a
group of students to Qumran across the Green Line not long ago, the
university only allowed us to go if we had one armed man for every 15
students in our group.

All in all, in those days without public transport and private cars, when
not everyone owned a horse or a donkey, people were experienced
walkers, and long journeys did not put them off. They knew how to
organize their travels, preferring the early morning hours and the late

afternoons to avoid the midday sun. There was no street lighting, people did not have pocket torches, and the roads were not lit by a full moon every night. It was essential to reach one's destination or a place of rest before it was dark. Therefore, the two Emmaus disciples invited Jesus into their house: 'Lord, stay with us, for the sun has set and it is about to get dark.'[6] Luke even inserts a moment of humour into his account: Jesus pretended that he was going to walk past their village. Where on earth did he want to go? There was no other village nearby. In human terms, this man, who had not been recognized as the risen Jesus at this stage of the journey, should have been more than happy to have reached a village before dark, even though he did not give the impression that this was his final destination. So they asked him in, perfect hosts, eager to offer hospitality to this odd man who knew so much about Jewish prophecy and the Messiah. The rest is history, as they say – and we will return to this part of our history later in the book.

Power games, or: How not to choose a biblical site

Luke knew where Emmaus was, and he expected his dedicatee Theophilus and other members of his original target group to know that there were at least two places of that name in the province. To avoid confusion, he provided them with the necessary pointers. His Emmaus was a village, and it was within convenient walking distance of Jerusalem. As we saw in the Introduction, there was another Emmaus on the same road between Jerusalem and the Mediterranean Sea. It was well known in Jewish and Greco-Roman history, thanks to the Maccabean battles of the late second century BCE. This Emmaus plays a major role in the first and second books of the Maccabees, which were written (in Greek rather than Hebrew or Aramaic) not long after the events they describe. Roman Catholic readers of the Bible will find them in the Old Testament; Protestant Bible editions have relegated them to the Apocrypha, the 'hidden' books, also called deuterocanonical writings: these are the texts which exist 'beyond (or outside) the canon', with 'canon' a technical term which literally means the 'yardstick' of what was thought to be inspired and authoritative. The Bible editors and translators of the Reformation era, beginning with Martin Luther, decided to follow the list of writings acknowledged by the Jewish, Hebrew Canon. Thus, Protestant readers will often know more about the famous Israeli Maccabee beer and the Jewish 'olympics', called the Maccabiad, than about the battles at Emmaus or the origins of the festivals of Purim and Hanukkah which are described in the Maccabean books. Music lovers may know more, however: there is Handel's oratorio 'Judas Maccabaeus', of which one chorus became the Easter hymn 'See, the Conquering Hero comes'.

Dramatic events happened at this Emmaus. In 167 BCE, pious Jews had had enough of the oppressive rule of the Seleucids, the Greek successors of Alexander the Great's general Seleukos, who had turned Jerusalem into a hellenistic city. Many Jerusalemites, however, liked what they saw. The attractions of Greek culture tempted them, and there were some Jews who even competed naked in Jerusalem's new gymnasium, having done their best to undo their circumcision by new-fangled surgical techniques: 'So they built a gymnasium in Jerusalem, according to Gentile custom, and removed the marks of circumcision, and abandoned the holy covenant. They joined with the Gentiles and sold themselves to do evil' (1 Macc. 1.14–15). But the orthodox realized that the Temple and the laws of the Mosaic covenant had been desecrated. A priest called Mattathias from Modi'in, with his sons Judas, Jonathan, Simon, John and Elazar, took the initiative. Mattathias refused to sacrifice at the Seleucid altar, killed a royal official and a Jew who had come to sacrifice: this initiated a revolt which soon grew into a popular uprising. His son Judas become the first hero of the anti-Seleucid revolution and soon earned his byname Maccabi, or latinized Maccabaeus, from the Aramaic *maqqaba*, 'the hammer'. In 165, Judas Maccabaeus carried out a pre-emptive strike against Gorgias, the commanding general of the Seleucid occupying power. While Gorgias had left his camp at Emmaus to attack the Jewish forces with his cavalry and several squadrons of foot soldiers, Judas outflanked him unnoticed, took Emmaus and put the enemy's main army to flight (1 Macc. 4.1–15).[7] It was the third in a series of victories which culminated in the reconquest of Jerusalem. On 14 December 164 the desecrated Temple was reconsecrated – the first festival of Hanukkah, which Jews worldwide celebrate for eight days in December to this day (1 Macc. 4.36–59).

After the death of Judas Maccabaeus in a later battle against the reorganized Seleucid forces under Bacchides in 161 BCE, his brother and successor Jonathan continued the struggle, but Bacchides took Jerusalem and retained the upper hand for several years. He turned Emmaus into a fortified city (1 Macc. 9.50). Far enough away – some 32 kilometres – to prevent the Maccabean freedom fighters from breaking through to Jerusalem too easily, it was now one of several cities and towns which formed a defensive circle around the City of the Temple.

Archaeologists have discovered remnants of the fortifications of this Emmaus, two kilometres east of the city centre, on a hill called Horvat 'Eqed. They excavated a circular wall which was some 1,050 metres long, with two towers flanking a southern gate. This confirms the description in 1 Maccabees 9.50, where 'high walls and gates and bars' are mentioned. The site was of the highest military strategical importance: it guarded the roads between Jerusalem and the coastal plain, and the water source, a spring called Ein Eqed, which supplied the city and the neighbouring villages. The conflict ended in 153 BCE, when inner Seleucid rivalries strengthened the position of the Maccabees as power-brokers in Judaea. Jonathan was appointed High Priest, and with the exception of Beit Tsur, six kilometres north of Hebron, the fortress cities were abandoned by the Seleucids. Emmaus remained an important and increasingly wealthy city at one of Israel's most important crossroads, but it was no longer a fortress and a garrison occupied by enemy forces.

By the time of Jesus, Emmaus had acquired the status of the chief city in the district of Gezer.[8] Between 57and 54 BCE, when Aulus Gabinius was governor of the Roman province of Syria (which included Judaea and other regions of Israel), Emmaus was probably elevated to the rank of one of five administrative centres or *synhedrions*. It seems to follow from all this that Emmaus was the most important Judaeo-Roman city in western Judaea when Jesus was born.

After the death of Herod the Great in 4 BCE, Jewish revolutionaries decided to use this opportune moment for their own purposes and started regional uprisings. The Roman governor of Syria, Quinctilius Varus, approached from Syria with two legions. Passing by Nazareth, where the eleven-year-old Jesus may have watched the Roman soldiers, some of his contingents destroyed the nearby town of Sepphoris. Nabatean auxiliary forces burnt down several towns and villages, among them the city of Emmaus, under direct orders from Varus.[9] The citizens managed to escape and returned soon afterwards, having been allowed to rebuild Emmaus. Its status as a city and regional capital was never questioned.[10] Like Sepphoris, it regained its wealth and importance in the years immediately after the destruction. By the time of the so-called first Jewish Revolt in AD 66–73, it was undoubtedly a major city. Rebuilt Sepphoris even became the new capital of Galilee under Herod Antipas, until this vassal king decided to build another new capital at the Sea of Galilee in AD 20, naming it after Emperor Tiberius. As Tiberias, it continues to bear the ancient imperial name in modern Israel.

There is no doubt: if we accept the two books of the Maccabees as part of the wider biblical canon then this truly is a biblical site. It illuminates a significant period of Jewish and Greco-Roman history. But is it Luke's Emmaus? International teams of archaeologists have been active at the site since the late nineteenth century. The French architect Joseph-Bernard Guillemot was the first to investigate the remains in 1879. He found ruins of a basilica, a baptismal font and a cruciform baptistry with fragments of an altar. Surveying the whole area, he saw a water basin and a courtyard paved with red stones on white marble, which had been replastered with black and white marble tiles in the sixth century. The water basin with its channelled outlet attracted his curiosity: he assumed that it was older than the basilica. Moving on, Guillemot found a small chapel and, under rubble, a severely damaged mosaic with three broken lines of a Greek inscription. He read them as 'We, the Bishop . . . have made . . . this work'. Finally, he took the measurements of the basilica. He worked out that the original building should be dated to the mid third century, to the period of the city prefect Julius Sextus Africanus, who was a Christian. If correct, this date would question the common assumption that Christians were not allowed to build churches before the reign of Emperor Constantine. But Guillemot was guessing, and the exact date of the ruins has remained a matter of scholarly debate. What he did recognize correctly, however, was the later activity of the Crusaders, who built a new church into the Byzantine remains in the twelfth century. The French architect trusted the prevailing tradition and was convinced that he had surveyed the Emmaus of Luke's Gospel – the courtyard marked, or so he thought, the place of the house of Cleopas.[11]

Guillemot had found two churches and other Christian remains, but nothing to prove that these buildings had been erected above a Jewish settlement of the first centuries BCE/AD. In his first published report (1882), he noted a personal experience: 'Amwas [the Arabic name of the nearby village, and clearly derived from "Emmaus"] is half way between Jerusalem and Jaffa. I have done this road several times on horseback. In the saddle, the distance between Jerusalem and Emmaus can be covered in four hours. It takes the same time from there to Jaffa.' It seems he never realized that he had demonstrated a striking improbability. If this was Luke's Emmaus, and if it took him four hours to get there on horseback, how much longer would the two disciples have needed to reach the city, walking as they did, and in deep conversation? Not only that, Cleopas and his companion returned to Jerusalem as soon as they had recognized the risen Christ. They left their house 'that same hour', which in Greek means 'at once'. Still hungry, and in darkness – the sun was about to set when they reached Emmaus – they are then supposed to have walked back to Jerusalem.

It would have been a remarkable feat even on horseback: eight hours with only a short break, and the return journey up hill. But they walked, and when I did it, a few years ago, it took me five hours, following as far as posssible the ancient Roman trajectory, walking fast and well-equipped with torchlight and ample supplies of water. The two disciples, however, made a return journey. If this Emmaus should qualify, they did ten hours there and back with hardly any time to recover in between, ignoring the fact that they would have reached Jerusalem at dead of night, when the city gates were closed. Luke is adamant: the two disciples reached Jerusalem while the gates were open and the other disciples were still fully awake, eager to talk and listen. Some 60 kilometres in ten hours – it would have been a deed worthy of an Olympic discipline. Literary sources and modern experiments have shown that even trained Roman soldiers managed a maximum daily distance of 30 kilometres.[12] The Greek geographer Strabo, who lived from c.63 BCE to AD 19, describes the distance between Sagalassos and Apameia in Bithynia, just over 30 kilometres and thus the exact equivalent of the distance between Jerusalem and Emmaus, as 'a day's journey'.[13] In another source from antiquity, where dates for court hearings were fixed in such a way that people travelling from afar would be able to arrive on time, a daily journey was calculated at 20 miles (about

30 kilometres).[14] Within the realm of the probable, and the humanly possible, this is the well-documented reality. It rules out the 60 kilometres in at least ten (practically uninterrupted) walking hours, even without the added problem of closed city gates.

Amazingly, neither Guillemot nor those who took over from him seem to have been perturbed by the obvious incongruity. They also happily ignored two further details: Emmaus, as we saw above, was a *polis*, a city, at the time of Jesus. Luke was aware of this fact, and thus he calls the Emmaus of Jesus and the two disciples a *kome*, a village. In other words, Luke, like most of his readers in the wider region (his dedicatee Theophilus included), knew that there was the famous city of Emmaus, and thus he makes sure that there is no misunderstanding. 'I know there is the city of Emmaus,' he implies, 'but I want you to understand that the one I am talking about is a village of the same name.' And if this was not enough, he even adds the distance: the city was 176 stadia (about 32.6 kilometres) from Jerusalem, the village just 60 stadia (about 11.1 kilometres).

Joseph-Bernard Guillemot may have been uncritical, but he merely took for granted what others had taught before him. It is a common phenomenon even today. A given opinion has become so widely accepted that no one thinks of questioning its basic assumptions. Everyone who read the Greek text of Luke's Gospel saw that the distance was given as 60 stadia, and even if one assumed that this was meant to be understood as a rough estimate, since Luke had not used a measuring wheel on an Ordnance Survey map, it was plain enough that his distance was about one third of that needed to reach the city of Emmaus. It was and is simply impossible to reconcile the Gospel text with the city of the Maccabean revolt.

Or is it? In the later fourth century, when the Byzantine Church had decided that the Maccabean Emmaus was also Luke's Emmaus, something strange happened: new Gospel papyri appeared on the market, and the distance had been changed. Instead of 60 stadia, it now read 160 stadia. In Greek, the change was from *hexekonta* to *hekaton hexekonta*, a single additional word easily inserted into the text. It still was not quite the exact distance of 176 stadia, but was close enough to look plausible. The oldest codex of the whole Greek Bible, the *Codex Sinaiticus* (now in the British Library in London, with some Old Testament leaves in the

University Library Leipzig and at St Catherine's Monastery on Mount Sinai), has this 'improved' reading, and a number of other manuscripts, including some Latin, Syriac and Armenian translations, follow it.[15] Just theoretically, one might argue that the opposite had taken place: an earlier reading of 160 stadia was later changed to read 60. After all, the fact that the oldest papyrus manuscript of Luke's Gospel, the P75 of the late second century, clearly has 60 stadia and is confirmed in this by numerous independent textual witnesses, among them several ancient translations into Latin, Syriac and Coptic, could be explained as 'accidental'. There is even a medieval scholarly myth that the eminent Christian librarian, theologian and textual critic Origen (c.AD 185–254) had supported the 160 stadia. As it happens, there is not a shred of evidence for this claim. And above all, why should the earliest extant textual tradition have invented a distance of 60 stadia? When the papyrus P75 was written, there was no rival site known as Emmaus anywhere within a radius of 11.3 kilometres around Jerusalem. The change would have been utterly pointless. As we shall see below, all knowledge of an Emmaus near Jerusalem was lost soon after AD 71, some hundred years before P75 was written. There is only one solution: the original distance of sixty stadia was manipulated and became 160, to suit a decision taken by the all-powerful Byzantine Church.

If we pause to wonder why the Christian Church, in its mid-fourth century incarnation, should have stooped to such measures, we realize that it is a rare, but certainly not unique incident. 'I can resist everything except temptation', Oscar Wilde famously said, and the temptation to alter the text of the New Testament has not always been resisted by people who have had a particular theological axe to grind. In the first centuries, it was comparatively easy to do. There were of course no printed editions, and a scribe or his masters could simply change a passage in a new manuscript, hoping that the change would catch on when this manuscript was spread and copied elsewhere. In modern times, textual critics have pursued a different course. They have relegated passages from the main text to the footnotes of their editions, hoping that no one would study these notes and realize that this is where the better text is to be found. Fortunately, we are not talking about hundreds of cases, so there is no need to be unduly worried if one relies on English translations; but these problems do exist and must be addressed. In passing, let us look at two examples which illuminate the vested interests of scribes – and the theologians behind them – who wanted to get their own particular message across, and who almost got away with it:

'Correctors' were quite uninhibited when they manipulated a passage about an expression of Christ's suffering and anguish. In Luke's Gospel (22.43–44), we read: 'Then an angel from heaven appeared to him and gave him strength. In his anguish he prayed more earnestly, and his sweat became like great drops of blood falling down on the earth.' Here, squeamishness set in early and forcefully. Christ suffering like this? It could not possibly be theologically correct, they thought. Two papyri, five codices, several ancient translations, and theologians such as Clement of Alexandria and Origen of Caesarea (plus Marcion, a mid second-century heretic) deleted these two verses. They did not even try to replace them with something else. Fortunately, we have the voices of early authors like Justin, Irenaeus and Hippolytus who intimate that these sentences were in the text originally. Another ancient, Epiphanius of Salamis, who wrote in the second half of the fourth century, realized that the omission had spread widely for doctrinal reasons and said so in no uncertain terms. But this evidence of their deletion has made some scholars uncertain to this day. After all, they have been taught – and some continue to teach – that ancient and widely diversified manuscript witnesses are a sufficiently strong argument. But this is not the case. A manuscript is either right or wrong, and there may be all sorts of reasons for the sudden emergence of an addition or a deletion.

In any given case of a variation in the transmission of a passage, the reader has to ask a number of questions, and the first two should always be 'How?' and 'Why?' Or, to put it differently, the evidence of each and every papyrus, codex, etc. has to be sifted carefully, and statistics cannot be used as a tool, even if they are based on a number of examples. If they could, we would soon end up judging the text like the infamous Jesus Seminar in the United States, where members decide about the authenticity or otherwise of a verse by dropping beads into a ballot machine and counting the result. Textual criticism is no democratic process, it is about rightness or wrongness. Or, to quote the classical scholar Martin L. West: 'That is what textual criticism is about: rightness! Which does not mean treating the external evidence in a cavalier fashion, but treating it critically, not giving systematic preference to some particular source or type of source. This brings us back to the axiom . . . that the editor should be a thinking being, not a puller of levers.'[16] The language of 22.43–44 is typical Luke, there is nothing odd about the way he tells this incident, and, above all, there is no reason why it should have been added to his text at a later date.

While Luke 22.43–44 may seem to be a minor controversy, as all English translations still have these verses (albeit mainly in square brackets), the attempts to alleviate the offensiveness of Christ's lonely struggle with his cries of utter loneliness and drops of sweat like blood were successful in Greek editions and translations of Hebrews 2.9: 'We do see Jesus, who for a little while was made lower than the angels, now crowned with glory and honour because of the suffering of death, so that apart from God he might taste death for everyone.' This is the original text, which echoes Psalm 22.2, but it proved indigestible to many readers and copyists. They simply changed the Greek *choris theou*, 'apart from God' or 'without God', into *chariti theou*, 'by the grace of God'. And this is how we read it in all modern translations – although thankfully, some at least offer an explanatory footnote, and point to where the original text can be found.

Again, as in the previous case, a sizeable number – in fact, the majority – of existing manuscripts have the 'grace' reading. But again, as philologists and textual critics know, majority is not a criterion in deciding between different readings. Even a supposedly good papyrus may contain one or several wrong readings, and a later manuscript, even if it stands completely on its own today, may well preserve the correct, original text. And indeed, things can change. Origen, studying the manuscript evidence for the whole Greek Bible in the early third century, knew that the vast majority had 'apart from God'. By the time of Jerome in the late fourth/early fifth century, the situation had changed, and the majority read 'by the grace of God'. Something must have happened. But what? It is obvious that the second reading was introduced, preferred and successfully imposed for dogmatic reasons – to such an extent that only three late Greek manuscripts have survived today which preserve the ancient original.[17] Since the first two depend on the last one, one might even go as far as claiming that only the manuscript 1739 remains as a textual witness

to Christ suffering 'divorced' from God. To those who rely on the arguments of early manuscripts and/or widespread evidence, this does not
look too good. And yet, thanks to Origen, we do know that the first stage
of the textual tradition had the words 'apart from God'. And if 'apart from
God' was the later, changed reading, you have to ask: who changed it,
and why? Bruce M. Metzger, in *A Textual Commentary on the Greek New
Testament*, which is the semi-official report on the findings of the editors
who put together the current Greek text of the United Bible Societies and
Nestle-Aland, does not have an even remotely persuasive answer.[18] A
scribal lapse, he suggests. But one hardly alters the whole theology of a
statement by a scribal lapse. Or was it perhaps, as Metzger also suggests,
'a marginal gloss' which was later introduced into the text by mistake?
But again: how and, above all, why? As the church historian Adolf von
Harnack noted as early as 1929, *choris* is typical of the letter to Hebrews. It
occurs no less than 14 times, as often as in all letters of Paul (the disputed
ones included) put together. 'Grace', *charis*, in Hebrews and always in
Paul, on the other hand, means the grace of God regained, and not, as it is
supposed to mean here, the cause of redemption by death.[19] Anyone who
reads the altered text carefully will wonder how it can be 'a *grace* of God'
that Christ suffered on the cross. In other words, let us admit the obvious:
Christ without God – this was not politically correct, and when certain
circles within the Church became powerful enough to influence the
manuscript tradition (in the mid-fourth century), such alterations became
feasible. Desperate to get the separation from God out of the text, they
weakened the powerful language of Hebrews.

Other examples of textual alterations discovered by classical philologists, some of them only quite recently, could be added.[20] Human frailty
did not stop at the door of the early Christian Church: but suffice it to say
that such instances are far less frequent than in non-biblical texts from
antiquity, and that they are not about secret, hidden messages. Experienced scholars have found them and will find them, to the benefit of
modern editions, translations, and their readers. Returning to Luke 24.23
and the altered distance between Jerusalem and Emmaus, we may still
look at such textual operations with a certain sense of amazement,
perhaps even bewilderment, but not without satisfaction that the few
cases which have occurred in the history of textual tradition of the New

Testament can be sorted out. Why, however, did the Byzantine Church come to this point in the first place? What made these people, devout Christians after all, who were keen to honour biblical places, choose an Emmaus which palpably is the wrong site?

Stones of contention

War and peace – this was, to all intents and purposes, the pattern of Roman hegemony. By the time of Augustus, conquering wars had ended, and peace prevailed, the famous *Pax Romana*. It was a unique period in human history. Augustus claimed to have done away with the destructive exploitation of the people by the aristocracy, he had ended civil war, freed the seas and the lands from pirates and robbers – in brief, he had created a peace which was unheard of and which lasted in some of the provinces (Asia for example) into the third century. If this sounds almost too idyllic, it nonetheless sums up life at that time and how it was experienced by the population at large. Particularly in the Greek-speaking east, Augustus was venerated as a god and saviour. Temples, inscriptions and papyri document how his veneration was so widespread that it went all the way from vassal kings like Herod the Great – who built several temples for the Emperor God Augustus (those in Caesarea Maritima, Caesarea Philippi and Samaria/Sebaste have been excavated) – to four lamp-lighting employees of two temples at Oxyrhynchus in Upper Egypt who took an oath in 29 BCE in the name of 'Caesar (Augustus), God, descended from a God'.[21]

At the borders, skirmishes continued: Germany and the Balkans were notoriously restless, and the adoptive son of Augustus, his later successor Tiberius, made his mark as a military commander by settling these affairs. Varus, the provincial governor who had quelled the revolts in Galilee and Judaea after the death of Herod in 4 BCE, suffered a devastating defeat in AD 9 against Germanic tribes under a Cheruscan chieftain called Arminius in northwest Germany, at Kalkriese near the Teutoburg Forest, where he lost two legions, his cavalry and his own life. Tiberius sorted out the ensuing mess, and the Roman Empire ended its eastward expansion, establishing its (threshold) *limes* near the river Rhine, the early central European equivalent to Hadrian's Wall. Thus, the emperor under whom

Jesus was born and the emperor under whom he was crucified both created and preserved an empire which was unprecedented and survived even the ugly – if unfounded – rumours about the alleged incompetence and licentiousness of Tiberius. His successors Claudius and Nero were more adventurous – Claudius conquered the south of England in AD 43, Nero consolidated the Armenian and Britannic conquests and managed to keep unrests in Judaea under control until the devastating revolt against Roman rule began in AD 66, two years before his death. Both Claudius and Nero were much maligned, Nero for good reasons and to great and lasting effect – countless movies on the Fire of Rome and his persecution of the Christians have proved the point. Robert Graves' *I Claudius* may have similarly damaged the reputation of Claudius, but achieved this certainly with stylistic flourish and legendary success on TV.

Galba, Otho and Vitellius, the hapless emperors of the brief period from AD 68 to 69, left no lasting marks on history. It was only with Vespasian, who was acclaimed emperor by his troops in Judaea in the third year of the Jewish revolt, that things began to improve throughout the Empire. Vespasian, whose outstanding career in Europe and Judaea will concern us in Chapter 6, left the Jewish revolutionaries to his son Titus and was in Rome when Jerusalem and the Temple were destroyed in AD 70. But he took one decision which changed the course of the Emmaus legacy, and here we find an answer to our question of why and how the Byzantine Church took the wrong decision about distances and identifications, and may even have done so in good conscience.

After the destruction of Jerusalem, Emperor Vespasian built a colony (in Latin a *colonia*) for veterans of the army which had destroyed the city in AD 70. There is one almost contemporary Jewish-Roman source, the *Jewish War* of Flavius Josephus, which was published between AD 75 and 79. Josephus does not mention the exact year of the colony's foundation, but he presupposes a date soon after the revolt. Since the last remaining fortresses of the revolutionaries (of which Masada near the southern end of the Dead Sea is the most famous) were not conquered in mopping-up operations until AD 73, 73/74 is the latest plausible year for its foundation, but 70/71 may be considered more probable, as it was a colony very close to Jerusalem and may have been chosen for veterans of the particularly difficult and cruel Jerusalem campaign which had ended in AD 70. This is the short text in the *Jewish War*, 7.216–18:

> At about this time, the emperor ordered Bassus and Liberius Maximus – the latter was the procurator – in writing to lease the whole land of the Jews.[22] For the emperor did not undertake the foundation of a proper city, he rather reserved the country for himself.[23] Only to 800 discharged members of the army, he gave a settlement area which was called Emmaus and which was 30 stadia from Jerusalem.[24] Furthermore, he imposed a poll tax on the Jews, wherever they may be resident. Every year, they had to pay two drachmae to the Capitol, corresponding to the tax they had previously paid to the Temple in Jerusalem. This was the situation of the Jews in those days.

These were decisions which altered the political and demographic land-scape. The poll tax, called *fiscus Iudaicus* in Latin, reminded the Jews everywhere, not just in Judaea, of the risk involved in opposing the Romans. In Rome, the Arch of Titus gave them the visual message with its depiction of Jewish slaves and Roman soldiers carrying the spoils of the Temple, among them the Menorah, the seven-branched candelabrum. And since the new tax took the place of the old Temple tax, the Jews were forced to remember that, as far as their taxes were concerned, the victorious Jupiter of the Capitol had replaced the God of the Temple. Domitian, a son of Vespasian and emperor from 81 to 96, enforced the Capitoline tax *acerbissime*, ruthlessly, as his biographer Suetonius puts it, taxing even those who only lived like Jews but had not converted (a phenomenon which was widespread: both the New Testament and Josephus refer to such people as 'Godfearers'), and searched out those who were hiding their Jewish origins. Suetonius mentions an event he had witnessed himself: 'I remember that I was present, as a very young man, when a procurator and his numerous Group of advisers examined a 90-year-old man, if he was circumcized.'[25]

The consequences of the Judaean land distribution were equally far-reaching. As a colony of veterans, the new settlement enjoyed a number of privileges. Such colonies were given city status, and in some cases the inhabitants were exempt from taxes. The sources do not tell us if this is what happened at Emmaus/Colonia, but there is a parallel case: Caesarea Maritima, the traditional seat of the Roman prefects and prucurators of Judaea, where the apostle Paul was imprisoned for several years (Acts 23.33–27.1). Vespasian turned it into a *colonia* with the full range of city privileges. Assuming that this is also what happened at Emmaus in about AD 71, we are faced with an interesting scenario. Most scholars continue to assume that Luke's Gospel was written in the late 70s or early 80s AD, or, in other words, *after* the colonization of Emmaus. If so, his unequivocal insistence on the fact that his Emmaus was a village may have been directed at two target groups – first, at those who knew that there also was a distant city called Emmaus, and second, at those who knew that Emmaus had acquired Roman city rights when it was turned into a veterans' colony by Vespasian, some 40 years after the incident he reports.[26] In any case, the ancient name Emmaus disappeared from the records and was replaced with the Latin Colonia. As usual, some specifications would have followed, to describe what kind of *colonia* it was, and a reference to the emperor and to the veterans may be assumed. The additions have not survived. But the name Colonia still exists, in the name by which the village is known today – Qaloniyeh. It was a Jewish-Arabic village until 1948, when Israel's struggle for survival against the attacking Arab forces in the War of Independence resulted in the almost complete destruction of the village. Among our very first finds, when we started excavating in 2001, was Russian ammunition dated 1948.

The Roman colony eradicated all memory of Emmaus so successfully that the Talmud returns to the name of the area as it was known from Old Testament times – Moza. Published in the sixth century, but compiled from source material which sometimes goes back to the first century BCE, the Babylonian and the Jerusalem Talmuds are difficult to date with any precision. But they are Jewish compilations, independent of Christian influences, and this means that their references to the site were not motivated by a preference for or against a location with Christian associations. Both Talmuds mention a debate among rabbis about the exact location of Moza. One of them explains that it is now called Qaloniyeh.[27] In the Mishna, the oldest part of post-biblical Jewish tradition that precedes the Talmud, we even read that Jews from Jerusalem came to Qaloniyeh below Moza to collect branches for the huts they built during Sukkot, the Feast of the Tabernacles.[28] All these sources agree that Qaloniyeh/Keloniya (there are several different spellings and transcriptions) was at or just below ancient biblical Moza, a place first mentioned in Joshua 18.26, where several places are listed which were given to the Israelite tribe of Benjamin.

The Hebrew name is Ha-Mozah. It is not difficult to see what happened: originally pronounced Hamotzah, it soon became Hamozah (with a soft 'z' sound), the initial 'H' was dropped, and the resulting Amozah then developed to Ammozah, Amaousah and, finally, to the Greek form Ammaous, which is the spelling we find in most manuscripts of Josephus' *Jewish War*. It is in fact a spelling development which is supported by the Greek translation of the Hebrew Bible, the so-called Septuagint of the third/second centuries BCE. Here, the Hebrew Ha-Mozah of Joshua 18.26 is translated into Am(m)osa. From there it is only a short step to Ammaôus (via a vowel shift), and finally to Ammaoûs/Emmaus. And noticeably, the surviving manuscripts of Josephus, who knows of at least two other sites called Emmaus (the one of the Maccabean wars and another one near Tiberias in Galilee), are flexible enough. They have the Greek spelling with an initial 'A', Ammaous, and also Emmaous with an initial 'E', for the site near Tiberias. Josephus tells his readers that the Emmaus at the Lake of Tiberias owes its name to a warm source, from the Hebrew *hammath* (with an initial 'ch' sound as in Scottish loch).[29] According to rabbinic sources, the name of the other Emmaus, the Maccabean one, was also said to be derived from the Hebrew for warm or hot source or spring, with variant Hebrew spellings like *hammatah* and *hammatan*. No one who read Luke's Gospel would have been surprised to see the Greek form, Emmaous, in 24.13: it was obviously well-known as a variant spelling for Ammaous. This third Emmaus was never linked with a warm source, however – neither by Josephus nor by the rabbis. And indeed, as we have confirmed during our excavation, there never was a warm one among the many springs which made this area so attractive to people from the Bronze Age to New Testament times and beyond. Its name describes not the quality of one of its water sources, but its ancient Hebrew origins: those of Joshua 18.26, 'Hamozah'.

Much later, when the writings of Josephus were translated into Latin, strange things happened to the text. Suddenly, we encounter manuscripts with weird readings which contradict earlier sources and betray a pretty far-reaching ignorance of Holy Land topography. For it looks as though Masada, the Jewish fortress near the southern Dead Sea which survived the Roman siege until the winter of AD 73/74, was confused with Emmaus by a scribe, who concocted the new Latin place name 'Amassada'. Scholars have tried to work out by which route that scribe may have arrived at his fictitious place name.[30] It seems likely, though, that the Latin scribe simply committed one of the mistakes which occur frequently in ancient manuscripts, and confused Masada, the fortress which was presented by Josephus in all the gory details of the final battle against the Romans, with the village of Emmaus, which he neither knew nor could make sense of – so that in his mind and in his writing hand, a confusion occurred which is not uncommon in ancient Greek manuscripts.[31]

For us, this somewhat technical description of the sources results in the straightforward conclusions outlined above. But Josephus was not read by Jews: they regarded him as a traitor who had changed sides after his capture by Vespasian in AD 67.[32] And Christians read him selectively, using him as a quarry of quotes for their purposes. Take Eusebius of Caesarea (c.260–339), the first Christian author who spread the alleged certainty that the Emmaus of 1 and 2 Maccabees is the Emmaus of Luke 24. Eusebius, adviser and court historian to Constantine the Great, director of the famous library at Caesarea and bishop of that city, had unlimited access to the imperial libraries and archives. He knew the writings of Josephus and quoted him at length. But he did not quote the reference to Emmaus in the *Jewish War* 7.217. There is only one reasonable explanation for this striking omission: Eusebius realized that there once must have been an Emmaus close enough to Jerusalem to fit Luke's account, although it no longer existed, and he decided to ignore the evidence by simply skipping it in his writings. Once he and, soon after him, the influential Jerome had persuaded the powers-that-be to establish a bishopric at the Emmaus of their choice, at this elegant, well-equipped Romanized city, this *fait accompli* was presented to potential pilgrims. From then on, the idea to look for the ruins of a place once called Emmaus as mentioned by Josephus did not cross anyone's mind. In fact, all knowledge and tradition of a once visible site near Jerusalem was not only lost by the second century at the latest (as we saw above), but there were no attempts to 'replace' it with another site, let alone with the site of the ancient, far-away city, before Eusebius entered the stage.

We know this thanks to the testimony of two exceptional men, Sextus Iulius Africanus and the Bordeaux Pilgrim. They occupy far more than a humble place among providers of information – they offer us a fascinating glimpse into the changing realities of the Roman Empire in the third and fourth centuries.

Should one ever need ammunition in defence of the intellectual qualities of early Christian thinkers and writers, the achievements of Sextus Iulius Africanus would do nicely. Born in the late first century AD, he grew up in Aelia Capitolina, the Roman military city which Emperor Hadrian had planted on the ruins of Jerusalem after the Bar Kokhba revolt of AD 132–5. An officer in the Roman army, he retired to become a Christian philosopher and philologist. Some of his writings have survived, among them a letter to Origen about text-critical questions, fragments of a *Chronography* in five volumes, and further fragments of a 24-volume miscellany on medicine, military topics, and non-Christian religious practices called *Charmed Girdles* (in Greek, *Kestoi*). His fame as a man of letters spread far and wide, and he attracted pagan admirers in spite of his avowed Christian faith.

In c.AD 220/221, he travelled to Rome to visit Emperor Marcus Aurelius Antoninus.[33] It was an extraordinary decision, for this emperor had begun his career as the priest of the 'Invincible Sun God' Elagabalus at Emesa in Syria, had taken the godhead's name, became known as Emperor Elagabalus and decreed that this godhead was to become the official deity of the Roman Empire, surpassing even Jupiter. Emperor Elagabalus was a shady character, to put it mildly. Having divorced his wife Julia Paula, he destroyed the sanctity of one of the most ancient Roman religious traditions, the cult of the Vestal virgins, when he married one of them to celebrate a 'sacred marriage' which united him, the Sun God, with a virgin of Juno. Hostilities broke out, he was forced to divorce the Vestal virgin and marry a descendant of Marcus Aurelius. Adulterous to the last, he returned to the Vestal virgin and was murdered in AD 222. His cult was linked with orgiastic ceremonials which disgusted everyone – the senate, the nobility, and the people. So why did the ex-officer and Christian philosopher visit him? As prefect of the District of Emmaus, he led a delegation to the Emperor's court for one purpose only: the people of Emmaus desired a new name for their city. They wanted it to be called 'Nicopolis', the city of victory. Elagabalus granted them their request. Henceforth, the ancient name disappeared from the official records, and Emmaus became Nicopolis.

It is of course unthinkable that a committed Christian like Sextus Iulius Africanus, whose disgust at the Emperor's behaviour should be assumed, would have gone to Rome to get his city's name changed if he had known or believed that it was the place where Jesus broke bread with two disciples. For his action helped to erase the biblical name from the imperial documents, and this would have been somewhat counterproductive if he and his community had venerated the place as a resurrection site mentioned as Emmaus in Luke's Gospel. Needless to say, commentators have been wondering why Sextus Iulius Africanus had desired this change of names in the first place. The most plausible explanation may be found in the rampant Christian anti-Judaism of the period, and the wish to gain imperial favour in times of regional and local persecutions. At Emmaus, the Romans had defeated Jewish revolutionaries and conquered the city during the first revolt, and if Jerusalem could be renamed Aelia Capitolina by Hadrian after the second revolt, the pro-Roman inhabitants of Emmaus now wanted their piece of the anti-Jewish, pro-Roman cake – and they got it. Whatever the reason, the fact remains that a Christian philologist and philosopher actively helped to delete the biblical name. It can therefore be safely excluded that he knew of any tradition linking this city with Luke's Emmaus.

More than a century later, in AD 333, and thus at the time when Eusebius was busy propagating his choice of the wrong Emmaus, an anonymous pilgrim reached the Holy Land. Because of where he came from, he has been called the 'Bordeaux Pilgrim'. Four manuscripts of his report, one of them complete, have survived.[34] The Pilgrim travelled from France to Constantinople, the new capital city of Emperor Constantine who was in residence at the time, and left for the Holy Land on 30 May 333. A year and a half later, on 25 or 26 December 334, he returned to Constantinople. A pious pilgrim, he also was a bone-dry, uninspiring writer who saw the sole purpose of his travelogue as painstakingly detailing every single stopover he made, complete with their distances in Roman or Gallic miles.[35] In Jerusalem, he described the desolate Temple Mount and a rite of mourning Jews in loving detail, and he generally preferred Old Testament quotations to those from the New Testament. Thus, some scholars have guessed that he was a Jewish Christian who was looking as much, if not more so, for his own roots as for those of his new faith. From time to time, the Bordeaux Pilgrim displays his hazardous acquaintance with historical facts: he mentions the birthplace of Alexander the Great and the burial site of Euripides correctly, but confuses the famous Carthaginian general Hannibal with a nephew of Emperor Constantine, thinks that Jacob fought God's angel at Bethel instead of Peniel near the river Jabbok, and commits other amusing blunders which make us appreciate that he mainly prefers to stick with the things he knows about – the names and distances of the sites he visited. Eventually, he reaches Rachel's tomb, Bethlehem, the terebinth of Mamre where Abraham had met three angels, and Hebron where the patriarch was buried. Here is an unabridged excerpt from Chapter 20 of his account, typical of his style and approach:

> From the terebinth to Mamre, it is two miles. There is a four-sided stone memorial of miraculous beauty, where Abraham, Isaak, Jacob, Sarah, Rebekka and Lea are buried. Then, from Jerusalem: the city of Nicopoli 22 miles – the city of Lidda ten miles – the coaching house (*mutatio*) of Antipatrida ten miles.

The sights of Jerusalem are described elsewhere, but here, it merely serves as a vantage point for names and distances of some places on the road to the Mediterranean coast, beginning with Nicopolis and moving westwards. Having heaped enthusiastic praise on the tomb at Hebron, he mentions Nicopoli(s) literally in passing, without so much as a hint at its previous name, Emmaus, let alone at a tradition that this might have been the site where the risen Jesus revealed himself to two of his disciples. In other words: in AD 333, Eusebius and his followers had not yet managed to spread their newfangled 'tradition'. The true Emmaus was lost, but the new and wrong one was unknown, as it had been unknown in AD 220/ 221, when Sextus Iulius Africanus persuaded Emperor Elagabalus to re-name the city 'Nicopolis'. All we read in the Bordeaux Pilgrim's account is the name and the distance, 22 miles (33 kilometres) from Jerusalem, which is remarkably accurate.[36]

At this point, those who have been to Emmaus-Nicopolis and have trusted their tourist guides may want to protest in bewilderment. It all looks so convincing over there, the archaeological remains are impressive, and why should we not trust an honourable church historian like Eusebius? Eusebius has always had a bad press in circles where anyone with a leading role in the Church is automatically under suspicion of having had vested interests and hidden agendas. After all, he was close to Emperor Constantine and was Bishop of Caesarea, the city where the Roman administration of Judaea had been based since AD 6. How neutral, how objective could he be?[37] On the other hand, there has also been a conservative backlash to this prejudice: it became fashionable to think that the so-called Church Fathers, 'patristric' writers like Irenaeus, Clement of Alexandria, Origen and Eusebius, could do no wrong. Their uttterances have often been treated as authoritative sequels to the historical texts of the New Testament.

The greatness of Eusebius lies somewhere between these extremes. He was indeed one of the most brilliant minds among the Christians of his era, fluent in several languages, the efficient director of the library at Caesarea, a circumspect textual critic and analyst of sources, the biographer of his Emperor, and a man who carefully observed and chronicled the spreading of the New Testament from its origins through periods of persecution to the triumph of its endorsement by the mightiest man in the world, the Roman Emperor. But he also had his pet hates and animosities, and often devised strategies to raise his own influence and prestige.

Take the example of the shifty way he dealt with Empress Helena's journey to the Holy Land in 326 (*Church History* 3.42–7). It was a political pilgrimage, culminating in her rediscovery of Golgotha, the Empty Tomb and the remnants of the Cross of Jesus with Pilate's headboard. Eusebius describes the journey of Emperor Constantine's mother to Jerusalem, he praises her rediscovery of the Tomb and how the first Church of the Holy Sepulchre was built above the site, but he ignores her discovery of the Cross. However, later legendary accretions apart, it is a fact that Helena did find at least one cross and a headboard with an inscription. This happened when her builders removed the temple of Venus which Emperor Hadrian had built above the area just before or after the end of the Bar Kohba revolt in AD 135 (in order to prevent pilgrims from venerating the site of Christ's death and resurrection).[38] So why does Eusebius decline to even mention this discovery? Interestingly, he does not mention another point about Helena's journey either: nowhere in her itinerary from north to south is there any reference to Emmaus-Nicopolis. Helena's guides, among them Bishop Macarius of Jerusalem, had obviously no knowledge of a resurrection appearance at this particular site, and although Helena did not overlook the churches even in the smallest towns, as Eusebius puts it, Nicopolis remains a blank space. As we saw, the correct Emmaus near Jerusalem was no longer a real presence, but it had evidently not yet been 'replaced' by the site so strongly favoured by Eusebius at about that time.[39] By why this silence about the Cross? Eusebius was no simpleton. He knew that the cross played in important part in the Emperor's religious and political plan. Before the decisive battle against Maxentius at the Milvian Bridge near Rome, in 312, Constantine had seen a vision in the sky, showing him the first two Greek letters of the word 'Christ', a 'Chi' and a 'Rho', shaped like a cross, with the message 'In this sign conquer'. Eusebius reports how Constantine described to his artists what he had seen: 'The sign was formed like this: A long, guilded shaft of a lance had a crossbeam and was thus shaped in the form of a cross. At the top, there was a garland attached, made from jewels and gold, and in it was the sign of the name of the saviour – two letters, the initial letters which signify the name of Christ, with the "Rho" crossed in the middle by the "Chi".'[40] Obviously, then, Eusebius did not sidestep the visual reality of the Cross. For him, it had become the 'trophy of the empire', a symbol of unity and of triumph. However, the Cross found by Helena was not a heavenly vision, it was a physical object. And this is where Eusebius begins to play his double role.

He praises Helena for her achievements, but subtly 'forgets' to mention her discovery of the cross, because if he had done so he would have strengthened the position of the Jerusalem bishopric, which was controlled by his archrival Macarius. Caesarea, his own seat, had nothing apart from a few references in the New Testament, the magnificent harbour which Paul had used on more than one occasion, and the praetorium where he had been been imprisoned. Jerusalem, on the other hand, had everything – and now the true cross, as well? It simply was too much for the proud, vainglorious courtier and historian. He knew that others would spread the message – as indeed they did – but it was not for him to add to the glory of this rival bishopric. The church of the Holy Sepulchre was there, the tomb was there and was empty, but the wood of the true cross and the power of Jerusalem's bishop to distribute portions of this relic, or at least to see it being kissed (which indeed happened) and venerated while he looked on – all this was more than Eusebius could stomach. Wherever he could, Eusebius even refused to mention Bishop Macarius by name; he does so only when he has no choice because he is quoting directly from Constantine's correspondence. Arrogant and petulant, the Bishop of Caesarea ignores and snubs the Bishop of Jerusalem.[41] In a nutshell then, Eusebius of Caesarea was a great scholar and historian, but also a devious tactician. The way he deals with the Emmaus 'scenario' is striking, but it was clearly not an isolated case; other scholars have assembled further examples of his strategies.

What exactly does Eusebius say, then, when he mentions Emmaus for the first time? In his *Onomasticon*, a biblical gazetteer which he wrote in c.AD 337, he does not sound too happy about the city's new name and explains that this is 'Emmaus, from where Cleopas came, which now is called Nicopolis, a famous city of Palestine' (*Onomasticon* 90.15–17). It looks as though Eusebius was testing the waters. Would anyone buy his unprecedented theory? When Empress Helena came in 326, she and her entourage had not heard of it; when the Bordeaux Pilgrim arrived another seven years later, nothing was known of the Bishop of Caesarea's plans to rebrand Nicopolis as the Emmaus of Luke. In any case, he seems strangely hesitant. Although he identifies Nicopolis with the Emmaus of Luke and calls it the hometown of Cleopas, he expects his readers to conclude for themselves, from their own biblical knowledge, that it was a resurrection site. A case of a bad conscience perhaps? Did Eusebius, who knew he was about to start a new local tradition, purposely stop short of claiming, expressly, unequivocally and in his own words, that this was where his Lord Jesus Christ appeared to two disciples?[42] In any case, for almost half a century, nothing happened. Then suddenly in 390, another great man of the Byzantine church, Jerome (c.347–420), translates the *Onomasticon* into Latin and renders the passage about Emmaus verbatim. Fourteen years later, Jerome is visited by a Roman lady called Paula. He takes her on a guided tour and sends a letter about the visit to her daughter Julia Euchstochia. Coming from Yafo, they reach Nicopolis, and in his letter, written 374 years after the historical event, he is the first Christian author to identify Nicopolis not only as the Emmaus of Cleopas and Luke's Gospel, but also to call it unequivocally the site of a resurrection appearance: 'We reached Nicoplis', he writes, 'which was previously called Emmaus and where the Lord, when he was recognized in the breaking of the bread, consecrated the house of Cleopas as a church' (*Letters* 108.8).[43]

This remains a useful source for all those who believe that the early Church may have been convinced that Nicopolis and the Gospel's Emmaus were one and the same, since Jerome not only quotes Eusebius and his own Latin translation, but adds the reference to the breaking of the bread. Unfortunately, he spoils it all by adding pure fantasy – the legend that Jesus turned the house of Cleopas into a church by consecrating it. Obviously, Jesus had done no such thing. On the contrary, he had disappeared from the house the very instant the two disciples recognized him (Luke 24.30–33). To put it differently, Jerome displays the cavalier fashion with which he so often approaches biblical topography. First, he merely quotes Eusebius, and when he tries to add something new, it turns out to be nonsense. Jerome was a great philologist, perhaps the outstanding expert in Hebrew, Greek and Latin at his time, and his brilliance as a translator remains unsurpassed. He almost single-handedly shaped the Latin text of the complete Bible, making use of earlier attempts by second- and third-century predecessors, and his version, later called the Vulgate, became normative for the whole Western Church throughout the Middle Ages, with only minor changes in later editions. In 1546, after the Reformation, the Council of Trent confirmed it as the authentic text of the Bible for the Roman Catholic Church. And yet the moment Jerome tried his hand at interpreting the text and localizing people and events, the results are often, to put it mildly, more than dubious. It was, for example, Jerome who thought that the site of the famous miracle at

Gadara, where Jesus drove demons into a herd of swine (Matthew 8.28–34), should be placed at Korazim, a town so far away from the Sea of Galilee that they would have had to be flying pigs to get anywhere near the shore in a hurry.[44] As Henry Chadwick once famously put it: 'Jerome was producing the biblical scholarship, but he was no thinker.'[45]

These were great men, who helped to shape the history of the Church. Thus we can easily understand why later authors copied them uncritically. Eusebius and Jerome had a committed following. For centuries, their vote on Emmaus was copied by other authors. One or two of them even tried to add something new. A priest called Hesychius of Jerusalem, for example, who died in c.AD 452, realized that the two disciples could not possibly have arrived at the distant Emmaus when it was almost sunset, then return in the dark, covering another 32.6 kilometres, mainly uphill, and still reach Jerusalem that same evening. If he still wanted to follow Eusebius and Jerome, what could he do? Having learned from these two masters that one may re-adjust the meaning of the text to fit one's own purposes, he simply changed the meaning of the Greek words. Luke's text is precise enough: Jesus and the two disciples arrive at Emmaus, Jesus apparently intends to continue his journey, and the two invite him in, exclaiming that 'it is almost evening and the day is now nearly over' (Luke 24.28–29). In Greek, as much as in English, this plainly means that they have timed their journey – a journey well-known to them, after all – in such a way that they would arrive just in time for the customary evening meal after sunset. Hesychius, however, desperate to accommodate Eusebius and Jerome's decision, tries to explain that 'evening' begins with the seventh hour (4 p.m.), and that the disciples left Emmaus for Jerusalem at about 3 p.m. This would allow him to reckon with a return to Jerusalem by about 9 p.m., presuming a departure from Jerusalem at about 9 a.m.[46] But apart from the physical impossibilty of doing all this, 3 p.m. in April, near Jerusalem, is bright afternoon, not the beginning of the evening. Ancient as much as modern customs are confusing only to those who do not know them or who want to confuse others in turn. When the French start saying *bon soir* instead of *bon jour* after lunch, they do not thereby imply that the evening begins at 12.30 p.m., nor would they assume that saying *bon soir* and inviting someone in at 3 p.m. involves an invitation to start eating supper. Jewish people likewise did not think of beginning their evening meal at 3 p.m. But Jesus enters the house, sits down at table and, as the honoured guest, he breaks the bread, signalling the beginning of dinner. The mid-afternoon theory of Hesychius is fancy, not fact. And so we could go on. Wherever one looks, the plain indications of Luke's text are ignored, and wishful thinking is put in their place.

Rabbis and Bishops: Representing Emmaus

As tourist guides, Jerome and the others may have failed. They went to the wrong Emmaus for the wrong reasons. But this is not the end of the story, for the area of the city of Emmaus-Nicopolis deserves a detour even today. As an ancient battle site, it will attract interested tourists in any case; and the Yad la-Shiryon Museum, at the Israeli Armoured Corps Memorial on the southern side of the road (near Latrun), displays maps and reconstructions of battles from those of the Maccabees to 1948. At this strategic site, where Jerusalem as well as the coast can be easily reached, untrained Jewish units battled for the fortress which had been occupied by Arab forces in the war against the new State of Israel in May 1948. In the end, they failed to take the fortress, left it surrounded, widened the Burma Road and reached west Jerusalem just in time before it would have fallen to the Arab onslaught. The memorial and the museum serve as stark reminders of the relentless determination with which this hillock has been fought over since biblical times. Many will have seen the area and scenes from the 1948 conflict in a popular Hollywood film *Cast a Giant Shadow* (1966), with Kirk Douglas as Colonel Mickey Marcus, the hero of the Jewish struggle, whom David Ben-Gurion appointed the first official general in Israel's history since Judas Maccabaeus.[47]

Opposite Yad la-Shiryon, the remains of the Crusader fortress of La Toron have been cleaned and partially restored only recently. When I was there in 2003 to help identify the chapel, my team quickly understood what it meant to be in possession of this area. Fertile, with ample natural water supplies, and in control of access routes in four directions, this is a place well worth fighting for. The medieval name of the fortress, La Toron, and the modern name of the area, Latrun, are probably derived from an early medieval tradition which identified the place as the home of the one penitent criminal crucified with Jesus (Luke 23.40–43): in the Latin Bible, the two criminals are called *latrones*, and the good one became known as *bonus latro*. His house therefore was called the *domus boni latronis*, and it is not difficult to see how Latoron and Latrun may have followed from this Latin appellation. Today, a Trappist monastery sells homemade wine close to the site, and nearby a Christian, evangelical retreat centre, the Community of Latrun, welcomes pilgrims. With all its biblical history, it is a Jewish and Christian area which is relevant to present times.

Back on the other, northern side of the A1 motorway, the Ayalon Park (sometimes also called Canada Park), a popular recreational area, encompasses most of the archaeological discoveries from the Roman period. The name reminds visitors of another famous biblical battle site which can be seen in the distance, three kilometres to the east: Saul defeated the Philistines at Ayalon (1 Sam. 14.31), where Joshua once had commanded the moon to stand still, on the day of the final battle against the Amorites (Josh. 10.12). The visible remains, spread over an area of 1,000 by 500 metres, recall the splendours of the city from the times of the Maccabees – represented by a vast, elaborate burial chamber, and the ruins of an administrative centre destroyed by the Romans (probably in AD 70, when the fifth legion was stationed here and left several inscriptions) – to the remains of the Romanized establishment, with two beautiful pyramid-shaped tombs and a system of aqueducts which was enlarged on several occasions to serve the growing city of Nicopolis. Recently, traces of a *nymphaeum* were discovered: a pagan shrine over a source, dedicated to the nymphs, the guardian spirits of sources of pure water.[48] Just outside Ayalon Park, a well-preserved Roman bath is hidden behind Muslim tombs. Built in its present form in c.AD 221, when Emmaus had become Nicopolis, it was partly destroyed during an earthquake in 498, rebuilt, and later used as a storehouse for wine and oil. In the thirteenth century, Muslims turned it into a shrine for Abu Ubaida, the legendary conquerer of Byzantine Palestine who had died during the plague which devastated Emmaus in 639.

The Crusaders, who had built the fortress of La Toron on the southern side of the road, built another one over here, Castellum Arnaldi, so as to better control the northern regions and the alternative access route to Jerusalem via Mount Joy (today's Muslim shrine of Nebi Samuil). A few walls remain, powerful enough to kindle memories of Richard the

Lionheart who led the Third Crusade in 1191–2, and began his march on Jerusalem from this fortress. He never entered Jerusalem: the Muslim defenders forced him to stop at the tomb of the prophet Samuel, Nebi Samuil in Arabic, which the Crusaders called Montjoie or Mount of Joy, as it offered them a clear view of the Old Town with its splendid walls. Modern visitors, who can still walk that route from Castellum Arnaldi to the Mount of Joy, will however be disappointed: the tomb is still there, inside a mosque, but the view is obstructed by the modern high-rise buildings of the suburb of Har Khotsvim. To summarize, strolling through Ayalon Park and its environs is like a holiday in history, from the Maccabees to the Crusaders.

And as if this were not enough, there is the Christian site of Emmaus-Nicopolis, built and enlarged in the period from the fifth century to the victorious arrival of Abu Ubaida and his Muslim forces in c.AD 637. Looked after by the French-speaking Communauté des Béatitudes, it is generally open to the public. Impressive ruins of a fifth-century Byzantine church remain, curiously altered by a Crusader church built into the central of its three apses during the twelfth century. Ever since Joseph-Bernard Guillemot conducted the first proper survey of these ruins in 1879, archaeologists have been digging in this compound. Two giants of early biblical archaeology, Louis-Hugues Vincent and Frédéric-Marie Abel, Dominicans from the Ecole Biblique et Archéologique in Jerusalem, excavated the site from 1924 to 1932, and published a book which has remained the benchmark for all future research.[49] Since 1993, renewed efforts by an international team, under the Finnish pastor Eero Junkaala from Helsinki and the archaeologist Mikko Louhivuori from Jerusalem, have resulted in a number of impressive finds.[50] A tomb was discovered with the skeleton of a third- or fourth-century lady who had been buried with three perfume bottles and golden earrings – neither Jewish nor Christian, but evidence for the wealth of the multicultural Roman city of Nicopolis before it was turned into the Byzantine bishopric of Emmaus. Mosaics were found, some of them with geometrical designs, and again of a remarkable quality and value.

Further away, unrelated to the Christian area and outside the ancient city's perimeter, two tombs were excavated – unfortunately, grave robbers had visited the area first. One of them was dated to the Herodian period, the other to the late Roman era. The Herodian tomb is definitely Jewish, a family tomb for six people; it was hewn into the rock, and has an opening which could be closed with a stone plate or a rolling stone. Although it was an ordinary tomb, it is well worth a visit (much more so than either the hideous kiosk which covers the invisible remains of the authentic tomb of Jesus in the Church of the Holy Sepulchre, or the scant remains of the so-called 'Tomb of Joseph of Arimathea' a few yards behind it). The Herodian tomb, discovered in 2000, may remind us of Jewish burials in New Testament times. In fact, even to visitors who may have preferred the Garden Tomb in Jerusalem to the Church of the Holy Sepulchre, this tomb at Emmaus-Nicopolis is a further improvement. The Garden Tomb is dated to the seventh century BCE, but this newly discovered burial site is roughly contemporary to the lifetime of Jesus. The discovery corroborates an earlier find of an ossuary from a tomb which apparently no longer exists (displayed in the garden of the Trappist Monastery of Latrun). Pious Jews used to rebury the bones of the dead, once the flesh had decayed, in such stone boxes, to prepare for the physical resurrection in the last days, according to the prophecy of Ezekiel (Ezekiel 37.7–14). Hundreds of them have been found in and near Jerusalem, among them the ossuary of the High Priest Caiaphas and that of a crucified man called Yehonan Ben Hazkul, but they are extremely rare at such a distance from the city of the Temple.[51]

Jews obviously lived here in Roman times, and although the tomb cannot be dated precisely, a coin minted by the Jewish vassal king Agrippa I (AD 41–4) found nearby may confirm the presence of pro-Roman Jews who enjoyed the privileges of city life before the Jewish revolt of AD 66–73. It is a conclusion which would justify the painstaking accuracy of Luke in his Gospel. Luke knew that there were two places called Emmaus where Jews lived at the time of Jesus – one was the distant city, where these discoveries have been made, and the other was the village near Jerusalem, where Jesus revealed himself to Cleopas and his companion.

One aspect of the archaeology and literary track record of Emmaus-Nicopolis remains puzzling, though. The Christian buildings belong to the fifth and sixth centuries, with some of the traces as late as the early seventh century. Nothing has been found which can be dated to the

National Gallery, London, UK. Out of copyright, courtesy of the Bridgeman Art Library.

The Supper at Emmaus, 1601 (oil and tempera on canvas) by Michelangelo Merisi da Caravaggio (1571–1610).

A mural at the Crusaders' 'Emmaus', Abu Gosh/Qiryat Yearim, recently restored, with a crucifixion scene, the 'ecclesia' – the Church.

The 'synagoga' – Jewry – at the cross; and a detail showing the 'Synagoga' held by an angel.

Partial Roman vault. Stone found in Square B, in the third layer of stone collapse from the Crusader building, bearing the inscription \LVI/.

A 'decanter' of the period before AD 70, documenting the quality of life at Emmaus; a new find from this season. The decanter was found under the aqueduct in Square D.

A 'terra sigillata' fragment with potter's mark and the Hebrew name 'Sh'ma', written in the handwriting of the Late Second Temple Period (i.e. the Emmaus period), before AD 70.

The 'Maltese Cross' wall tile with the oldest eight-pointed cross of the Hospitallers ever found anywhere in the world, discovered in our Area A in 2001 and datable to (roughly) between 1125 and 1150 as discussed in Chapters 6 and 7.

The fragment of a 'Klall', a 'stone water jar for the Jewish rites of purification' (cf. John 2.6) – one of the conclusive finds which prove this was a Jewish settlement before AD 70 (when Vespasian's colony was put in its place and the tradition of 'klall' usage ended in Israel).

Beginning the excavation, Summer 2001.

The Hill Colonia.

A coin of Justinian I (AD 527–565), mentioned as proof of a Byzantine settlement – Carsten Thiede found it during our 2001 season. Used with kind permission of the Israel Antiquities Authority, Jerusalem.

fourth century, let alone to the third decade of that century (when Eusebius started his campaign). But on the other hand, we do have a list of bishops who attended the first official council of the Christian Church under Emperor Constantine, which took place in AD 325 in the Phrygian city of Nicea. And on this list we find more than 200 bishops, among them 19 from the Roman province of Palestine. One of them is Peter (Petrus Longinus), Bishop of Nicopolis.[52] Could it be that Eusebius chose to improve the status of the bishopric of Nicopolis by inventing the link with Luke's Emmaus? Unlike Jerusalem, where Bishop Macarius and Helena's discovery of the True Cross were seen as a threat to his own privileges, Nicopolis was harmless, and by 'identifying' it with the Emmaus of Luke, Eusebius could elegantly outplay the rivals in Jerusalem: they might possess the Cross and the Titulus, but Nicopolis, which belongs to Eusebius' metropolitan district, had a resurrection site. Since Eusebius preferred the theology of the Resurrection to the theology of the Cross anyway, this would have come in handy.

Peter of Nicopolis and his successors probably lived in humble circumstances, perhaps still using the traditional house churches, meeting places in private homes. The first proper church building was not built for another 80 years after the Council of Nicea. It seems that Eusebius and Jerome's advocacy of Emmaus-Nicopolis as a resurrection site failed to convince those people at the time who were willing to invest in majestic buildings. And for Emperor Constantine, the building programme his mother Helena had initiated and supervised in AD 326 was sufficient: a church in Bethlehem to commemorate the birth of Jesus, a church at Golgotha to commemorate his crucifixion and resurrection, and a church on the Mount of Olives for the ascension. A second resurrection church would have had to be based on solid evidence, as provided by the unbroken local tradition and archaelogical finds at Golgotha and the Empty Tomb in the emperor's eyes, and such evidence was not forthcoming at Emmaus-Nicopolis.

Bishops came and went. It seems that all of them, beginning with Peter Longinus, were gentile Christians. The Jewish heritage of the city was not represented in the choice of bishops, and as far as we can see the once thriving Jewish community had all but disappeared by the early fourth century. This is all the more surprising because the rabbis had cherished

Emmaus. It occurs frequently in their writings, and one of the most famous among them, Rabbi Akiva – who had proclaimed the revolutionary Simon Bar Kokhba as the true Messiah – seems to have lived there during the revolt of 132–4.[53] At the turn of the second and third centuries, just before the arrival of Sextus Iulianus Africanus in the city, Rabbi Jacob ben Korshai of Emmaus gave instructions on trading at the market of Emmaus: 'The merchant shall not embellish what he wants to sell, neither a slave, nor a piece of cattle, nor tools, and one shall not say to the slave: "Paint yourself".' We may gather from this dictum that there were Jewish salesmen at Emmaus who sold slaves, and this in turn implies that they participated in a multicultural city life where not everything that was orthodox and kosher was practised by every Jew.[54] The last of the rabbis linked with Emmaus whom we can trace in the sources is Rabbi Akha. He seems to have lived in the early fourth century, before or at the time when the city became a bishopric. Interestingly, the Jewish texts never call Emmaus by its new name Nicopolis; Jews may have refused to do so because the name had been changed through the intervention of a Christian, Sextus Julius Africanus.

In any case, the rabbis disappear from the sources, and the only non-pagan, non-Gentile Christian group to carry on living under the bishops was the Samaritans. The Jews did not recognize them as Jewish, but they were favoured by Jesus in several of his parables, and early gentile Christians appreciated their presence. In the context of increasing anti-Jewish tendencies in the Eastern Church, Samaritans played a useful role: they were the good ones. It is a development which should sadden, but not surprise us: ever since Bishop Melito of Sardes introduced the teaching that the Jews who killed Jesus had murdered God,[55] the Church was moving towards a hatred of the Jews which it has all too often failed to call a sin and a crime.

Searching with the Crusaders

Then as now, three centuries is a long time. Bearing in mind the average life expectancy of people in late antiquity, we are talking about six to eight generations. Eusebius, Jerome and their followers had achieved their objective. Emmaus-Nicopolis had become the one and only Emmaus of

Luke 24.13, and everyone happily believed in the new tradition, at least until the Muslim invaders under Abu Ubaida arrived at the scene in AD 637 and expelled the Christians. But by then, the Emmaus equation had been firmly entrenched in their minds, even though they no longer had access to the site. Sozomen of Constantinople, who published a *Church History* in 450, embellished the stories of his predecessors and told the legend of a miraculous water source at Nicopolis, where Jesus had washed his feet. This was a welcome addition to the panoply of early Christian novelties which were meant to fill the gaps left by the all-too-sober, all-too-historical Gospel accounts. Other authors took it up, and the medieval Church never looked back. Eventually, Christian pilgrims were allowed access to their holy sites. In 723, Willibald of Eichstaett reached Emmaus-Nicopolis, now called Amwas in Arabic, saw the unused church still intact, quoted the story of the miraculous source and thought that the church had been built above the house of Cleopas. It was a hollow glory, and by 1009 the church had disappeared: the mad Fatimid caliph of Egypt, al-Hakim bi-Amr Allah, had ordered Yaruk, the Governor of Ramla, to destroy all Christian sites. Beginning with the Church of the Holy Sepulchre (called the Church of the Resurrection in the accounts of the demolition), Yaruk, his son and their men plundered, burnt down and demolished up to 30,000 churches in the territories under Fatimid rule. The church at Emmaus-Nicopolis was one of these.

This Muslim barbarism, along with other acts of suppression which followed them, eventually gave rise to the desperate pleas for help which reached the Western Church, and they were the major cause for the First Crusade of 1099. It may be true that later Crusades were feudal campaigns about fiefdoms in the Holy Land, about riches to be gained and the outdoing of rivals like the Eastern Church with its centre at Byzantium but the First had different aims. Saving the Christian sites and guaranteeing free access to them was paramount. Solid economical interests eventually persuaded European rulers to support the enterprise – the merchants at the Mediterranean ports were seeking protection and expansion – and Pope Urban II wanted to help the Byzantine Christians in their struggle against the Turkish Seljuks – not quite unselfishly, as he hoped to achieve the goal of reunification of all Christian churches under the supremacy of Rome. Modern historiography tends to emphasize the wanton savagery which accompanied the conquest of Jerusalem on 15 July 1099, as though this were unusual in medieval warfare; but for many of the knights who volunteered for the First Crusade, the thought of standing at the Tomb of Christ (which Caliph al-Hakim had in fact almost completely destroyed) was a decisive motive for undertaking the journey and risking their lives.

One group of Crusaders soon formed a new knightly order which became known as the Hospitallers, a byname derived from the hospitals and hospices they built to look after the wounded and sick on both sides. The Pope gave them statutes, and as the Knightly Order of the Hospital of St John at Jerualem, they established the only medieval order which has survived to the present day, as the (Roman Catholic) Sovereign Military Order of Malta – the Maltese Knights, and the (Protestant) Most Venerable Order of the Hospital of St John in Jerusalem, the Knights of St John (whose St John Ambulance is an everday sight in modern Britain). In the early twelfth century, they introduced the eight-pointed cross, often known today as the Maltese Cross, which has been interpreted as a symbol of the eight beatitudes in Jesus' Sermon on the Mount. Symbolisms apart, these knights began to build churches, hospices and hospitals in Jerusalem and throughout Galilee, Samaria and Judaea, protecting them with fortifications, castles and fortresses. Both castles near Emmaus-Nicopolis, La Toron and Castellum Arnaldi, were part of this elaborate building programme.

When these Crusaders arrived at the ruins of Amwas-Nicopolis, on 5 June 1099, they immediately realized its strategic importance, and recognized it as a former place of Christian worship. Building their own church into the central apse of the ruins, they may have been aware of the widespread legend that this was the place where Jesus had entered the house of Cleopas. But they came with their own Latin Bibles, and the Latin versions had withstood all attempts to change Luke's distance of 60 stadia to 160. Jerome, with all his influence over the Latin text, had apparently not dared to alter the manuscripts, as some of the Greek scribes had done before him. Was this a kind of precautionary measure, or just one of the cases where Jerome the textual critic realized the quality of the correct manuscript tradition and preserved it in his Latin version, whereas Jerome the unreliable topographer sided with Eusebius and opted for a city 176 stadia from Jerusalem? We will probably never know, but it certainly underlines the deep insecurity felt by a scholar who, despite the evidence from his manuscripts, felt drawn towards an identification imposed by the Bishop of Caesarea, because it appeared so attractive among the sumptuous Roman buildings of the city of Nicopolis. The Crusaders, however, not only knew their Bible; as experienced travellers, they also realized that the distance from Amwas-Nicopolis to Jerusalem ruled out the popular identification straightaway. Unlike the bishops, who preferred to stay within their immediate spheres of influence and who, if they went to Jerusalem at all, would not have dreamt of testing the possibility of doing the ten-hour walk there and back, the Crusader knights would have had to make such return journey regularly as a matter of military necessity, sometimes on horseback, sometimes on foot, and so realized that it could not be done in the time presupposed by Luke's account. Thus, they had two good reasons to rule out Nicopolis. But what could they do? As far as they had been told, there was no alternative site still known as Emmaus which was closer to Jerusalem. So they soon began to look for a candidate themselves.

First of all, they looked at the alternative routes leading to and from Jerusalem. There were, as we have seen, two approaches from the west: the more northerly one, which would have led them via the Tomb of the Prophet Samuel and from there to the city, and one from due west, a straight route which climbed up towards Jerusalem just beyond Moza-Qaloniyeh (the true but then unknown Emmaus), on a stretch which is still called in Hebrew the Ma'ale Roma'im, the 'Ascent of the Romans'. It was, as the name betrays, the ancient Roman road between the Mediterranean and Jerusalem. This Roman and indeed pre-Roman road linked the port of Yafo (called Joppa or Jaffa in many Bible translations) via Lydda (near Lod, today the site of Tel Aviv airport) with Emmaus-Nicopolis. Immediately to the east, 'it climbs a series of abrupt hills, next it ascends the precipitous western escarpment, descends to Abu Gosh, makes the sharp climb to Qastel Hill, following which it has to cross the steepest ravine of the region, Nahal Soreq, before making the final ascent to Jerusalem.'[56] Anyone driving by car from the Tel Aviv airport to Jerusalem these days, using the A1 motorway which partly follows the ancient road, will still sense the steep climbs and descents which are of course even more noticeable to walkers. This is the road travelled by the Bordeaux Pilgrim who, as we saw above, gives the distance as 22 miles (33 kilometres).

The alternative northern road from Emmaus-Nicopolis to Jerusalem, via the ascent of Bet Horon and the Tomb of Samuel, was less difficult to negotiate, but much longer – 18–19 kilometres from Emmaus to Bet Horon, and another 19 kilometres to Jerusalem. In walking time, they both pretty much amount to the same, roughly five hours (with an added 'bonus' for walking in darkness), as I have found out by walking both roads fast, on more than one occasion. Thus, the Crusaders had the choice of two roads, and we know that the northern road was known to them, since they built a magnificent fortress on the hillock of Samuel's Tomb, their Mount of Joy (which was only recently excavated and is worth a detour in its own right). But in their search for Emmaus, they obviously preferred the central west–east approach.

What they were looking for was simple: it had to be a location close enough to Jerusalem to accomodate Luke's specification of 60 stadia. It had to be at a site which was inhabited in the early first century; and, given the ancient traditions which linked Emmaus with the place of a source, such a source should be evident as well. Walking the road to Jerusalem and checking the sites on the way, they did not have to look for long. They found the hill of Qiryat Yearim, called Qiryat el-Anab in Arabic, where the Ark of the Covenant had rested for 20 years before David took it to Jerusalem (1 Sam. 6.19–7.4; English translations tend to spell it Kiriath-Jearim). Today, there is a convent with the church of Notre Dame de l'Arche de l'Alliance on the site, displaying a late fourth-century Byzantine mosaic. Immediately below this biblical hill, they found a Muslim *karawanserei* at a major source, with several wells in the vicinity. The Abassids had built it in the early ninth century, when Christian pilgrims came in growing numbers (thanks to an agreement between Charlemagne and Caliph Haroun al-Rashid), and needed a place of refreshment on their way to Jerusalem. It may have been one of the fleeting periods in the history of the Holy Land when Muslim travellers and Christian pilgrims rested at the same guesthouse.

The Hospitallers even found a few remains of a first-century Roman presence: an officer's sarcophagus, and an inscription of a contingent belonging to the Tenth Roman Legion 'Fretensis', which helped to conquer Qumran in AD 68 and Jerusalem in AD 70. The stone slab can still be seen, now encased in a wall near the main entrance to the Crusader church.[57] What the Hospitallers did not know was the date of these finds: the Tenth Legion put up quarters at the site only after the destruction of Jerusalem, and stayed here for two centuries: the latest Roman coins found *in situ* are dated 251, the last year of Emperor Decius' reign. At that time, the *vexillatio* was despatched to Elat at the Red Sea. In a way, this is a parallel to what happened at Colonia-Emmaus, when Vespasian established a veterans' colony in AD 71. A vexillatio was no colony, however, but technically speaking a special detachment with a specific task. Here at Qiryat Yearim, this was to protect the main route between Jerusalem and the Mediterranean. The Romans were in fact the first to tap the main water source systematically, and they constructed two water reservoirs for their soldiers. The central one has survived to the present day, and can still be seen under the crypt of the Hospitallers' church.

Two problems with this site apparently did not bother the Crusader knights. First, they did not find a single trace of pre-Roman Jewish life near the road or the water sources: the Israelites had preferred to stay in the hillcountry, as did the Byzantine Christians, who arrived after the departure of the Romans, built a church up there (to commemorate the Ark of the Covenant), and called the area Kariathiarim, which simply was the Greek form of Qiryat Yearim in the Septuagint, their Greek Bible. And second, the place was never, at any stage in the history before the arrival of the Crusaders, known by the name of Emmaus. Both facts should have ruled out their identification straightaway, but they either did not know about them, or ignored them, happy to have found a Roman site with an Arab *karawanserei* and biblical history nearby, at a realistic distance from Jerusalem.[58] But even so, like Emmaus-Nicopolis, it was a holy site of Christendom; many pilgrims came here to venerate the place where, or so they thought, Jesus had appeared to Cleopas and the unnamed other disciple.

In 1141, the Hospitallers bought the area, which until then they had merely used as a site on which to build a hospice and a hospital with a small chapel. Raimond du Puy, the first Master of the Order after the death of Gerard in 1120, signed a treaty with Robert de St Gilles, the

Crusader knight who 'owned' the territory. They called it 'terra de Emmaus' in the document, which was signed and sealed in the presence of the King and Queen of Jerusalem. Even the Patriarch of Jerusalem was present at the ceremony, and thus the church of Jerusalem gave its blessing to the Hospitallers' activities.[59] They immediately began to build a church over the spring and cistern. Apart from the Church of St Anna in Jerusalem, it is the most magnificent Romanesque church in the Holy Land. Forced to leave the Holy Land after the defeat at the Horns of Hattin in 1187, they may have returned between 1229–44, after the treaty between Emperor Frederic II and Sultan Melek al-Kamil that gave the Christians the territories of Jerusalem, Bethlehem, Nazareth and Acre. The victorious Saracens finally turned the church into stables for their *karawanserei* and built a mosque next door. And although the beautiful frescoes were damaged and partly destroyed by the acid evaporations of the animals, this secondary use of the building guaranteed its survival. Today, the compound is a Benedictine monastery, and the town is called Abu Gosh, after a nineteenth-century 'Robin Hood' who levied tributes on wealthy travellers (with the permission of the Ottoman rulers who did not feel threatened by his antics).

Visitors, who are always welcome to attend the daily sung services, will enjoy the breathtaking acoustics, and especially the unique, fragmentary frescoes which have only recently been restored. When they were presented to the public in April 2001, one of the frescoes stood out with a mould-breaking theological message. These Hospitallers probably arrived with the same anti-Jewish interpretation of the New Testament which was *de rigueur* in medieval Europe. One of the archetypes of this thinking, seen frequently in medieval art, was the confrontation between 'Church' and 'Synagogue', usually represented by two women. One of them, the 'Church', is depicted as triumphant at the side of Jesus, while the other, 'Synagogue', is lonely, expelled from his company, with lowered head, a broken staff, and often blindfolded or driven away by an angel: this is the image that dominated the decades before the First Crusade, and remained the prevailing imagery in illuminated manuscripts, stained glass windows, ivory panels and sculptures for many centuries. The Crusades were accompanied by anti-Jewish excesses all over Europe. But this was not always so. At the beginning of the First

Crusade, Emperor Henry IV called on his knights to protect the Jews. It did not really change the general situation, and yet, some of those devout Christian knights who soon after their arrival in the Holy Land formed the Order of the Hospitallers to help the sick and injured among the local population as much as the pilgrims and fellow knights, may have become critically pensive. When they commissioned the master artists who painted the frescoes, they altered the usual message: there is still the woman representing the Church, the *ecclesia*, who is led towards the crucified Christ by an angel, and there is the woman representing the Jews, identified in Latin as *synagoga*. Synagogue still has the customary broken staff, she has turned away from the cross, as though she thinks she has to go – but her head is turned backwards, towards the cross, and the expression on her face is of a moving, heartbreaking sadness. Behind her, there is the traditional angel. But the angel is not driving her away. With tender kindness, he has his hands on her shoulder, with the fingers of the left hand touching her gently: stay, the angel indicates, do not go away. There is a place for you under the cross of Jesus.

The Hospitallers' artist was able to convey the unmanipulated theology of the Apostle Paul. Paul, himself a Jew from the tribe of Benjamin, and also a Pharisee, had written about his fellow Jews who had refused to accept Jesus as their Messiah, and had described the 'hardening which has come upon a part of Israel until the full number of the Gentiles has come in' (Romans 11.25). And he had added: 'And so all Israel will be saved, as it is written.' While pogrom after pogrom brutalized Christian Europe, the Hospitallers understood Paul's teaching and enshrined it in one of the most remarkable works of art of the Middle Ages. In fact, the artist adds another element from Paul's teaching: as 'Synagogue', who is not blindfolded, turns her head backwards, to look at the cross, one is reminded of a sentence in 2 Corinthians 3.15–16, 'Indeed, to this very day, whenever Moses is read, a veil lies over their [the Jews'] minds; but when one turns to the Lord, the veil is removed.' The Hospitallers chose the wrong Emmaus, but they left us a fresco which retains a message rarely understood in those days, and all-too-often neglected in the anti-Jewish history of Christendom.

The Hospitallers were a group of independently minded knights. Under Gerardus (Gerard), the rector of a hospital in Jerusalem which was already in existence when the Crusaders reached Jerusalem – it had in fact existed since the days of Charlemagne, when the Abassid Caliph Haroun al-Rashid and the Emperor had agreed to cooperate rather than fight each other – they formed a community which was recognized by Pope Paschalis II with the bull *Pie postulatio voluntatis* on the 15th February 1113. Having established their first hospital by enlarging Gerard's building in the quarter of the Old Town (which today is known by its Persian name *muristan*, 'hospital'), they took the name of the patron saint of the fifth-century church next door, John the Baptist, and became formally known as the Order of the Knights of the Hospital of St John at Jerusalem. Six years later, Pope Callistus II confirmed their privileges with another bull, *Ad hoc nos*. Finally, in 1135 Pope Innocent II officially confirmed what these Knights had been assuming anyway: they were now formally outside episcopal jurisdiction. From time to time, it seems this independence annoyed the ecclesiastical leaders in the region. A trace of these inner conflicts has survived: in 1180, Willam of Tyre, Chancellor of the Kingdom of Jerusalem and since 1175 Archbishop of Tyre, wrote a history of the First Crusade and its aftermath. It is full of source material and eyewitness accounts. But when he talks about Nicopolis, he cannot help following the line of the earlier medieval tradition. Forty years after the establishment of the Hospitallers' 'Emmaus' at Qiryat Yearim, with its Latin name Castellum Emmaus, he still maintains that Nicopolis was Luke's Emmaus.[60] It is however obvious that the bishop is merely defending the earlier tradition, and never researched the matter himself: he quotes Luke 24.13 correctly by giving the distance of 60 stadia but must have known, as a man of the region, that Nicopolis was not 60 stadia from Jerusalem by any stretch of the imagination. And he quotes Sozomen of Constantinople with the remark that the Romans called Emmaus Nicopolis after the destruction of Jerusalem and their victory over the Jews, which is nonsense, as we know. Two wrongs do not make a right; William's apologetic propaganda exercise is easy to discount.

William's misguided defence of Nicopolis appears all the more strange because one of the participants of the First Crusade had been the first to reappraise the position of Emmaus half a century earlier. Fulcher of Chartres, who was a chaplain to the Crusaders and became chaplain to Balduin I, the King of Jerusalem, witnessed the march from the coast via Ramla to Jerusalem. In his *Historia Hierosolymitana* ('History of Jerusalem'), which he wrote in 1127/28, he describes how the Crusaders left Ramla and reached a village 'which was called Emmaus and which was near Modin, the city of the Maccabeans'.[61] In those days, the Maccabean city of Modi'in was (wrongly) placed near Tzuba, where the Crusaders eventually built a castle called Belmont, 'beautiful hill', which has been excavated and can be visited by walking up the hill from the modern Kibbutz Tzuba. Belmont/'Modi'in' is halfway between Qiryat Yearim/Abu Gosh and Moza-Qaloniyeh. Thus, if we do not want to assume that Fulcher of Chartres knew where the true Emmaus was to be located (at Moza-Qaloniyeh), he was obviously referring to the new site chosen by the Hospitallers, their Castellum Emmaus below the hill of Qiryat Yearim. In other words, by 1128, only 29 years after the arrival of the Crusaders, their choice of a site for Luke's Emmaus was known to a contemporary observer, and it became accepted by most. (It is the description of the site near Modi'in which is decisive, not the name Castellum Emmaus, which was merely the name which the Crusaders found in the Latin version of Luke 24.13.)

Thirteen years later, in 1141, the Hospitallers' Emmaus is documented in the treaty mentioned above, as the 'terra de Emmaus' with its farm-steads and agricultural produce. The Hospitallers agreed to provide the Canons of the Holy Sepulchre in Jerusalem with wheat, oil, chickpeas and other items, and the amount they agreed to deliver was 'half of the tithe'.[62] It was a generous agreement, since Christians in Jerusalem had no agri-cultural land of their own, whereas the area of Castellum Emmaus was wealthy and produced much more than the Knights needed. By 1172, eight years before William of Tyre tried in vain to turn back the clock, Theoderic of Wuerzburg described the state of affairs as it was then: near the hill country of Modin, 'which is called Belmont, there is Castellum Emmaus which the people of today [*moderni* in the Latin original] call Fontenoid. This is where the Lord appeared to the two disciples in the day of His Resurrection.'[63] Fontenoid, an alternative name for the Hospital-lers' site – most of them had originally come from French-speaking Europe – translates as 'place of the source'. The source of Emmaus, *fons Emmaus*, one of the reasons for the Hospitallers' decision to locate their Emmaus below Qiryat Yearim, is mentioned in a report about the Third

Crusade by Vinisauf, an aide-de-camp of Richard the Lionheart. Here, 'the Turks' had set up camp, but on 12 June 1192 Richard defeated them, killing 20 of the enemy singlehandedly.[64] In other words, by the end of the twelfth century, the new Emmaus, of the Hospitallers' choosing, was firmly established in the records. In 1210, even the bishops, or at least one of them, were in agreement. Bishop Jacob of Acre listed a number of holy sites and mentioned 'Castellum Emmaus, 60 stadia from Jerusalem near which there are Modin and Gabaon [as we know, 86 would have been correct; but Jacob, like the Hospitallers before him, placed it within what he thought was an acceptable range of tolerance to Luke's 60].' Thus, he agrees with Fulcher of Chartres and Theodoric of Wuerzburg and applies his bishop's seal, as it were, to the Crusaders' conclusion that Qiryat Yearim/Fontenoid/Castellum Emmaus is Luke's Emmaus.[65] It was an identification which persisted until 1291, when the Crusaders' lost Acre, the last of their fortifications, to the Mamelukes and left the Holy Land for good.

A rescue operation: The Franciscan circle

No one knows why, but by the sixteenth century, the Muslims appear to have left Qiryat el-Anab, as they called it, and Christian pilgrims returned to visit the area. They no longer regarded it as Emmaus, for the Franciscans had changed the tradition in the meantime, and bowdlerized an Arabic name. As a result of the mulberry trees which grew near the source, the name Ain el-Tut, 'Source of the mulberries', had come into use, and the pilgrims turned this into 'Anatot', the birthplace of the prophet Jeremiah (Jer. 1.1; the real site is to be found northeast of Jerusalem). In 1573, Boniface of Ragusa published his guidebook to the Holy Land, *De perenni cultu Terrae sanctae*, with a prayer to be said at the cenotaph of Jeremiah. And funnily enough, the name of St Jeremiah remained associated with the place until the mid twentieth century. In 1957, the French Consulate in Jerusalem and the French Foreign Office referred to it by this name in documents about Abu Gosh.[66]

By then, of course, Luke's Emmaus had been relocated once more. After the final departure of the Hospitallers in 1291, 'Emmaus' was no longer accessible, and when the Franciscans were entrusted with the Custody of the Holy Land (the *Custodia Terrae Sanctae*) by Pope Clement VI in his bull *Gratias agimus* of 21 November 1342, with the Muslim authorities conceding to them permission to look after holy sites, there was a new Christian Order to take charge. Trying to establish their own Emmaus, they realized that the old Byzantine site at Nicopolis was no alternative, as the distance was wrong. They took a pair of compasses and drew a circle with a radius of 60 stadia around Jerusalem. And perhaps to their surprise, they realized that there was a place near that perimeter, at 65 stadia, where canons of the Church of the Holy Sepulchre had established an outpost in the twelfth century: Parva Mahumeria, Latin for 'little Mohammed[an] site'.

The Crusaders had been there before, using it as one of their posts on the access routes to Jerusalem.[67] No one had identified it with Emmaus, and for a reason. Regardless of whether one calls it Parva Mahumeria, or by its Mameluke name of El-Qubeibe ('little cupola'), it simply never was called Emmaus in first-century records, nor at any time before or after the period of Luke's account. But the Franciscans saw the (almost) fitting distance; they saw the Roman road and what they thought were Roman remains; they could not think of any other site on their perimeter, and so they made it their Emmaus. In 1485, a Franciscan custodian of the Holy Land, Francesco Suriano (1450–c.1530), provided the first surviving account which refers to the place as Castellum Emmaus.[68] Remains of a Romanesque church were found and reincorporated into a new church in 1901. The Franciscan archaeologist Bellarmino Bagatti, who dug at the site from 1940–44, believed that some further traces which he found actually belonged to a building of Roman times, and thought that the oldest walls were those of the house of Cleopas.[69] It was a classic case of wishful thinking. So far, and in spite of repeated efforts, no early Roman traces have been discovered, and above all, not a single Jewish object, let alone one that could be dated to the Herodian or Late Second Temple period, the time of the Emmaus disciples.[70] Even so, El Qubeibe has remained a remarkable place of Christian worship, not least in these turbulent days: the only one of the traditional contenders for the true location which now is in the territory of the Palestinian Autonomy, it is difficult to reach in spite of being within easy walking distance from Nebi Samuel and the real Emmaus at Moza-Qaloniye, lying as it does beyond Israeli checkpoints and within the sights of Palestinian Arab gunmen on the other side of the border.[71] It deserves a visit not least because of the courageous presence of the nurses at the old people's and nursing home of Beit Emmaus, and for the view across biblical landscapes towards Jerusalem.

From time to time, other locations for Emmaus have been suggested, but they lie well and truly in the realm of fiction. Artas near the so-called Pools of Solomon south of Bethlehem; Beit Ulma, one kilometre north of Colonia-Emmaus; el-Hamman near er-Ram, ten kilometres north of Jerusalem; Hamassah (Khirbet Ain el-Kinseh) southwest of Bethlehem; and Nakkuba, one kilometre north of Abu Gosh. All have found someone who thought that the name or the presence of a warm source or some other reason might look convincing. But they do not. None of them was called Emmaus in the first century, none of them appears in any of the ancient records. We have come full circle. Only one site meets all the relevant criteria: the Emmaus below the terraces of Moza, the Emmaus of Josephus, Vespasian's colony, the place where the Jews from Jerusalem collected the branches for their Sukkot tabernacles.

Notes

1   For the birth of Jesus under Augustus, see Luke 2.1. According to Luke 1.5 sq. and Matthew 2.1, Jesus was born before the death of Herod the Great in 4 BCE; the winter of 7/6 BCE has been calculated thanks to cuneiform tablets from the Babylonian observatory at Sippar, which calculate a specific stellar movement and so predict the birth of a Saviour in Judea for this period – this is the background to Matthew's story of the 'wise men from the east' (*magoi* in Greek, which means astronomers: the three kings are a later Christian legend unrelated to the text of the Gospel) – and the Star of Bethlehem. Thus, Jesus was born before his attributed birth date, but the year '0' of the modern Christian calendar is based on the miscalculations of a sixth-century monk and cannot be attributed to the Gospels. The most detailed study of the evidence, with charts and photographs of the tablets (some of which can be seen in the British Museum), was published by the leading Austrian astronomer, Konradin Ferrari d'Occhieppo, Emeritus Professor of Theoretical Astronomy in Vienna, as *Der Stern von Bethlehem in astronomischer Sicht*, Giessen/Basel, 4 edn 2004. As for the pirates, Augustus proudly notes: *Mare pacavi a praedonibus*, 'to the sea, I have given peace from the pirates'. It is one of the feats he mentions in his autobiographic *Res gestae* (25.1).

2 There are some New Testament scholars who doubt that the flight into Egypt and Herod's murder of all male children under the age of two ever happened. This is not the place to discuss the matter; suffice it to say that modern historical research has substantiated the historicity of both events.

3 For a detailed analysis of the traditions linking Ein Karem with John the Baptist and his parents, see S. Gibson, *The Cave of John the Baptist*, London 2004, 25–43.

4 The historicity of the Roman census mentioned in Luke's Gospel is disputed. Recent research, including the discovery and analysis of a testified Roman census document from the Babata Archive discovered in the Cave of Letters at the Nahal Arugot near the Dead Sea, confirm Luke's accuracy; cf. C.P. Thiede, *The Dead Sea Scrolls and the Jewish Origins of Christianity*, Oxford 2000, 85–8; C.P. Thiede, *The Cosmopolitan World of Jesus. New Light from Archaeology*, London 2004, 18–19, with further literature. For the question of whether Luke mistook a later census of AD 6 for an earlier one at the correct time of Jesus' birth, see C.P. Thiede, *Jesus. Der Glaube, die Fakten*, Augsburg 2003, 20–2.

5 The two swords are described as *machairai*, short swords (some have called them long daggers). Peter could easily have hit the right ear of the High Priest's Servant with this kind of weapon. A priest was not allowed to serve at the Temple with physical blemishes (cf. Lev. 21.28), and the servant, probably a man of noble Nabatean descent himself (his name Malchus is derived from the Nabatean root *mlk*, 'king'), represented the High Priest. Thus, Peter's action was meant to signify that Caiaphas was rendered unfit for office. The high priest's rule had ended and the final messianic battle should begin. When Jesus healed the wound, he not only performed the last of his earthly healing miracles, he also underlined – not for the first time – that he was not the military Messiah, but the suffering Messiah of Isaiah 53.

6 Here, 'Lord' is not yet the devout form of address for Christ. It could be used to address anyone who was high-ranking or who was thought worthy of polite appreciation. The Greek equivalent *kyrios* is used in both senses throughout the New Testament: Emperor Nero, for example, is called *kyrios* (Acts 25.26).

7 Flavius Josephus confirms the account in his *Jewish Antiquities*, 12.305–8, with some additional details.

8 C.f. A. Schalit, König Herodes, *Der Mann und sein Werk*, Berlin 1969, 183–211; see also J. Schwartz, 'Once More on the "Boundary of Gezer" Inscriptions and the History of Gezer and Lydda at the End of the Second Temple Period', in *Israel Exploration Journal* 40 (1900), 45–57.

9 Josephus, *Jewish War* 2.69–71.

10 Emmaus may not have possessed formal city charters at the time (unlike Ashkelon, Caesarea Maritima or Gaza) but there is an interesting parallel in Josephus, *Jewish Antiquities* 20.130 and *Jewish War* 2.515. In the former

passage, Josephus calls Lydda, another seat of district administration, a village (in Greek, a *kômê*) which however was 'in size not inferior to a city', and in the latter reference, he simply calls it a city (in Greek, a *polis*). In other words, Josephus knew that Lydda, in view of its status, was not really a simple village, the lack of city charters notwithstanding. The same obviously applied to Emmaus.

11   Guillemot continued to work at the site after his first visit and published the results in 1882: 'Emmaus-Ammous', *Les Missions Catholiques* (3 March) 1882, 103–6.

12   See M. Junckelmann, *Die Legionen des Augustus. Der römische Soldat im archäologischen Experiment*, Mainz 1986, 233–4.

13   Strabo, *Geographia* 12.6.5.

14   Gaius, *Digesta* 2.11.1, etc.

15   There is one later reading which has seven stadia (*hepta* in Greek, c.1.4 kilometres), but in a rare case of scholarly unanimity, this has been recognized as a scribal error.

16   *Bryn Mawr Classical Review* (2001).

17   They are 0243 (= 121b) in Venice, 424 in Vienna, and 1739 on Mount Athos, all dated to the tenth century.

18   B.M. Metzger, *A Textual Commentary on The Greek New Testament. A Companion Volume to the United Bible Societies' Greek New Testament*, 2nd edition, Stuttgart 1994, 594.

19   A. von Harnack, *Studien zur Geschichte des Neuen Testaments und der alten Kirche, I. Zur neutestamentlichen Textkritik*, Berlin / Leipzig 1931, 236–45.

20   See U. Victor, 'Textkritik – Eine Einführung', in U. Victor, C.P. Thiede and U. Stingelin (eds), *Antike Kultur und Neues Testament*, Basel 2003, 171–252.

21   The papyrus P.Oxy. 1453, dated to 30/29 BCE.

22   M. Aemilius Bassus was praetorian legate of the newly established province of Judaea; Liberius (or Laberius) Maximus was his procurator, in charge of all financial matters.

23   Vespasian had decided to keep the new province as his personal property; Bassus and Liberius were asked to re-divide the land and to lease it to pro-Roman Jews and non-Jews who could afford the rent. This measure also helps to explain why the old name 'Emmaus' was not remembered; none of the previous inhabitants of the region was left to preserve the memory over against the new *colonia*, and the new ones were plainly uninterested. In Samaria, Vespasian had established a city – a *polis* – Flavia Neapolis. In Judaea, however, he intended to keep matters firmly in his own hands, and the city rights of a Roman *polis* would have limited his powers. At one stroke, he kept his privileges and showed the Jews that he was not willing to give them any new concessions by allowing building activities. They had been firmly put down, and they were to suffer the consequences.

24 As we saw and shall discuss again later, the distance was 46 stadia; Josephus
    noted it from memory and underestimated it by three kilometres.
25 Suetonius, *Domitian* 12.2.
26 On Luke as an historian and the dates of his writings, see Chapter 4 below.
27 Jerusalem Talmud jSukk 54 b; Babylonian Talmud bSukk 45a.
28 Mishna Sukka 4:5a.
29 *Jewish War* 4.11.
30 G. Schmitt, for example, suggested a linguistic route from Greek 'Ammaous'
    via a mis-spelling like 'Amaaous', then 'Amaas' to 'Amaasa' and 'Amadasa'
    to 'Ammasada' as we find it in the faulty Latin tradition: see *Siedlungen
    Palästinas in griechisch-römischer Zeit. Ostjordanland, Negev und (in Auswahl)
    Westjordanland*, Wiesbaden 1995, 52–4. This is entirely possible, of course, but
    remains hypothetical. Equally hypothetical, and occasionally simply wrong,
    are the philological reconstructions attempted by F.M. Abel, in L.H. Vincent
    and F.M. Abel, *Emmaüs. Sa basilique et son histoire*, Paris 1932, 284–384. But in
    spite of the presupposition shared by his team that the other Emmaus, the
    city, was the right one, Abel referred to a twelfth-century tradition that
    assumed the 'source of Emmaus' at Moza (383–4); in AD 520, Cyril of
    Scythopolis had already mentioned a 'source of Colonia' (in his *Life of St Saba*,
    67). Other scholars remain uncommitted; in the latest critical edition of
    Josephus' *Jewish War* in Greek (*De bello Judaico* – *Der jüdische Krieg*, II/2,
    Darmstadt 1969, 258–9 note 109), Otto Michel and Otto Bauernfeind decide
    that the Emmaus of Josephus and the Emmaus of Luke are one and the same
    village near Jerusalem, but they also suggest that the Latin tradition of
    Josephus' text is superior to the Greek one. It is not easy to see how and why
    this should be so, since Amassada would have made 'perfect' sense to a Latin
    scribe without any linguistic and etymological games en route.
31 For a list of selected New Testament examples, see U. Victor, 'Textkritik – eine
    Einführung' in U. Victor, C.P. Thiede and U. Stingelin (eds), *Antike Kultur und
    Neues Testament*, Basel 2003, 171–252, here at 200–51.
32 See Chapter 4 below.
33 Jerome, *On Famous Men* 3.23.
34 For an edition of the Latin text, see *Corpus Christianorum Series Latina* 175
    (1965), 1–26.
35 A Roman mile was 1.5 kilometres, a Gallic mile (*leuca*) was 2.25 kilometres.
36 According to most modern measurements, it is 32.6 kilometres, but this
    minute variation can be understood easily enough: it was not determined
    where exactly in Jerusalem the measuring should begin, and where in
    Nicopolis it should end. The 'ten miles' after the name of Lidda (Lydda, Lod)
    is the distance from Nicopolis; the 'ten miles' after Mutatio Antipatrida is
    the distance from Lidda to Herodian Antipatris, ancient Pegae. It has been
    suggested that the lack of any reference to Nicopolis and Emmaus being

identical is not significant, since the Bordeaux Pilgrim does not mention New Testament events at Lydda (Acts 9.32–35) or Antipatris (Acts 23.31) either, but this is beside the point: the Pilgrim does not even know that Nicopolis once was called Emmaus. In other words, he is not aware that it could even theoretically be a New Testament site, whereas Lydda and Antipatris are the very names which occur in the Greek and Latin texts of the book of Acts, so that every reader of his account could associate them at leisure with Peter's healing of Aeneas and Paul's stopover en route to Caesarea (respectively).

37   In his *Eusebius as Church Historian*, Oxford 1980, 37, R.M. Grant calls him 'not only a mediocre stylist, but a depressingly unobjective historian'.

38   For a detailed discussion of the evidence, see C.P. Thiede and M. d'Ancona, *The Quest for the True Cross*, London 2000, 38–58.

39   It is of course true that Eusebius does not give a complete itinerary in his *Church History*, but it remains noteworthy that a decision he himself propagated to such lasting effect – the placing of Luke's Emmaus at Nicopolis – had apparently not caught on by 326. Seven years later, as we saw above, the Bordeaux Pilgrim was equally unaware of the new fashion.

40   *Vita Constantini* 31.1–2.

41   Fortunately, Eusebius quoted Constantine's correspondence from time to time, and he did not dare to delete the Emperor's reference to the 'token of that holiest Passion', i.e, the existence of the true cross, in his *Vita Constantini*. When he spoke in the presence of the Emperor in 336, to celebrate Constantine's thirtieth imperial jubilee (published as *In Praise of Constantine*), he also obliquely but inescapably referred to the existence of the Cross when he called the Church of the Holy Sepulchre a 'temple of the saving sign' (cf. P. Walker, *Holy City, Holy Places? Christian Attitudes to Jerusalem and the Holy Land in the Fourth Century*, Oxford 1990, 258; S. Borgehammar, *How the Holy Cross Was Found: From Event to Medieval Legend*, Stockholm 1991, 106).

42   A few scholars believe that Eusebius was not the first to link Nicopolis with Luke's Emmaus. They suggest that Origen had already made the equation in c.AD 230. But there is no trace of this in Origen's writings, and his trusted correspondent Sextus Iulius Africanus had only just persuaded Emperor Eliogabalus to change the name to Nicopolis, without any recognizable awareness of a tradition identifying it with the Emmaus of the Gospel. Origen therefore had no reason to suggest a baseless equation. One single, late comment, an anonymous *scholion* on Luke 24.13, claims that Origen allegedly supported the (new) manuscripts with the distance of 160 stadia instead of 60. It is unlikely that he, the circumspect philologist, could have done so, and we certainly have nothing from his own pen about Luke 24. Unfortunately, the most recent defender of the city of Emmaus, Rainer Riesner, presents his conclusions in a way which is as typical of this school of thought as it is illogical: there is this single unattributable comment on

Origen, with no parallel anywhere in Origen's writings, but even so, 'it should be correct'. Then (!) 'already Origen († 254) identified the Lukan Emmaus with Emmaus/Nicopolis' (R. Riesner, 'Die Emmaus-Erzählung [Lukas 24,13–35]. Lukanische Theologie, judenchristliche Tradition und palästinische Topographie' in K.-H. Fleckenstein, M. Louhivuori and R. Riesner (eds), *Emmaus in Judäa. Geschichte – Exegese – Archäologie*, Giessen 2004, 150–208, here at 188).

43   In Latin: '... *apud quam in fractione panis cognitus dominus Cleopae domum in ecclesiam dedicavit*'.

44   For the history of Chorazin as the location of this miracle, cf. D. Baldi, *Enchiridion Locorum Sanctorum*, Jerusalem 1955, 278–9; for the original and correct reading of Gadara in Matthew, Mark and Luke, see C.P. Thiede, *The Cosmopolitan World of Jesus. New Light from Archaeology*, London 2004, 41–7.

45   H. Chadwick, *The Early Church*, Harmondsworth 1967, 216. 'He is proverbially careless and inaccurate', commented A.C. McGiffert on Jerome, in 'The Life and Writings of Eusebius' in *A Select Library of Nicene and Post-Nicene Fathers of the Christian Church, Second Series*, Vol. 1, Edinburgh/Grand Rapids, repr. 1997, 3–56, here at 42.

46   Hesychius, *Questiones et responsiones, ad loc.* (*Patrologia Graeca* 93, 1444). There is an interesting case study in a Greek manuscript of the Old Testament: in Judges 19.9, a Levite intending to return from Bethlehem to Gibeah is asked by his father-in-law to stay with the family overnight, because it is no longer full day (literally, 'the day has weakened'). The Levite however decides to risk the journey and reaches Gibeah when the sun had just set (19.14). He had to cover a distance of some 14 kilometres, for which an average walker would have calculated about two and a half hours. The Levite would have left Bethlehem when the sun was beginning to set; indeed, this is what the story in Judges implies, for when they were near Jerusalem, 'the light was going fast' (19.11). In brief, it is a straightforward account which confirms that the distance from the real Emmaus to Jerusalem, 8.6 kilometres, was just about 'safe' for fast walkers who wanted to get to Jerusalem before it was too late, but that the 32.6 kilometres from the wrong Emmaus would not have been considered realistic even by the fast, intrepid Levite walker. However, Christian editors of the Greek Old Testament saw a chance to link the text of Judges with that of Luke. The *Codex Alexandrinus*, written after Eusebius, Jerome and Hesychius in the fifth century, altered the Greek text of Judges 19.9, so that it reads just like Luke 24.29. Most modern translators have also seen a parallel, so that the sentence now appears identical in both passages. But if Judges 19.9–14 offers us anything, it is yet another clue to the conclusion that the distant city of Emmaus must be ruled out, in favour of the closer village mentioned in Luke's Gospel and in the *Jewish War* of Josephus.

47   Cinema buffs have called this one of the best films on the brutality of the War of Independence and the battles over territories in the Middle East at the end of the British Mandate. In view of the present political disputes, it still has a thought-provoking message; in any case, the cast of supporting actors, from Frank Sinatra and John Wayne, Yul Brynner and Haim Topol to Angie Dickinson and Senta Berger, makes it highly watchable.

48   For a brief account of the aerial photography which led to these discoveries in the area of the Roman city of Emmaus-Nicopolis, see A. Söderlund, 'Die Entdeckung eines römisch-byzantinischen Stadtgeländes bei Amwas (1999)' in K.H. Fleckenstein, M. Louhivuori and R. Riesner (eds), *Emmaus in Judäa. Geschichte – Exegese – Archäologie*, Giessen 2004, 299–310.

49   L.H. Vincent and F.M. Abel, *Emmaüs, sa basilique et son histoire*, Paris 1932.

50   M. Louhivuori's preliminary report has been published in German: 'Ausgrabungen in Emmaus/Nicopolis 1993–2002' in K.-H. Fleckenstein, M. Louhivuori and R. Riesner (eds), *op. cit.*, 238–66.

51   Cf. C.P.Thiede, *The Cosmopolitan World of Jesus. New Light from Archaeology*, London 2004, 92–5.

52   For the complete list of attending bishops see H. Gelzer, *Patrum Nicaenorum Nomina*, Leipzig 1894. Nine of the 'Palestininan' bishops came from cities which had no links with New Testament sites (e.g. Longinus of Ascalon, Marianus of Jamnia, Patrophilus of Sythopolis = Bet-Shean). Nicopolis, like Bet-Shean, had become a bishopric because of its importance as a Romano-Christian city. The convenors of the Council of Nicaea did not know that the Bishop of Caesarea had just finished writing his *Onomasticon* with its attempt to change biblical topography.

53   Mishna Keritoth 3.7–9. For a detailed discussion of the rabbinic sources about Emmaus, see R. Deines, 'Emmaus in der jüdischen Tradition' in K.-H. Fleckenstein, M. Louhivuori and R. Riesner, *op. cit.* 40–86. The quotation from Rabbi Jacob of Emmaus following in the main text above is taken from Deines' article, 80–1.

54   Buying and selling (Jewish) slaves was usually left to non-Jews; cf. 1 Macc. 3.41; 2 Macc. 8.11; Josephus, *Jewish War* 7.208, etc.

55   Melito of Sardes (c.120–90) wrote his Easter Homily in c.160. Lines 710–39 are an antisemitic diatribe, and in line 734 he declares that God was killed on the Cross; in lines 735–6 he adds that the right hand of an Israelite destroyed the King of Israel. It is a classic example of manipulation, since nowhere in the Gospels is there a hint of this, let alone a factual statement that a Jew killed Jesus; every single source emphasizes that it was the Roman prefect Pontius Pilate and his soldiers who did it. In fact, Emperor Constantine made sure that the Christian world heard that message when he convinced his bishops at the Council of Nicea (Eusebius of Caesarea and Macarius of Jerusalem were present) that the Nicene Creed should not blame the Jews. Today still,

Christians proclaim that Jesus was 'crucified under Pontius Pilate', not by the High Priest Caiaphas and the Jews. But Melito's message was more persuasive and helped to 'justify' two millennia of persecutions, pogroms, and attempted genocide.

56 From the description of the survey in M. Fisher, B. Isaac and I. Roll, *Roman Roads in Judaea II. The Jaffa-Jerusalem Roads*, Oxford 1996, 87. The authors work out that the distance between Emmaus-Nicopolis and Jerusalem was 27 kilometres (18 Roman miles, or 146 stadia), but this is the distance by car, from the eastern perimeter of Nicopolis to the Old Town of Jerusalem, and if one takes the detours necessitated by the alignments in the landscape into account, 32.5 kilometres (22.5 miles, or c.176 stadia) come closer to the actual course of the road. As mentioned above, absolute precision will remain elusive, since we simply do not know where the ancients began and ended measuring the distance in Jerusalem and the area of Nicopolis (the city measured at least two kilometres in diameter). Jerome Murphy O'Connor worked out that 31 kilometres was correct (*The Holy Land. An Oxford Archaeological Guide from Earliest Times to 1700*, 4th edn Oxford/New York 1998, 320). In any case, the fact, ascertained by topographical experiment, remains: the time needed to cover the distance is at least five hours, or up to one hour more, depending on the time of day, physical fitness, etc.

57 It reads *'Vexillato Leg X Fre'*, with a missing second 'i' in *vexillatio* – perhaps a ligature, but probably a scribal error: the scribe had run out of space and dropped the letter. It was a clever move: whenever I take students to the site, I ask them to read the first line, and so far not a single one has noticed the missing second 'i'. They all read the text 'correctly', knowing what should be there – but is not.

58 In 2003, my colleague Rafi Lewis of the Israel Antiquities Authority conducted the most recent survey in the area of the church, but no Jewish remains or objects could be found.

59 See J. Delaville le Roulx, *Cartulaire générale des Hospitaliers de Saint-Jean de Jérusalem*, Paris 1894, 113–15, nos 139–40; see also note 62 below.

60 William of Tyre, *Historia rerum in partibus transmarinis gestarum* 7:25.

61 Fulcher of Chartres, *Historia Hierosolymitana* 1.25.

62 R. Röhricht (ed.), *Regesta Regni Hierosolymitani. Additamentum*, Innsbruck 1904, 50 (no. 201).

63 See T. Tobler, *Theodirici Libellus de Locis Sanctis editus ca.* AD 1172, St Gallen/ Paris 1875, 86.

64 D. Baldi, *Enchiridion Locorum Sanctorum*, 3rd edn, Jerusalem 1982, 715, note 1.

65 Against all the evidence, M. Ehrlich recently suggested that Fontenoid/ Castellum Emmaus/Abu Gosh are not the same site ('The Identification of Emmaus with Abu Gosh in the Crusader Period Reconsidered' in *Zeitschrift des Deutschen Palästina-Vereins* 112 (1996), 165–9). Misunderstood references

and a vagrant grasp of linguistics take him on a contorted journey at the end of which he concludes what was evident before he even started: that the Crusaders' Emmaus was at the site (or, more precisely, below the hill) of Qiryat Yearim. This, after all, was one of the reasons why they chose the location in the first place.

66 See O. Englebert, 'Abu Ghosh' in Communauté bénédictine d'Abu-Gosh (ed.), *Abu Gosh. De l'Emmaüs des Croisés au Monastère de la Résurrection*, Nantes 1995, 7–32, here at 31.

67 See A. Boaz, *Crusader Archaeology. The Material Culture of the Latin East*, London/New York 1999, 65–8.

68 Francesco Suriano, *Trattato di Terra Santa e dell'Oriente*, Venice 1524; see the English translation in T. Bellorini and E. Hoade (eds), *Francesco Suriano: Treatise on the Holy Land*, Jerusalem 1949, 36–40; 151–5. Suriano was Custodian of the Holy Land from 1493–95 and from 1512–15.

69 B. Bagatti, *Emmaus-Qubeibeh: The Results of Excavations at Emmaus-Qubeibeh and Nearby Sites*, Jerusalem 1993. Bagatti's report contains excellent documentation, with photographs, of the Crusader finds.

70 These results notwithstanding, some commentators have defended the Fransciscan choice. See, among others, J.N. Geldenhuys, *Commentary on Luke*, London / Edinburgh 1950, 636; W.J. Harrington, *The Gospel According to St Luke*, London 1968, 272–3; S. de Sandoli, *Emmaus – El Qubeibeh*, 2nd edn, Jerusalem 1980.

71 I have been there several times and have not always enjoyed the circumstances of the journey.

3

People of Action: Jesus and Those Who Saw Him

The myth appeal

We have assumed that there actually is a case to be investigated. But the quest for the true Emmaus would be nothing but a footnote to the history of the Early Church if the Emmaus story as such had never happened. Could it have happened? Did Jesus really appear, after his crucifixion, alive, risen from the dead, walking and talking, not as a vision, but with a real body, able to break bread, but also able to disappear as he liked? We have heard it said often enough: this story, as so many other stories in the Gospels, is a myth, a legend, a pious fairy tale. Allegedly, the Resurrection, like the Nativity, is steeped in ancient near-Eastern cult legends, emulating Egyptian and other religious myths. We have heard those claims, and we will hear them again, but as historians have worked out, in painstakingly detailed, comparative analysis, nothing could be further from the truth. Let us look at the story from a different angle, for a change: what actually was the world of myth, religion and philosophy in New Testament times? What did the first readers of the Gospels, Acts and the Epistles know of these, what did they expect to learn, and where did the differences between the ancient world-view and that of the New Testament begin?

In antiquity, people were as inquisitive as they are today. And then as now, their intellectual abilities made a difference. If we read that there are more witches today than priests and more people who read their daily horoscope than their daily Bible notes, we should be healed instantly of the faith in our intellectual superiority over the people of New Testament times. To understand how low the level of critical intelligence has actually sunk in our present age, we only have to look at the most successful hardcover novel ever sold, Dan Brown's *The Da Vinci Code* (2004). Brown has written a novel, and no-one expects a novel to be an historically accurate description of past or present events. Most of those who read it will enjoy a good yarn (in spite of its cliché-ridden style), and laugh at the harebrained assumptions which the heroes apparently take for granted on every other page, finally putting it aside without giving it a second thought. However unfortunately, millions of readers seem to believe what Dan Brown stated in an interview: everything is based on serious research, and the documents cited are rendered accurately and truthfully. It sounds impressive, but only plays to the superficiality of modern reading habits. When Hitler's diaries were published in 1983, and renowned scholars like Lord Dacre of Glanton (aka Hugh Trevor-Roper) pronounced them to be authentic, they had certainly been quoted, photographed and reproduced in facsimile as accurately as modern techniques allow, and yet they soon turned out to be abysmal forgeries. But, the real problem with the *The Da Vinci Code*, in the context of our quest for accurate and trustworthy sources, should be seen in the claims Brown made about documents which do exist and are undoubtedly not forged: the Gospels, the Nag Hammadi Codices, the Dead Sea Scrolls, and others.

According to *The Da Vinci Code*, Jesus survived the crucifixion, married Mary Magdalene, had a child with her and established a dynasty whose successors are alive and kicking in present-day France. If this sounds familiar, you only have to turn to a worldwide bestseller from the 1980s to find it: *The Holy Blood and the Holy Grail* by Michael Baigent, Richard Leigh and Harry Lincoln. It is all there, in all its mind-boggling naffness. Brown adds a mystery cult of his own: the Holy Grail is not a chalice, but the womb of Mary of Magdala, the womb which carried the bloodline of Christ. Obviously, to anyone who creates such myths and legends, the Gospels are a hindrance. Baigent, Leigh, Lincoln and their successor Brown have had to distort, manipulate and generally explain away what these documents say. In his novel, Brown claims that Emperor Constantine the Great (274–337), the first Christian Roman Emperor, destroyed literally thousands of original manuscripts which allegedly told the story of a merely human, far from immmortal Jesus. The evidence provided? None. There is not even a shred of suspicion anywhere in the sources. By the time of Constantine, in the first half of the fourth century, Gospel manuscripts had reached every corner of the Roman Empire, and the Emperor would not have had the chance to destroy them, even if he had tried. Some 100 pre-Constantinian papyri have survived, in more than

20 libraries from Jerusalem to Cairo, from Oxford to Cambridge, from
Berlin to Ann Arbour, from Dublin to Cologne, and in none of them
is there any trace of editorial changes. As Ulrich Victor, a classical
philologist from Berlin's prestigious Humboldt University, recently put it:
ordinary human scribal errors apart, we have the Gospels as they were
written, they are early historical records in the mould of hellenistic
historiography.[1]

As always in such books, the Vatican is presented as the evil power,
trying to prevent access to the truth. We have already had this in
another Baigent/Leigh 'classic', *The Dead Sea Scrolls Deception*. It is conveniently ignored that the Vatican never had access to the scrolls in the
decisive years after their discovery. Not a single Vatican scholar ever
joined the editorial teams when the scrolls were collected, photographed and handed over to scholars for the painstakingly difficult process of deciphering, transcribing and publishing. The Scrolls, which do
not mention Jesus at all, and the fourth-century Nag Hammadi Codices,
named after their place of discovery in Egypt, along with the so-called
Gospel of Thomas (a late collection of sayings which cannot contain
historical narratives about Jesus by any stretch of the imagination) are
praised as the real evidence.[2] In other words, *The Da Vinci Code* is a
book for people who enjoy reading about conspiracy theories. It should
worry us that, apparently, there are so many of these people around, in
our 'enlightened' era, but it should not deflect our attention from the
real issues. So how then did people in antiquity approach myth and
reality?

There certainly were mysteries and mystery cults. Ancient mysteries
were purveyors of 'good news', concerned with the life of people on
earth, and the different aspects of their future (if any) after death. If this
sounds familiar, then that is how it should be: in the eyes of first-century
beholders outside Judaism, the message of the Christians was, at first
glance, just another mystery. In their eyes, it was the function of their own
particular 'myth' (*mythos* in Greek), to tell the story. In other words, a
Greek-speaking man or woman in the Roman Empire of that period did
not treat a 'myth' as something negative. It simply was the oral and
literary form of any given mystery cult. And mysteries were anything but
secret affairs: contrary to what most of us assume, none of the ancient

mystery cults was restricted to a small circle of select followers. We know from ancient sources that over the centuries literally millions of people were initiated into (for example) the Eleusinian Mysteries, celebrated in the Greek city of Eleusis in honour of the female godhead Demeter and her daughter Persephone. This cult existed until AD 395 and was therefore known and indeed popular during the first four centuries of Christianity. It is true that the adherents of these Eleusinian Mysteries, and of the Orphic Mysteries, and so forth, had to swear to secrecy. But if, as the Greek historian Herodotus (c.485–425 BCE) tells us, every Athenian and any other other Greek person who desired it was free to be consecrated, one might say that a vast number of people knew the 'secret' anyway.

An atheist of the fifth century BCE, Diagoras of Melos, betrayed the secret of the Eleusian mysteries to all and sundry, without it having any effect whatsoever on the popularity of the myth as such.

To put it differently, if Christians today say 'Let us proclaim the mystery of faith' just before receiving Holy Communion, and go on to say that 'Christ has died, Christ is risen, Christ will come again', then this was and is, formally speaking, quite in tune with what a message of 'mystery' meant to the ancients. Origen, that ubiquitous theologian of the early to mid-third century, was happy to accept the term 'mystery' as a description of Christian teaching when he refuted the anti-Christian polemics of a certain Celsus. This man, an otherwise unknown philosopher, had published a diatribe against the Christians in about AD 178–80 entitled 'True Knowledge', wheeling on the full array of neo-Platonist arguments, and often using the teaching of pseudo-Christian sects and gnostic movements against orthodox Christianity. Apart from everything else, this makes his book a useful source for late second-century Greek thinking. Most of the 'True Knowledge' has survived thanks to the extensive quotes in Origen's reply, *Against Celsus*. Origen rebutted the accusations, but he had no problems with the term 'mystery'.[3]

However, Origen, like the Jewish-Roman author Flavius Josephus in the late first century, did emphasize a vital difference. The ancient mysteries were confined to a small number of festive days. Judaism and Christianity, on the other hand, involve their adherents' whole life, every day, not merely on the Sabbath or on Sundays. As Josephus put it: 'Could

God be more worthily honoured than by a scheme under which the true veneration of God is the aim of the whole community . . . and the whole administration of the state is set out like a sacred ceremony? Practices which, under the name of mysteries and initiation rites, other peoples can only observe for a few days, unable to persevere, we keep them up with delight, and with unwavering determination, all our lives.'[4]

What Josephus said about Jewish practice is precisely what any Christian might have said and continues to say even today – about the Christian faith. It is not a matter of a few special holy days, but a whole lifestyle. Admittedly, modern practice often enough resembles the ancient 'special day' mysteries: once a week, or once a year, at Christmas and perhaps also at Easter, many people enter a church and join in the proclamation of that mystery of the faith which for the rest of the week (or year) is of no particular concern to them. Neither the Jew Josephus nor the first Christian thinkers agreed with the idea, produced by pagan writers like Celsus or Lucian of Samosata (c.AD 120–185), that Christianity was just another mystery – albeit a new-fangled one with dubious credentials. What all 'mysteries' had in common was the concept of a message meant to shape a believer's life and to imbue it with meaning. Celebrating this message was a daily necessity and a joyous obligation for Jews and Christians, but an occasional observance for all the others.

To live with joy, and to die in the hope of something better to come, as the Roman philosopher Cicero put it in 44 BCE (*On the Laws* 2.36), was the good news of the ancient mysteries. It was this, rather than any particular initiation rites, which made both these cults so popular, and Christianity a dangerous rival in their eyes. Christianity, in finally going beyond the basis it shared with Judaism, introduced a decisive change: the ancient 'myths', i.e. the stories told about Demeter and Persephone at Eleusis, or about Isis and Osiris and their cult (which had permeated the whole Roman Empire in New Testament times), were unhistorical. They were tales told about gods and demi-gods who never existed, which were refuted by most philosophers (beginning with Plato) and by historians as early as Herodotus. This is the stage at which 'myth' acquired its modern, colloquial sense of something untrue, untrustworthy. The Gospels are 'myth' merely from a technical, classical perspective, as stories about a mystery. But that is all. The message of the Gospels is explicitly historical (cf. Lk. 1.1–4; Jn 19.35, 21.24, etc.), about a person who really lived and was seen by many. He was at no-one's disposal, quite unlike the many cultic deities of the Roman Empire, simply because it was impossible to invent or re-invent, use or misuse him – the real-life personified God – according to one's own tastes. The teachings about Jesus and his message may have been misinterpreted again and again in the history of the Church, but this happened (and continues to happen) not because Christianity is a free-for-all mystery religion, but because readers and interpreters deviate from the message of the historical accounts.

To understand what this meant in those days, we can look at the Roman practice of taking over other peoples' gods. When they laid siege to a city, they called on the city god and demanded that he join them. It was an act for which there even existed a technical term, the famous *evocatio*. Obviously, no godhead appeared in person and did anything of the sort. But when the Romans successfully conquered the city, they saw this as proof positive that the god had indeed changed sides, and in gratitude, they built him a temple in Rome. This happened again and again. In New Testament times, the God of the Jews and Christians and Jesus himself was never within reach of such attitudes. Jesus did not join others, whether in victory or in defeat; he was joined by those who decided to follow him. It was all completely new, entirely unheard of, and in fact went too far for those orthodox Jews who refused to acknowledge Jesus as the Messiah. God on earth, fully man and fully God, seen by thousands of eyewitnesses, documented in writings during the eyewitness period: nothing like it had ever happened before.

At this stage, we can understand why the first Christians happily used the term 'mystery' in their conversations and dialogues with non-Christians. After all, it was a welcome starting-point. You begin with the similarities, and from that shared ground, you proceed to explain the differences. In his dealings with the Athenian philosophers, the apostle Paul used the stones of all those altars erected to known and unknown gods in the city of Athens and in the surrounding landscape to tell the philosphers that he knew where they were coming from. He quoted the Greek philosopher Aratus (c.315–239 BCE) about the one God: 'We are of his kind'.[5] Only then, in a second step, did he introduce his audience to the decisive differences. And Paul was well aware of what had gone on before he arrived on the Christian scene. Nicholas Orme, Professor of History at Exeter University, recently asked: If none of the Gospels had been published before the apostle Paul wrote his letters, how could he afford to say so little about the life and the sayings of Jesus?[6] This is an historian's question – quite a few New Testament scholars, convinced of their world-view which allows the Gospels only to have been written two or three decades after Paul's letters, would not even understand what he is saying.[7] With Orme's justified question in mind, we may wonder if a Jewish library like the one at the synagogue at Beroea (Acts 17.10–12) did not contain a copy of an early Christian writing. Paul and his colleague Silas (who like him was a Jew with Roman citizenship) lectured at Beroea in AD 47/48. Their Jewish audience, decided to 'examine the Scriptures every day to see whether these things were so'. By then, Mark's Gospel could have been in circulation for up to seven years.[8] And while the debate about the exact or most likely date of Mark's Gospel continues, we would have to admit that even the fourth decade of the first century are not an early, but a late dating.

No one, so far, has produced a single convincing reason why the Christians should have waited for ten years or more before they set pen to paper, given the fact that their neighbours, the rival messianic eschatological movement of the Essenes, produced, copied and distributed scroll after scroll to proclaim their own messianic vision. It should be obvious enough that a new movement which proclaimed the fulfilment of these Jewish hopes and expectations had to write down what they knew and believed. An oral tradition was valuable, but on its own it was inadequate. The incident at Beroea proves the point: those pious Jews listened to Paul and Silas (to the oral tradition, as it were), but afterwards they studied the Scriptures to find out if it were true. The Scriptures meant the prophetic writings of the Old Testament, first of all, but also other Jewish literature which was widely read but did not belong the canon of the Jewish Bible.[9] And, needless to say, the first Christian writings were regarded as Jewish Messianic, eschatological literature, written by Jews and with a Jewish (and non-Jewish) readership in mind. When Mark, Luke and Paul wrote, there was no fixed literary genre of 'gospels', nor was there a 'New Testament'. But imagine for a moment that the Christians had no scrolls of their own to be placed and studied next to the scrolls of the common Jewish heritage, not even by AD 47, when Paul spoke at Beroea: would those Jews have taken their claims seriously? Writing, producing scrolls, was of the essence. Nicholas Orme's question certainly points in the right direction.

Let us look in another direction. At Qumran near the Dead Sea, three of the caves, numbered six to eight, could only be accessed through the main settlement. Anyone who wanted to read their contents had to pass a 'face check'. Small and largely destroyed, the mixed scrolls of caves 6 and 8 do not offer any clues as to the reason why they were so close to the settlement. Cave 7, however, appears to have been a 'poison cabinet' of exclusively Greek writings made only on papyrus – a unique phenomenon at Qumran – which many scholars have described as a collection of texts used and written by Jewish Christians. It seems the Qumran Essenes, who had heard about the new messianic movement, wanted to study their first writings, and as the jar with the Hebrew inscription 'Rome' implies, they got these scrolls from the large Jewish community in Rome (some 60,000 Jews lived in the city at the time), probably just before AD 68, rather than causing suspicion by buying them in Jerusalem. If at least two of the tiny Greek papyrus fragments found in Cave 7 really are Jewish Christian texts (Mark and 1 Timothy), then this unique cave would confirm the ongoing interest, from all sides, in the inner-Jewish debate about the true Messiah. And, as we shall see, this included the question of Messianic miracles, culminating in a bodily res- urrection. One of the leading Jewish Qumran scholars, Shemaryahu Talmon, was among those who suggested that the Essenes at Qumran were the most likely people to collect these rival writings from the beginning.[10]

It was in the best interests of these two messianic, eschatological movements – the Essenes and the Christians – to spread their thoughts as quickly and as widely as possible. Everyone, after all, should have a fair chance to learn and change their ways. The Essenes, it seems, restricted their missionary activities to Jewish communities throughout the Roman Empire. They were not interested in reaching the gentile world.[11] But the Jewish Christians targeted Jews and non-Jews alike, as Jesus had done from the very beginning of his ministry. Their teaching was not confined to a closed community, and their texts were to be made available to a wider readership: both the old scripture – the Torah, the Prophets, the Psalms and the Historical Writings of their Jewish heritage – and the new. Every member of the community, not just the initiated elite, but everyone who could hear or read, was included: 'Greet all the brothers and sisters with a holy kiss', Paul writes in 1 Thessalonians 5.26–27, 'I solemnly command you by the Lord that this letter be read to all of them.' Writings are passed on and exchanged: 'And when this letter has been read among you, have it read also in the church of the Laodiceans. And see that you read also the letter from Laodicea' (Col. 4.16). Even the book of Revelation insists on the importance of an accessible, written form of teaching and communicating: John is not told to visit the seven churches in Asia Minor and to have a cup of tea with them, he is told to send them letters (Rev. 1.9–3.22).

What matters most in our immediate context is that, 'even' the faith in a bodily, physical resurrection was shared by Essenes and Jewish Christians: the vast majority of Jews were expecting a resurrection. Only one Jewish movement, the Sadducees, remained on the sidelines, as they refused to believe anything they failed to find in the Torah (the five Mosaic books). Flavius Josephus and the New Testament concur in their accounts: the Sadducees, the priestly caste of the Temple, did not believe in the Resurrection. It was of course a problem entirely of their own making, as God's capability to raise the dead is unmistakably mentioned in the last book of the Torah, Deuteronomy (at 32.39). Everyone else was able to trace the line that went from Deuteronomy to Isaiah 26.19, Ezekiel 37.7–14, Daniel 12.2 and Hosea 6.2, looking forward to a triumphant resurrection in the last days. The Essenes set down their hopes in one of their writings, which has survived as fragments in their caves at Qumran. It is the scroll 4Q 521, fragment 2. Here it is, quoted with square brackets around damaged words which have had to be reconstructed:[12]

[For the heav]ens and the earth will listen to His Messiah, [and all w]hich is in them will not turn away from the commandments of the holy ones. Strengthen yourselves, you who seek the Lord, in His service. All you who are hopeful in your hearts, will you not find the Lord in this? For the Lord will seek the pious and call the righteous by name. Over the humble His spirit will hover and will renew the faithful in His strength. And he will honour the pious on the throne of his eternal kingdom. He will set prisoners free, opening the eyes of the blind, raising up those who are bo[wed down]. And f[or]ever shall [I] hold fast [to the h]opeful and pious … And the fr[uit] will not be delayed. And the Lord shall do glorious things which have never been achieved, [just as He promised]. For He shall heal the pierced, He shall revive the dead, and bring good news to the poor.

The final fragment underlines the bodily resurrection: 'And He will open the tombs.' Another Qumran scroll, the Thanksgiving Hymns, confirms the continuous presence of the age-old prophetic spirit among the contemporaries of Jesus:

You [the Lord] have purified man from sin, so that he may be holy for you, with no abominable uncleanness and no guilty wickedness, so that he may be one with the children of your truth and share in the lot of your holy ones, so that bodies gnawed by worms may be raised from the dust, to the counsel of your truth.

(1QH 19[11]. 10–14)

Later, in the Talmud, the erroneous teaching of the Sadducees is contradicted from a Pharisaic perspective: 'And you shall know that I am the Lord, when I open your tombs, and bring you up from your graves, O my people' (Taanit 2a/2b). The Talmud thus interprets Ezekiel 37.13, which it quotes and expands, as the prophecy of a bodily resurrection. Another Talmudic text, Ketubboth 111b, likens the rising bodies to grain which is buried naked but will rise clad in splendour. The writings of the Talmud contain some teachings that go back to the time of Jesus and before, but they were published long after the resurrection of Jesus, in the sixth century. This is remarkable, for the Talmudic collectors could easily have excluded or deleted all of the references to the physical resurrection if the resurrection of Jesus had bothered them. The spontaneous reaction of some of the High Priest's people who claimed that the disciples must have stolen the body of Jesus (Matt. 27.62–66; 28.11–15) did not lead to a revision of the ancient conviction that there will be a resurrection, and that it will not be spiritual, but physical.

All these Jews believed something crucial: a risen body is a new body, and whereas this body is a physical reality, able to speak, walk, eat, and drink, it is also a new creation. No-one had been raised to this new life before. When Jesus brought Lazarus back to life, and the young man from Nain and the daughter of Jairus, these were reawakenings of people who would have to die a normal human death eventually. His followers would simply have to come to terms with the unknown reality of a risen Messiah. Only one thing, as readers of Ezekiel 37.7–14, could they be sure of: they would not be able to recognize the risen Christ from his physical appearance, since the old bones would be covered by new sinews, new flesh and new skin. They took that for granted. We may be surprised that they did not recognize him, but they themselves – at least on reflection – would not have been. When the two disciples on their way home to Emmaus, Cleopas and his nameless companion, meet the risen Christ, they do not recognize him until he is at home with them, takes the bread as the honoured guest, breaks it and blesses it in a characteristic manner (Lk. 24.30–31). Mary of Magdala takes him for a gardener, and only when he pronounces her name in a way she recognizes does she turn round and address him as 'Rabbuni' (Master: Jn 20.14–18). 'Doubting' Thomas, who was not present when Jesus revealed himself to the other disciples, wants to see the marks of the nails in his wrists[13] and the wound in his side (Jn 20.24–25). The others had seen these marks of the crucifixion already, but Thomas applies the art of lateral thinking: a risen body is pure, the new flesh will not show any traces of the person's life, no wounds, no warts, no scars.

In those days, Jews practised the second burial. After several months, when the flesh had decayed, the tomb was reopened, and the bones were placed in an ossuary, awaiting the bodily resurrection according to Ezekiel 37.7–14, when new, pure flesh and skin would be put on them. These ossuaries were often inscribed with the name of the re-buried person. The ossuary of a contemporary of Jesus, Yehonan Ben Hazkul, included the heelbone along with a nail of his crucifixion – the nail had fishhooked and could not be pulled out. This is the only archaeological evidence to date, although there are numerous literary references, of a Roman crucifixion.[14] So even a crucified man was not excluded from the preparations for the resurrection in the last days.

Jesus, however, had risen before his bones could be placed in an ossuary. What would his new body look like? Had the others merely imagined that the old wounds were still there? On a newly created resurrected body, they should not be visible, after all. Thomas wanted to see for himself. The risen Christ had entered the room although the doors were shut. Miraculous perhaps, but then again even the most observant of Jews did not know what a resurrection body would be able to do. Enlightened as they were, they accepted what they saw. The next step was decisive: Jesus parted his cloak, and Thomas saw the wounds. He knew that they should not have been there, on the pure skin of a risen person's body, but there they were. And so he understood that Jesus, the Risen One, still remained the Crucified One. His Resurrection does not negate or nullify his crucifixion. The risen Christ remains the crucified Jesus. Thomas does not even have to touch the wound – John in his Gospel does not say he does, it is merely the interpretative addition of many famous works of art which has made us think otherwise. Overwhelmed by this sudden insight, he said what no Jew had ever before said about another Jew: 'My Lord and my God.' Some critics have opined that this is the Evangelist's theological invention. But, having looked at the context of the crucifixion from a Jewish perspective, we know better. The words uttered by Thomas turn out to be a very devout, a very Jewish statement. In one moment, old prophecies and experienced truth fell into place and became one.

It is impossible to escape the sober insistence, free of all those legendary additions one so often finds in Egyptian and Greek myths, of the observed reality of these events. There is Simon Peter, who is mentioned in Luke's Emmaus account when the two disciples joyously return to Jerusalem to tell the others about their experience, and are interrupted with the exclamation, 'The Lord has risen indeed, and he has appeared to Simon' (Lk. 24.33–34). This Peter, a fishing entrepreneur from Capernaum, who clung on to his human hopes so firmly, not wishing Jesus to die, that he raised a sword in the Garden of Gethsemane to defend him, was both courageous enough to follow him into the High Priest's courtyard and humanly frail enough to deny him three times. The same Peter met the Roman centurion Cornelius in Caesarea Maritima and gave this experienced professional soldier an eyewitness testimony which included an unmistakable reference to the physical body of the risen Christ: 'We are witnesses to all that he did both in Judaea and in Jerusalem. They put him to death by hanging him on a tree; but God raised him on the third day and allowed him to appear, not to all the people but to us who were chosen by God as witnesses, and who ate and drank with him after he rose from the dead' (Acts 10.39–41).

Luke, the author of the book of Acts, knew what he was doing when he included this snippet of information about food. In his Gospel, he had made the same point when he reported that the risen Christ was given a piece of broiled fish 'and took it and ate in their presence' (Lk. 24.42–43). For a man like Cornelius, a Roman officer educated in the Greco-Roman mould, there was no life after death, nor a resurrection of the body. All he, and people like him, could envisage was a separation of body and soul and the possibilty that the soul might hover on a kind of 'island of the blessed'. Evidently, the testimony of the eyewitness convinced him. Jesus was different: his resurrection was real, not just spiritual. He could eat and drink. Cornelius was baptized, and his whole household with him. And Theophilus, the dedicatee of the Gospel, who is addressed as 'Your Excellency' (*kratiste* in Greek, a term reserved in Jewish-Greek writings for high-ranking Roman civil servants), obviously understood and accepted that the Gospel was written for him so that he may 'know the truth concerning the things about which you have been instructed' (Lk. 1.4).[15] He was convinced by the eyewitness accounts, too, for he agreed to allow the sequel to the Gospel, the book of Acts, to be dedi-cated to him as well (Acts 1.1) (he would have refused to accept that dedication, and Luke would not have written it for him, if there had been any doubts). Two educated Romans in leading positions, Cornelius and Theophilus, were convinced by what they had heard and read, although it went against everything they had learned during their Greco-Roman upbringing.

Christian teaching had to deal with the many 'myths' sooner rather than later. The debate began in New Testament times, early on in the controversies betweeen Christianity and its rivals. The Greek word *mythos* is used five times in the New Testament: 1 Timothy 1.4 and 4.7; 2 Timothy 4.4; Titus 1.14; and 2 Peter 1.16. Each of these passages deals with real, observable and well-documented conflicts. The myths of the mystery cults celebrated in Ephesus and elsewhere (1 Tim. 1.4 and 4.7); early stories about a different, philosophical rather than divine Jesus (2 Tim. 4.4 – a myth re-told and believed by certain New Testament scholars, particularly those of the Jesus Seminar in the USA today); extra-biblical Jewish stories deviating from Old Testament teaching as Christians saw it (Tit. 1.14) – among them were some of the popular tales contained in the Sibylline Oracles, or even some Messianic ideas contained in the Dead Sea Scrolls which were known, of course, to many Jews and Jewish Christians, thanks to their wide distribution.

The last of these five passages about myth in the New Testament, 2 Peter 1.16, is particularly interesting. The message of Jesus is directly contrasted with the real 'myths' prevalent in rival religions and cults. No, Peter implies, ours is not a mystery cult based on 'cleverly invented myths': unlike all the others, it is historical truth – 'We had seen his majesty with our own eyes'. Peter of course is referring to the so-called Transfiguration on a mountain in northern Galilee (probably Mount Hermon): 'We ourselves heard his [God's] voice from heaven, when we were with him [Jesus] on the holy mountain.'[16] This is it, in a nutshell: so many aspects do look similar, at first glance. Many made an ideal starting-point for the Christian message. But Peter – and the others – are uncompromising. Beware the temptation of becoming syncretistic in your theology, they said. The similarities end where the historical message of Jesus the Son of God begins. The 'good news' of a godly life on earth, of the Kingdom of Heaven and eternal life in Christ is not yet another myth. In unequivocal words, Jesus himself expressed this in John's Gospel, speaking 'to the Jews who believed in him': 'If you make my word your home, you will indeed be my disciples; you will come to know the truth, and the truth will set you free' (Jn 8.31–32). The Resurrection accounts in all four Gospels and in Paul's first letter to the Corinthians must be seen in this contemporary context, and Luke's Emmaus story is no exception.

Luke the eyewitness?

Luke's account of the walk to Emmaus is remarkably restrained. There is no speculation about the nature of the sudden appearance and disappearance of Jesus, as we would find in the myths of gods and demi-gods in Greek or Roman literature. And yet, for all his restraint, the author slips one or two details into the text which hint at a personal knowledge of the event. An historian would assume that Luke had done what he had promised to do in his Prologue to his Gospel (1.2–3) – namely to interview eyewitnesses – and had actually spoken to Cleopas. In the early Middle Ages, however, pilgrims and commentators thought that Luke himself had been there, as the second disciple, and had humbly declined to mention himself by name. Willibald, later a Bishop of Eichstaett, who visited the Holy Land between 723–6, was merely the most eminent of those supporting this idea and a handful of modern scholars have agreed with him.[17] While it is impossible to dismiss this out of hand, it is unlikely, since we have no reason to suppose that Luke was in or near Jerusalem in AD 30. He joined the group around Paul several years later, and would certainly have referred in his Prologue to his own eyewitness status if he had had one. We can in fact still see the method he used in his writings, when he wanted to make sure that his readers knew he had been present himself: for example, in the famous 'we' passages in his second volume, Acts, which bear all the hallmarks of eyewitness accounts.

Even so, the two disciples, Cleopas and the unidentified other, were indeed eyewitnesses. It seems Cleopas became a well-known man in the early Church: a continuous tradition, which began with the church historian and apologist Hegesippus in c.AD 160, has identified him as being a brother of Joseph, the adoptive father of Jesus.[18] Any sober-minded historian will make the point that nothing depends on the truth of such an identification. Whoever this Cleopas may have been, he was known to Luke by name, and this should be adequate. But the consequences of a family relationship are of course intriguing. It would appear that Cleopas was not only an uncle of Jesus by adoption, but also the Cleopas/Clopas whose wife Mary stood at the cross of Jesus (Jn 19.25).[19] Again according to Hegesippus, he had a son called Simon/Symeon who became the second leader or bishop of the church in Jerusalem, after the murder in AD 62 of James, 'the Lord's brother', as Paul calls him (Gal. 1:19).

Both the tradition handed down by Hegesippus and the comments added by Eusebius are unfortunately full of the additions of legend.[20] This makes it difficult to disentangle historical truth from apologetic make-believe. On the other hand, one may enjoy the thought of a family 'caliphate' in the church of Jerusalem, and it is by no means impossible to accept the authenticity of the names and relationships. Luke, therefore, even if he had not himself been on the road to Emmaus, could have interviewed the son if the father had been unavailable (or dead by then) to find out what the family knew. It has even been suggested that the son was the second traveller. But if this was the case, it would be all the less explicable as to why Luke should not have named him.[21] Others have suggested that the second disciple was Simon Peter. But again, Peter, as the first among the apostles, would have been mentioned by name – and he cannot have been on the road to Emmaus anyway, as the Emmaus disciples are greeted on their return to Jerusalem with the message that elsewhere, 'the Lord has risen indeed, and he has appeared to Simon' (Lk. 24.34).

The list of candidates is almost endless: Philip the Deacon; James the brother of the Lord; and Nathanael the Pharisee who helped to bury Jesus; the daughter of Cleopas; and an otherwise unknown Ammaon have been suggested, although the latter name is probably nothing but a spelling mistake for 'Symeon' in two manuscripts of Ambrose (the late-fourth-century Bishop of Milan). There is only one conclusion left: the second person must have been someone whose name would not have been of singular importance in his or her own right. This would appear to rule out the son of Cleopas, since he, the second 'bishop' of Jerusalem, became even more important than his father. But Luke's Gospel was written before the appointment of Simon in AD 62, and there are no later Gospel manuscripts which add his name once he had become famous. So should we go back to Simon, son of Cleopas, after all? Many scholars today appear to be convinced that it was him. There is a much more likely candidate, however: the wife of Cleopas. Women are not always mentioned by name, and this is the case particularly when they appear in the company of men. Far from being a case of misogyny, it was just a habit. Jewish, Greek and Roman attitudes hardly differed in this respect.[22]

Remarkably though, the four Gospel authors emphasize the importance of women wherever possible. Against the prevailing attitude of their time, they even mention them as the first witnesses to the empty tomb and to the physical resurrection of Jesus. In legal terms, this was absolutely counterproductive: no court would have accepted the witness of women. This is why Paul in his first letter to the Corinthians assembles his list of resurrection witnesses without mentioning a single woman (1 Cor. 15.5–8): the Corinthians needed a list they could use to defend the Resurrection accounts, and women would have spoilt such a list for this specific purpose. The four Gospel authors, however, wrote history, not documents which could be used for legal purposes, and thus they insisted on the priority of the women. To the historian, that is one of the most persuasive reasons for accepting that this is exactly what happened. All four Gospel authors chose to mention the women they and their target readership either knew or knew of, and thus the lists differ; but even John, who refers to only one by name (Mary of Magdala), tells us that she was not alone – 'We' she says when she tells Peter what she had seen (Jn 20.1–2).

In spite of this insistence on the leading role of women, which we find in all four Gospels, their names are not always mentioned in mixed lists. Perhaps the most striking case of this occurs in Mark and Matthew's Gospels, where the names of Jesus' four brothers are given, but the sisters remain an anonymous group.[23] Thus, although we may find it unusual from our modern perspective, the most likely explanation is simply that the unnamed traveller was a woman and so, by inference, the wife of the named male traveller.[24] If, as looks most probable, the unnamed companion was indeed Mary, the wife of Cleopas, the plot thickens. There would have been a complete family tradition, husband, wife, and son, to guarantee the trustworthiness of the Emmaus incident.

Digging at Moza-Qaloniye/Emmaus, we jokingly thought of another reason why the unnamed companion must have been the wife of Cleopas. When the group with Jesus arrived at their home, dinner was not ready. Jesus disappeared immediately after the breaking of the bread, the customary beginning of the evening meal. Would he not have stayed on had there been a delicious plate of exquisite fish – we found scales of imported Nile perch – or even an 'ordinary' three-course dinner? Apart from bread, the table was empty, as the housewife had not been at home to prepare anything for the family, let alone for the unexpected guest, and so Jesus simply left, as did the two disciples, who immediately returned to

Jerusalem. Simon, the son, was a young boy, old enough to stay at home on his own, but not brought up to be the cook of the family.

Scholarly and anecdotal speculations aside, one basic fact should be emphasized. Luke's main source was a man known to the early Church. And we may even find a 'hidden' hint at the eyewitness quality of his report. Although the distance, and the insistence on the status of Emmaus as a village rather than a city, may have been the result of Luke's own research, there is the further detail that the two disciples did not recognize the risen Jesus because 'their eyes were held', or, as the New Revised Standard Version of the Bible translates it, 'their eyes were kept from recognizing him' (24.16). How? As we saw above, there was a reason known to all Jews: a resurrection body was a new creation, using the old, dry bones (which of course could not be seen and identified) with new sinews, new flesh and new skin (Ezek. 37.5–6). Observant Jews may not have expected anyone to rise from the dead prior to the last days, when God would raise the pious from among the people of Israel (Ezek. 37.11–14; Isa. 26.19; Dan. 12.1–3; Qumran Scroll 4Q 521, etc.), but even when they understood that Jesus was the first to be raised by God, they would of course have seen this in the context of these resurrection prophecies. As for the changed physical appearance, Ezekiel had been specific enough. The surprise about the inability of Mary of Magdala and the male disciples (Thomas, Peter and others included) to recognize the risen Christ immediately is entirely ours. The women and men concerned would not have been surprised at all. They all needed some form of proof that it was indeed Jesus, and they all got such proof. In the case of the Emmaus disciples, it was in the way he broke the bread.

In other words, we have a prophetic explanation – a risen body is not recognizable as such; and we have a theological, eschatological explanation – only Jesus himself decides when and how he wants to be recognized. But Luke wrote for a man with a Greco-Roman background, 'His Excellency' Theophilus, and he expected other readers from a similar background to pick up his Gospel. Thus, he underlined the physical reality of Jesus' resurrection body: 'They gave him a piece of broiled fish, and he took it and ate it in their presence,' he wrote when he describes the scene where Jesus appears to the disciples in Jerusalem immediately after the return of the Emmaus couple (24.42). 'We are witnesses who ate and drank with him after he rose from the dead,' Peter explains to the Roman centurion Cornelius in Caesarea, as depicted in Luke's second volume (Acts 10.41).

Jesus himself knew of course that they would not recognize him. In Jerusalem, when the Emmaus disciples and the others were together, he lowered the sleeves of his garment and uncovered his feet: 'Look at my hands and my feet; see that it is myself. Touch me and see; for a ghost does not have flesh and bones as you see that I have' (Lk. 24.39). This was the miracle behind the miracle. The whole point of the bodily resurrection, in Jewish thought, was the new creation on the old bones, bereft of any traces of the previous life, with its scars and everything else now gladly shed for good. Jesus, however, still showed the marks of his crucifixion. It was Thomas who fully understood the message: the resurrection of Jesus does not negate his crucifixion. The risen Christ remains the crucified Christ, who died, as the New Testament writings agree, for the sins of mankind. Thus, the so-called 'Doubting' Thomas, who asks, sees and understands, exclaims 'My Lord and my God' when he recognizes the old wounds on the new body (Jn 20.28).

To all this, Luke adds a snippet of local detail.

Walk from Jerusalem, following the ancient Roman trajectory from the western gate, along today's Yafo Road, through Giv'at Sha'ul, the Jerusalem Forest and 'Ma'ale Roma'im', past Ramat Moza, to the source of Ein Moza and the newly excavated remains of Vespasian's Colonia and the Emmaus of Luke and Josephus, and arriving just before dusk, you will find yourself walking for one and a half hours straight into the setting sun. We have done it several times, and we noticed that our eyes were indeed held: held down – looking at the road. For when you look up, your eyes are blinded by the sun, and the further you walk, the more it sinks to eye level. If you look up, you become dazzled and are in danger of stumbling on the uneven surface of a Roman road. If you notice someone moving up beside you, and you want to see who he or she is, your eyes, immediately blinded by the sun, are unable to focus, and before you can even attempt to establish who the person is, you have stumbled again. So you do not even try, and concentrate on the road ahead. 'Their eyes were held' is an accurate description of such a situation.

The Greek word used by Luke, *ekratounto,* is the grammatically appropriate form of *kratéo,* which literally means 'to control', 'to lay hold of' or 'to get possession of' someone or something. Luke uses it only one other time in his books, in Chapter 8.54 of his Gospel, when Jesus firmly grasps the hand of the dead daughter of Jairus, takes control of her and resuscitates her. Thus, for a brief but decisive moment, Luke combines all three elements of the story: there is the prophetic angle, represented by Ezekiel; there is the sovereignty of Jesus who decides when and how he wants to be recognized; and there is the eyewitness experience of the walkers, who are not in a position to recognize anyone, whoever he may be, because the setting sun keeps their eyes firmly on the road.[25]

Luke was not only a Christian believer and a Jewish expert in Scripture, he also was a researcher, interviewer and historian and, as he had set out to be (1.3), a literary artist aiming to produce an 'ordered narrative'. Reconstructing the route taken along the Emmaus road, and walking it at the same time of day and under the same circumstances, helps us to see that he achieved what he set out to do.

Notes

1   U. Victor, 'Was ein Texthistoriker zur Entstehung der Evangelien sagen kann', *Biblica* 79 (1998), 499–513. See also *id.,* 'Textkritik – eine Einführung' in U. Victor, C.P. Thiede and U. Stingelin, *Antike Kultur und Neues Testament,* Basel 2003, 171–252.
2   On the historical background of these scrolls, see C.P. Thiede, *The Dead Sea Scrolls and the Jewish Origins of Christianity,* Oxford 2000.
3   Cf. *Against Celsus* 3.59; 6.24.
4   Josephus, *Against Apion,* 2.185.
5   Aratus, *Phainomena* 5; Acts 17.28.
6   N. Orme, review of *The Bible: A History, Church Times,* 16 May 2003, 22. Orme also asked why so many scholars assume that the Gospels should be dated to the late first century, against the fact that they do not even reflect, clearly and unmistakably, the destruction of Jerusalem and the Temple in AD 70.
7   But see, on the evidence of Gospel publishing prior to Paul's letters, P.E. Hughes, *The Second Epistle to the Corinthians,* Grand Rapids 2nd edn 1986, 311–16, discussing 2 Cor. 8.18 as a reference to Luke's Gospel (*ton adelphon hou ho epainos en to euangelio,* 'because of the Gospel', not, as most modern translations interpret, because of his proclamation of the Gospel, or his

service to the Gospel). Early Church Fathers recognized Luke in this reference; see also J. Wenham, *Redating Matthew, Mark, and Luke. A Fresh Assault on the Synoptic Problem*, London 1991, 207–9, 230–8; H. Riesenfeld, 'Neues Licht auf die Entstehung der Evangelien. Handschriften vom Toten Meer und andere Indizien' in B. Mayer (ed.), *Christen und Christliches in Qumran?*, Regensburg 1992, 177–94, here at 182, *et al*. The use of 'Gospel', 'Euangélion' for a specific genre of literature can also be found in two of the earliest writings of post-New Testamental literature, the letters of Ignatius, who was martyred in c.AD 109, to the Smyrnaeans and to the Philadelphians. In 'To the Smyrnaeans', he describes those who deny Christ and writes: 'The words of the prophets did not convince them, nor the law of Moses, nor, so far, the Gospel' (5.1); see also 7.5 and 'To the Philadelphians' 8.2. From quotes and allusions in his letters, it transpires that his favourite Gospel was Matthew, closely followed by John. For a characteristic summary and defence of the current majority position, which prefers a much later date for the introduction of 'Gospel' as a technical term for a book about Jesus, see J.A. Kelhoffer, ' "How Soon a Book" Revisited: ΕΥΑΓΓΕΛΙΟΝ as a Reference to "Gospel" Materials in the First Half of the Second Century', in *Zeitschrift fuer die neutestamentliche Wissenschaft* 95 (2004), 1–34.

8   AD 40 is the date suggested by a Jewish expert in hellenistic literature, the late Guenther Zuntz (Professor of Hellenistic Greek at Manchester University): 'Wann wurde das Evangelium Marci geschrieben?' in H. Cancik (ed.), *Markus-Philologie*, Tübingen 1984, 47–71. See also for a date in the 40s of the first century J.A.T. Robinson, *Redating the New Testament*, London 1976; B. Orchard and H. Riley, *The Order of the Synoptics*, Macon 1987; J. Wenham, *op. cit.* C.P. Thiede and M. d'Ancona, *The Jesus Papyrus*, London 1996. For a summary of the traditional arguments for and against a date in the 40s, see D. Guthrie, *New Testament Introduction*, Leicester/Downers Grove 4th edn, 1990, 81–9.

9   If the plural 'Scriptures' (*graphai* in Greek) is used, as it is here, (Jewish) literature beyond the generally accepted books of the Old Testament is included; if only the Torah (the books of Moses), the Prophets, the Psalms and the Historical Writings of the Hebrew Bible are meant, the singular *graphê* is used. See C.P. Thiede, 'The Apostle Peter and the Jewish Scriptures in 1 & 2 Peter', *Analecta Bruxellensia* 7 (2002), 145–55, here at 150–5.

10   Professor Shemaryahu Talmon, former President of the Hebrew University Jerusalem, and Professor Joan M. Vernet of Cremisan College Bethlehem, speaking in the public debate during the Dead Sea Scrolls Conference at the Notre Dame Centre Jerusalem, 3 January 1999. Recently, E. Puech and E. Muro have tried to link 7Q4 with passages from Enoch, but using their method and checking the original fragments, the result is in fact the opposite: five new fragments from 1 Timothy have come to light. Another fragment,

7Q19, appears to be a lost commentary on Paul's letter to the Romans. For a detailed description of the procedure and all aspects of the debate about Cave 7, its jar and its papyri, see C.P. Thiede, *The Dead Sea Scrolls and the Jewish Origins of Christianity*, Oxford 2000, 124–81, 237–44.

11   See more generally on Jewish reticence in these matters, M. Goodman, 'Jewish Proselytizing in the First Century' in J. Lieu, J. North and T. Rajak (eds.), *The Jews Among Pagans and Christians in the Roman Empire*, London/New York 2nd edn, 1994, 55–78.

12   See C.P. Thiede, *The Dead Sea Scrolls and the Jewish Origins of Christianity*, Oxford 2000, 204–9.

13   'Hands' is a mistranslation: the Greek word *cheir* can mean both hand and (lower) arm, but since we know that a crucified person was not nailed through the palms (which would be torn apart immediately under the weight of the body), 'wrists' or broadly 'arms' would be a more accurate rendering of the Greek word.

14   See J. Zias and E. Sekeles, 'The Crucified Man from Giv'at ha-Mivtar: A Reappraisal', *Israel Exploration Journal* 35 (1985), 21–7.

15   Apart from Theophilus, the Greek word *krátistos* is used by Luke only when he talks about the two procurators Felix and Festus (Acts 23.26; 24.3; 26.25). As a contemporary Jewish author writing in Greek, Flavius Josephus confirms the use of this term as an address of influential Romans when he uses it to address Epaphroditus, the wealthy and influential private secretary of Emperor Nero (*Against Apion* 1.1). Epaphroditus was the dedicatee of Josephus' *Jewish Antiquities*, *Against Apion*, and of his autobiography.

16   2 Peter 1.17–18; cf. Mark 9.2–13.

17   E.g., F. Godet, *Commentaire sur l'Evangile de Saint Luc*, 3rd edn, Neuchâtel 1889; F. Rienecker, *Das Evangelium des Lukas*, Wuppertal 1959.

18   Hegesippus, *Hypomnemata*, quoted in Eusebius, *Church History* 3.32.6.

19   Cleopas/Clopas, or in Greek Kleopâs/Klôpâs (a semitic Greek form preferred by John), are shortened variant spellings of Greek Kleópatros. See R. Bauckham, *Jude and the Relatives of Jesus in the Early Church*, Edinburgh 1990, 15–18.

20   See R. Bauckham, *op. cit.*, 88–94.

21   Origen seems to have been convinced that this son Simon was the second traveller. For a discussion of his references, see Th. v. Zahn, *Das Evangelium des Lucas*, 4th edn, Leipzig/Erlangen 1920 (repr. Wuppertal 1988), 711–13.

22   Cf. R. Bauckham, *Gospel Women. Studies of the Named Women in the Gospels*, London/New York 2002, 269–77.

23   Mark 6.3–4; Matthew 13.53–56.

24   Richard Bauckham has put it succinctly: 'Nothing in Luke's account is inconsistent with this suggestion, whereas if the other disciple were known to Luke to be such a well-known early Christian leader as James the Lord's

brother or Symeon the son of Clopas . . . it is indeed incredible that he should not have named him' (*op. cit.*, 212, note 45). Bauckham goes on to analyse the role of Mary, the wife of Cleopas, in the early Church ('Her role in the Mission of the Church in Palestsine', *ad loc.*, 213–223).

25 A few minutes later, in the next sentence, 'they stood still, looking sad', and talked with the stranger (Lk. 24.17). By then, Luke the expert writer had made his point, combining prophecy, christology and topography, and he now takes up the thread that will lead his readers to verses 37–40, where all the disciples, including the two arrivals from Emmaus, are gathered in Jerusalem, and thought 'they were seeing a ghost' when Jesus enters the room, but eventually recognize him in spite of his changed appearance.

4

Luke and Josephus – Two Historians of their Time

Lucky Luke: The right man in the right place

Throughout this book, we have treated Luke, the author of a Gospel and of the first church history, as a trustworthy source and a person of integrity. Had it been otherwise, the quest for the true site of a resurrection event would have been somewhat pointless. Historians are amused by the steadfast refusal (still) of quite a few New Testament scholars to trust Luke. They treat him as a purveyor of legends with a purely theological message, crediting him only occasionally as having given accurate information. It is not only Luke who has suffered this fate; the other Gospel authors have been similarly treated, Matthew and John perhaps more than the other two. Obviously, they all have a message, and they tell us what their intentions are. Luke explains why he makes the effort to verify eyewitnesses, collect and read the written sources and 'investigate everything very carefully': 'So that you may know the truth concerning the things about which you have been instructed' – in other words, to strengthen the faith of Theophilus, his addressee. Historical investigation and faith in Jesus were not irreconcilable opposites, as Luke and Theophilus knew.

Mark successfully employs a similar introductory strategy. In the first verse of his Gospel, he explains that he is about to begin the *euangelion* of Jesus Christ, the Son of God. To modern readers, this smacks of pure theology: *Euangelion*, 'evangel', (or in plain English, 'Gospel') is, after all, the very genre which these days is the target of disbelief and suspicion. But when Mark was writing, this literary genre did not exist – he was the first to introduce it. *Euangelion* meant something different to an ancient reader. The Greek word was in fact quite common, and every citizen of the Roman Empire would have recognized it: *Euangélia*, 'good news', were the birthdays of the emperor and the anniversaries of his accession to power. An inscription found at Priene in Asia Minor and dated to the year 9 BCE, is one of many documents containing the term which have survived: 'Anniversary of the God Augustus, beginning of the good news for the whole world which were announced by him.' Readers of classical literature would also have remembered the word from Homer's epic *Odyssey*, where it refers to the reward for the messenger who brings the good news.[1] By 424 BCE, some three centuries before Augustus and the succeeding Roman Emperors were using the term, the word *euangelia* had become so inflationary that the Greek comic poet Aristiphanes mockingly described how the *euangelia* are called out when the price of sardines has been cut.[2] With Augustus, Tiberius, Claudius and Nero (the four Emperors who ruled between the time of Jesus' birth, death and resurrection and the publication of Mark's Gospel), the word had acquired a solemn meaning within the Imperial Cult, as a part of the veneration of the Emperor as a Son of God and as a god in his own right.

As for Mark's Jewish readers, they would have encountered the word in the Greek Septuagint (the translation of the Hebrew Bible into Greek, by Jews and for Jews, in the second/third centuries BCE). The Septuagint has different names and places for some of the Old Testament books, so the Greek references have to be translated into our terminology. Thus, we find the word four times in 2 Kings (which in Hebrew Jewish and modern Christian Bibles is 2 Samuel) at 18.20, 22, 25, 27, and once in 4 Kings (which is 2 Kings) at 7.9. Each time, it is used in the plural. The singular is used only once, in 2 Kings (2 Samuel) 4.10. It simply means 'good news', without any prophetic or messianic overtones. Even those readers of Mark who had only read the Latin classics would have recognized the terminology of the great orator and philosopher Cicero (106–43 BCE). In his letters to his friend, the wealthy editor and bookseller Titus Pomponius Atticus, he employs the Greek word in the otherwise Latin text: 'First, the – as I think – euangelia', he writes.[3]

Mark appeals equally to his Jewish and to his pagan readership. Homer, Cicero, the cult of the emperor, 2 Samuel and 2 Kings – wherever one looked, a world of expectation was linked to the *euangélia*. It is a statement of purpose: this book of mine, Mark implies, is not about legends, it is about a person whose life was firmly a part of the reality of the Roman Empire. You know the word, and you know its meaning because you can see it on inscriptions, in papyri, in public places and in the temples of the

Emperors. But I will tell you, in this new scroll, that things have changed and that the word has obtained a new meaning.

What makes Mark's use of the word so outstanding is the use of the Greek singular, *euangelion,* as opposed to the Emperors' *euangelia.* Attentive readers would have noticed the difference straightaway; for others, it would become apparent in the course of the text. In his book, the panoply of good news was abolished. In place of the whole inflated range, there now was only one piece of good news worthy of being singled out: one and only *euangelion* – the Gospel of Jesus Christ, the Son of God. And indeed, by referring to the Son of God, Mark again reinforces the fact that his Gospel is unequivocally placed in the real world of real people of his time. Jewish readers may have recognized the term from the writings of Philo of Alexandria, the great Jewish philosopher who died in c.AD 50, who called Abraham a 'Son of God'.[4] In the Old Testament, the idea that a successor of David will be God's son is first expressed in 2 Samuel 7.14 (in the Greek Bible = 2 Kings 7.16): 'I will be to him a father, and he shall be to me a son.' Whether or not the Jewish writers of these books envisaged a Son of God conceived by God the Holy Spirit, God's only begotten Son (as Christians proclaim him in the Creeds) is of no concern at this point. Every Jew would, at the very least, have seen the term in the context of God acting among men. But for Greco-Roman readers, the answer was even more unambiguous. They all knew who the Son of God was, from inscriptions, coins, and papyri: the Son of God was the Roman Emperor.

Ever since Augustus had persuaded the Senate to style his deceased adoptive father Julius Caesar 'the divine one' (*Divus*), the practice flourished, and the son of such an elevated ruler became 'the son of the divine one', the *Filius Divi*. In the Greek-speaking parts of the Empire, 'divine' and 'God' were the same word, so the son of the divine one became the Son of God, in Greek the *hyios Theou*: exactly the same terminology which we find in the New Testament writings when they speak about Jesus. In Luke's Gospel, for example, it arises in the annunciation story (1.32–35). Jesus was born under a Son of God, Augustus, and he was crucified under a Son of God, Tiberius. Greek and Roman readers seeing the words 'Son of God' at the end of Mark's first sentence, or finding it in the first chapter of Luke, had no choice: they had to think of the Roman Emperor. And it was not just a polite title. The Imperial Cult was a serious matter, particularly in the east – there were 37 temples dedicated to Augustus while he was still alive (at least three of them built by Herod the Great, at Caesarea Maritima, Caesarea Philippi, and Samaria/Sebaste), and 19 more after his death.[5] Thus, those readers of Mark's Gospel would have understood that the new dramatic beginning, the hitherto unheard-of good news, did indeed concern a rival to the Emperors. The unknown Jewish Jesus was a force to be reckoned with: not a myth, not a legend, but a religious and political challenge to the established system.[6]

To put it differently, Luke was not alone. He was one of a group of authors and communicators who knew they were transmitting historical events with a theological message. And all four gospels' authors have something else in common: they saw themselves as servants of their hero, not as masters of their craft who wanted to be hailed as literary artists. Their own personalities did not come to the fore; there is no auto-biographical cameo at the beginning of their books. This does not mean that their personalities and identities were of no consequence. Luke, in particular, must have been a writer who was well known at the time of the publication of his two scrolls. Since both books contain dedications, it follows that the dedicatee, Theophilus, and his wider circle, knew who the author was (there were no anonymous dedications in antiquity). Then, as now, the name of the author is not mentioned in the main part of the book; today, we find it on the title page, the flyleaf and the spine, while in classical antiquity, scrolls had a *sittybos*, a parchment or leather strip attached to the handle of the scroll with the information for anyone browsing in a library or a bookshop about author, title and subject. Sometimes, it was written on the outside of the rolled-up scroll; later, when scrolls fell into disuse, the information 'travelled' from the *sittybos* strip or the outside of the scroll to the cover and the first page of the 'codex', the new format for books which was used by practically all of the Christian scribes and Roman authors from the last quarter of the first century onwards. Thus, from very early on, the names of the Gospel authors were made public, not once but twice, on the scrolls and in the codices.[7]

In brief: the gospels were not written anonymously. This in turn made it almost mandatory for the reader to find out more about this humble author who 'left' nothing but his name and the name of the dedicatee of his two books. Notably, there never was a rival tradition about any other individual called Luke who might have written the Gospel and its sequel, the book of Acts. There always was only one candidate: the 'physician' (in Greek the *iatrós*) whom Paul calls his dear friend and whom he names 'Loukâs' in his letter to the Colossians (4.14), and who is mentioned twice more by Paul, in his short letter to Philemon (24) and his second letter to Timothy (4.11). This is not the place to go into all the technical details, but the fact that Loukâs is a very rare name in Greek antiquity, and that he is the only Christian in the first century referred to by this name, limits the possible options to the one who was always identified as the author, right from the first commentators writing about the authorship of the third Gospel: not a famous man whose name could have been invented to impress his readers, not even an apostle of the first or second generation, but a man close to the circle of Paul.

As a member of the medical profession, Luke belonged to the educated classes (in the fourth century BCE, Aristotle may have been the first to see physicians as erudite beyond their chosen profession).[8] By the time of Jesus, the medical profession had become highly specialized: there were ophthalmologists, dentists, ear specialists, and army doctors, both as civilians and as medical officers. Since Homer's days, medics often were itinerant practitioners; Luke could combine practising his profession with his journeys in Paul's entourage, or on his own.[9]

We do not know where Luke came from, but there is at least one indication of a place where he settled for a while: in Philippi, a city established by Philip II, the father of Alexander the Great, in 356 BCE. In 42 BCE, Octavianus – later Emperor Augustus – and Marcus Antonius defeated Brutus and Cassius, two of the murderers of Julius Caesar at Philippi; the city was developed as a veterans' colony, the Colonia Augusta Julia Philippensis. Luke arrived with Paul and Silas, having joined them at Troas (Acts 16.10) in about AD 49, but after the dramatic events in Philippi, Paul and Silas left without him (16.40). Years later, in about AD 56, Luke joined Paul's team once more, coming from Philippi (20.6). These seven or eight years in Philippi were certainly not wasted in idleness. The city had a large library with several buildings (remnants of which were discovered at the east end of the Forum), and there were all the other modern conveniences associated with a Greco-Roman city.

Luke's description of Philippi as a city and colony (*pólis* and *kolônía* in his Greek text) is as accurate as his description of the architectural ensemble of forum and public judgement seat (16.19–20), which has been excavated by archaeologists.

Philippi would have been a convenient place for Luke to order his material: the eyewitness interviews from Jerusalem, Judaea and Galilee, and the written sources about Jesus, ranging from collections of his sayings which had been circulating for some time, to Mark's Gospel. The works of the great Greek historians could be consulted in the city library, above all, Herodotus and Thucydides (it can hardly be disputed, for example, that Luke read the *History of the Peloponnesian War*, from about 404 BCE, and used some of its literary techniques for his Gospel and Acts).

Many scholars have assumed that a passage in Paul's second letter to the Corinthians refers to Luke as the author of a completed book about Jesus: 'We are sending the brother who is famous among all the churches because of the Gospel; and not only that, but he has also been appointed by the churches to travel with us . . .' (2 Cor. 8.18–19).[10] The only problem with this is the date which follows from such a reconstruction. Luke's Gospel would have been available by around AD 56. A majority of New Testament scholars find this difficult to accept. But is it impossible? Most of those who date Luke's Gospel to the 80s or 90s of the first century assume that he knew about the destruction of Jerusalem and the Temple in AD 70. They base this mainly on the prophecies of this destruction by Jesus (Lk. 19.41–44; 21.20–24), and since, according to their world-view, Jesus could neither perform miracles nor prophesy, the predictions must have been put into his mouth after the event. The facts tell a different story, however. In not a single New Testament text is there a reference to the destruction of Jerusalem, apart from the prophecy of Jesus, which can only be disputed by those who are predisposed against his prophetic abilities – and this, needless to say, is ideology, not scholarship.[11] The impossibility of the allegedly late date of Luke's Gospel grows when one looks at his second volume, Acts. It ends with Paul in Rome, under house arrest but free to welcome visitors and to teach 'with all boldness and without hindrance' (Acts 28.30–31). This means that Luke concludes his book in AD 61. There is not the minutest trace anywhere, in the papyri or in the comments of early Christians, that Luke ever considered, wrote or published a third volume.

But not only does he end with Paul teaching in Rome, there also is no reference to the destruction of Jerusalem, which early Christianity soon interpreted as a punishment according to the will of God, acted out by the Romans. Had this happened by the time of Acts, it is quite inconceivable that Luke would not have made use of it.[12] The Jewish-Roman historian Flavius Josephus, writing a couple of decades after Luke, had no qualms about the justification of Jerusalem's destruction. As we shall see, he even regarded the Roman Emperor Vespasian as the true Messiah, the saviour of the world who had defeated the godless uprising of the Jewish revolutionaries against the Romans. In Luke's Acts, there is not even a hint of the destruction of the Temple which, after all, continued to be visited by the first Jewish-Christians as a place of prayer and worship.

A year after the last stage mentioned in Acts, a catastrophic event befell the church in Jerusalem: James, the brother of Jesus, was executed in a wanton case of lynch justice by a group of members of the Sanhedrin, under the high priest Ananus. When the new Procurator of Judaea was informed, he immediately punished the murderers. Again, it is inconceivable that Luke, who dedicated the longest single passage of Acts to the accusation, defence and killing of Stephen (6.8–8.2), would not have mentioned the killing of the man who had been 'bishop' of Jerusalem for 20 years (after the departure of Peter for Rome in AD 41), and who played such an important role in previous chapters of Acts. Again, it is Flavius Josephus who tells us about this murder.[13] This should place Acts in AD 61/62. And if you think that James on his own may have been overlooked by Luke (unlikely as this would be), the martyrdoms of Paul himself, and of Peter, are conspicuous by their absence. Most historians suppose that Peter and Paul were killed in the early stages of Nero's persecution, which began in the months after the fire of Rome (19 July 64), but in fact they may have died later. In Peter's case, a date in late AD 67, during the last year of Nero's reign, is more probable. Be this as it may, even the latest possible date implies that Luke's Acts were written before the watershed year of AD 70. To be sure, this is so obvious that scholars noted it long ago. The famous church historian and philologist Adolf von

Harnack, for example, who had originally taken a liberal position which put the Gospels and Acts in the late, second- to third-generation period of early Christianity, changed his mind and published his results in a study which should be obligatory reading material for all those who still think that Luke wrote late.[14] And if Acts was published by AD 62 or just after, it follows that the Gospel, must be earlier still. There is no historical reason to exclude a date around AD 56. In fact, the classical philologist and textual critic Ulrich Victor put it succinctly: 'There simply is not a single piece of evidence, of any kind whatsoever, that the Gospels were written later than the mid-first century AD.'[15] Until recently, scholars who argued in favour of Luke's credibility and early date were accused of apologetics, if not of fundamentalism. The tables have been turned. The apologetic fundamentalists now are those who still maintain their anti-historical ideologies and claim that Luke was a late and rather unreliable writer.

In passing we have stated that Luke was a Jew, perhaps with a Greek, non-Jewish background. This, too, has been disputed. Back in the fifth century, Jerome invented a new identification which has remained fashionable in some circles: Luke was not a Jew, but a Gentile who converted to the Christian faith without making the 'detour' via Judaism. To anyone who reads both of his books carefully, this is highly implausible. Here is an author who is deeply immersed in Jewish thought, theology and language. No gentile convert to the Christian faith, not even the pagan 'godfearers' who attended synagogue services and followed some Jewish rites, could have acquired this to the extent and ease displayed by Luke. He is equally at ease with Greek terminology, calling non-Jewish foreigners *barbaroi*, barbarians, a word commonly used in Greco-Roman literature for anyone who did not belong to the Romanized peoples of the Empire (Acts 28.2–4). Like his famous contemporary Philo of Alexandria (but with the decisive difference that Philo did not have any Hebrew, whereas Luke undoubtedly did) Luke came from a cultivated hellenistic background. Born in Alexandria, as some early sources have it, but probably resident in Philippi.

Suspicions about the allegedly pagan identity of the pre-Christian Luke are caused, not least, by the very late and very sudden emergence of this hypothesis. Apparently, until Jerome appeared on the scene, no-one connected Luke with non-Jewish origins. In his *Questiones hebraicae in Genesim*, Jerome claimed that Luke was a proselyte from paganism, who did not know much about Jewish literature but became a Jew before he converted to Christianity. He obliquely refers to earlier sources, of which however no trace has remained.[16] The reference may allow for the possibility that Luke converted via Judaism, but this is far from clear. In any case, Jerome's was the first authoritative voice to declare that Luke was not a Jew by birth. The single source used by anyone who has subscribed to this opinion since then is a passage in Paul's Letter to the Colossians (4.10–14), where the apostle first mentions several companions who are 'the only ones from the circumcision among my co-workers' and then names a few others, among them Luke, who is singled out as the beloved physician. Adding one and one, people have deduced that Paul must have kept two separate lists and that Luke did not belong to those 'from the circumcision' and thus was not a Jew. But Paul says no such thing.[17] He merely talks about a number of committed Jewish Christians who adhered to orthodox Jewish practice, and he was grateful that they had joined him in spite of his advocacy of a mission among people who, in his opinion, should not have to be circumcised first in order to become Christians – this, after all, was the whole point of the so-called Apostolic Council in Jerusalem (AD 48), and its unanimous decision to allow Paul to continue his work among gentiles without requiring them to be circumcised, whereas those 'from the circumcision' would continue to be valued and looked after by other missionaries (Acts 15.1–29).

Paul did have problems with 'people from the circumcision' on other occasions. To see how deeply he felt about this, one only has to remember how he opposed his colleague Peter in Antioch, whom he mistakenly thought to have been influenced by pro-circumcision hardliners from Jerusalem (Gal. 2.11–15). And thus, in his valedictory greetings at the end of his letter to the Colossians, he gratefully acknowledges the fact that at least some of those Christians who were and remained orthodox Jews had joined his team, among them Aristarchus, Mark (the cousin of Barnabas and author of the first Gospel), and Jesus Justus. This does not in itself imply that the three men and the one woman who are mentioned afterwards (Epaphras, Luke, Demas and Nympha) are gentile Christians. To put it differently: making out that Luke was a gentile on the sole basis of this – to put it mildly – inconclusive passage is yet another case of wishful thinking. By the fifth century, the Church had become anti-Jewish. Jerome's hint, void of any anti-Jewish overtones, was welcome: at long last, they had at least one New Testament author who was not a Jew. It was a late victory for Marcion, who in c.AD 140 had tried to 'purify' the New Testament by accepting only one Gospel, Luke's, in an edited version without the pro-Jewish passages. Marcion failed in his attempt, and the other gospels remained: but in the process, Luke had been changed into a non-Jewish Christian.

Restoring Luke's Jewishness, we can see the outlines of an individual who was a multilingual historian with practical experience in medicine – and as such a highly valued, well-educated professional. He has often been compared to the Greek physician Galen (c.AD 129–99), who influenced the history and practice of medicine until the late Middle Ages almost as much as Luke influenced the history and practice of Christian historiography. Just as anything Luke may have written on medicine has not survived, Galen's historical and philosophical treatises are no longer extant, give or take a few fragments. But scholars have found numerous hints at Luke's medical expertise in his Gospel and in Acts. In the former, the incidents where Luke goes into health aspects not mentioned by the other Gospel authors come to mind, such as the high fever suffered by Peter's mother-in-law (Lk. 4.38); the medical portrayal of a leper (5.12); the type of sweat on Jesus in the Garden of Gethsemane (22.44); the healing of the High Priest's servant's ear (although all four Gospel authors know of Peter's swordsmanship, only Luke mentions the healing, at 22.50–51); and, conversely, the omission of a woman's complaint about the incompetence of doctors which precedes a miracle told by Mark (5.26) but is conveniently dropped in Luke's account of the same incident (8.43).[18] In Acts, there is the story of the snake which bites Paul on Malta (Acts 28.3–6), expertly told and combining a description of a type of snake technically called *coronella leopardinus*, with the popular belief that any snake which bites must also be poisonous – a superstition decidedly not shared by Luke, but described by him in loving detail (28.6).[19] All of this is, at best, circumstantial evidence, but it should not be discounted, since it is part and parcel of Luke's approach to his sources.

Luke the learned physician and skilled historian is anything but an illiterate legend-monger – so much should be obvious. He is not responsible for the pious tales which were told about him in later centuries. The most touching of these sees him as a painter. Visitors to the Syrian-Orthodox monastery of St Mark in the Old Town of Jerusalem – a site which the monks claim to have held the house of Mark's mother, one of the two centres of the Jerusalem community (Acts 12.12–17) – will be shown his painting of the Virgin and the Child. It is far too late to be even remotely acceptable as a first-century work of art, but as an example of Byzantine paintings, it is worth a closer look. Even so, the claim is not unique. Rome asserts its own original, in the church of Santa Maria Maggiore. In the Cappella Paolina, the *Salus Populi Romani* ('Salvation of the people of Rome') is on display – the Virgin Mary painted by Luke. The painting has been dated to the thirteenth century, and is a few centuries younger than the one in Jerusalem. Both represent a belief in the complete artistry of Luke, the physician, historian and painter, revealing to us how an authentic nucleus of reliable information can develop into folk religion and veneration. Luke became the patron saint of painters, in fact of all artists, and (obviously) of doctors, especially surgeons. For the classicist, these – and other – later additions to the picture of Luke will not deflect from what was the ascertainable core. He was a master historian, one of the greatest of his art in antiquity.

Finding the Messiah: Josephus the religious historian

Flavius Josephus is an indispensable source. Apart from the four Gospel authors and, to a certain extent, Philo of Alexandria, he is the only Jewish writer on historical matters in the first century. And he acknowledges the existence of not just two, but three sites called Emmaus: the city of Emmaus-Nicopolis; the village which became Vespasian's veterans' colony; and a third one near Tiberias at the Lake of Gennesaret. He is also the only first-century author to differentiate between these three places. This third one is called Hammat in the Old Testament (Josh. 19.35). It is to be pronounced with an initial 'ch' as in Scottish loch, and is decribed as 'a fortified town' belonging to the territory of the tribe of Naphtali. Parts of it have been excavated just south of the modern city of Tiberias, and it is not surprising to visitors that Josephus explains the name of this site as a derivation from the Hebrew biblical name which means 'hot/warm spring(s)'[20]: the steaming water can be seen near the magnificent mosaic floor of a fourth-century synagogue. There is a Turkish bath nearby and, on the other side of the road, a modern spa is frequented by up to 2,000 visitors per day. It was famous in antiquity, and Josephus knew people who went there to take the hot baths for health purposes.[21] In one manuscript of Josephus' *Jewish War*, his Greek spelling Emmaous/Ammaous was changed to Ammathous, to make it closer to Hammat.[22] But regardless of the inevitable variant spellings, the conclusion is plain enough: Josephus knew of three places of the same name, and for only one of them did he provide the etymology from the Hebrew *hammat*, 'warm or hot spring(s)'. Archaeologists have shown that he was quite right to link only one of the three to a warm source. There is none among the many springs and sources at Emmaus-Nicopolis, and there is none at Emmaus-Colonia either, although the area is literally overflowing with natural water supplies.[23] And as we saw in previous chapters, 'hot spring(s)' is not the only conceivable origin of the Greek word Emmaous/Ammaous; in the case of Emmaus-Colonia, the demonstrable root is Ha-Moza, as in Joshua 18.26. In brief, Josephus apparently knew his local geography.

However, even Josephus has had his detractors. Who was he, and what did he know about Jesus and early Christianity? Someone writing a work called *Jewish Antiquities*, with a scope ranging from the creation of the world to the reign of Nero, could not easily ignore the Jewish Christians who had been actively spreading their message for 38 years by the end of Nero's reign. And indeed, Josephus does mention them. He refers to many of the people known from the Gospels – John the Baptist and his execution, the Herodian family, Caiaphas and Pontius Pilate – but above all, there are James and Jesus. James, the brother of Jesus, appears in an account of some character defects ascribed to the High Priest Ananus. In AD 62 – and as we saw above, this date helps us to date Luke's Acts and, by inference, his Gospel – Ananus convened the Sanhedrin to have James and others sentenced to death by stoning, on the trumped-up charge of a 'transgression of the law'. Albinus, the newly appointed Roman procurator, had not yet arrived, and Ananus exploited the interregnum to get rid of a devout but dangerously effective missionary. When Albinus arrived, the High Priest was ousted by King Agrippa, acting on the instructions of the procurator.[24] Josephus notes that not all of the observant Jews in Jerusalem were happy with the stoning:

> Those of the inhabitants of the city who were considered to be particularly fair-minded and keen observers of the law, sent messengers to King Agrippa, asking him to make sure that Ananus would desist from further such actions, for this was not the first time that he had acted unjustly. Some of them even went to meet Albinus, who was on his way from Alexandria, to inform him that Ananus had no authority to convene the Sanhedrin without his consent [to impose a (death) penalty].

Obliquely, Josephus hints at an observation no-one could escape in Jerusalem: among so many enemies, the Jewish Christians had friends and supporters. And since Josephus the Jew accuses Albinus of being 'one of the school of the Sadducees who are indeed more savage than any of the other Jews', we may assume that he, who was after all a Pharisaic priest himself, saw the supporters of justice as being from the ranks of the Pharisees in Jerusalem. This coincides perfectly with the image of the Pharisees presented in Luke's Acts: Rabbi Gamaliel in particular is portrayed as a model of justice and wisdom (Acts 5.34–42). It is also Luke who reports how the apostle Paul spoke of himself as a Christian and a Pharisee in the same breath.[25]

The sentence in Josephus's passage about James that usually attracts people's attention reads like this: 'And so he [Ananus] convened the judges of the Sanhedrin and brought before them the brother of Jesus called Christ, by name of James, and certain others.' It is a remarkable way of putting it, for James is identified by his status as Jesus's brother. Jesus is mentioned first, and only then the name of the man to be stoned by the Sanhedrin, James. And since Jesus was the third most common first name in Judaea and Galilee at the time, Josephus specifies which Jesus he is talking about – Jesus called Christ (*Christós* in Greek). Again, it is a striking formulation. Writing in Greek, Josephus uses the word *legomenos*, which does not mean 'so-called' (as if Josephus was distancing himself from the title Christ). It means that this is what Jesus was called. Obviously, we may want to add 'by his followers', but this is not what Josephus says. He plainly accepts that Jesus, the brother of James, was called Christ or, in Hebrew, 'Messiah'. How could he, the Jew who became a Roman and even an adopted member of the Roman imperial family (the Flavians), but never a Christian, make such a matter-of-fact statement?

The solution can be found several pages earlier, in Book 18 of the *Jewish Antiquities* (18.63–4). This is what we find:

> At this time, there lived Jesus, a wise man, if one should call him a man. For he performed surprising feats, and as a teacher of people who gladly accepted the truth, he won over many Jews and many Greeks [i.e. Gentiles]. This one was the Christ. And when Pilate, who had heard the accusations of the most prominent among our people, condemned him to be crucified, those who had come to love him at the beginning did not give up their affection for him. On the third day, he appeared to them restored to life, something which, among 10,000 other miraculous things, the prophets of God had said about him. And to this day, the tribe of the Christians, so called after him, has not disappeared.

This passage has been called the Testimonium Flavianum, which is a bit of a misnomer, since Josephus became a Flavian only by late adoption – but admittedly, it sounds nicer than the more appropriate Testimonium Josephinum. And 99 per cent of scholars have argued that all, most, or some of this statement must be a Christian addition, an interpolation by Christian scribes, since a Jew who remained a Jew could never have written like this. It is a curious majority position, since the single most 'offensive' statement, the central sentence that 'He was the Messiah', could never have been added by a Christian scribe. To Christians, then as now, Jesus *is* the Messiah – in the present, not the past tense. But could a non-Christian Jew talk about Jesus as the Messiah even in the past tense, and could he, as it seems he did, accept that Jesus appeared, risen from the dead, on the third day after his crucifixion?

Jehosaph Ben Mattityahu, alias Flavius Josephus, certainly is the first Jewish author outside the New Testament who mentions Jesus. Let us recapitulate: Josephus was born in AD 37, seven years after the death of Jesus, and his fame rests on two major writings, the *Jewish War*, published in about AD 75, and the *Jewish Antiquities*, published in about AD 94. This means they were known at a time when both members of the first Christian communities in Jerusalem, Rome and elsewhere, and some of the opponents of Jesus, were still around. His Testimonium looks straightforward enough, but there are whole shelves full of conjectures about the original text and about later Christian changes and additions. Even a Slavonic translation of Josephus has been adduced to 'restore' the original, and hardly anyone dares to suggest that the Greek text which exists today is identical to the original. The problem is, however, that all of the existing manuscripts of the *Antiquities* include these lines. Speaking from the perspective of the textual critic, there is no evidence whatsoever that Josephus's words were tampered with. And judging them by the standards of his time, and his own position, there is no 'theological' reason why he should not have said what he said. Let us look at the text as we have it today.

Josephus began his public career as a priest of the Pharisees and a commander of the Jewish forces in the revolt against the Romans, which started in AD 66 and ended in the destruction of Jerusalem and the Temple in AD 70, followed by some mopping-up operations like the conquest of the Masada fortress in AD 73/74. In the early stages of the revolt, he was taken prisoner by the Romans, told their commander Vespasian that he would become Emperor, and was freed and honoured by Vespasian when the prediction became true in AD 68. Vespasian adopted him into the Imperial Flavian family, and the Pharisee and Revolutionary General Jehosaf Ben Mattityahu became Flavius Josephus. The rabbis regarded him a traitor; to this day, his writings are shunned by observant Jews, do not feature in most Jewish encyclopedias and are not included in the curriculum of schools in Israel. He himself tried hard to explain both Jewish values to the Romans, and Roman concepts to the Jews. Strictly speaking, therefore, his writings cannot be understood as Jewish ortho-doxy, nor as Roman state propaganda. But he did not become a Christian either.

Most of our passage should be uncontroversial. Josephus underlines the formal legality of the process taken against Jesus. There were the accusers (in Latin, *delatores*), and there was the judge, the Roman prefect Pontius Pilate, who found the accused guilty and condemned Jesus to the customary method of execution for non-Romans, crucifixion. Writing at the court of the Roman Emperor, Josephus underlines that it was the Roman prefect, the Emperor's man, who executed Jesus. Other elements of the passage in the *Antiquities* should be equally uncontroversial. Josephus reports what he found in his sources. The miraculous feats performed by Jesus were well attested: even Caiaphas had not doubted them, and had used them as his starting point for the decisive question: 'Are you the Messiah, the Son of the Most High?' His followers accepted his truth gladly: this is a statement of fact, not necessarily an endorsement. Truth was relative, in philosophical terms, and Josephus, writing as Vespasian's court historian, knew this as much as Pilate, who had concluded one of his hearings with the philosophers' question: 'What is truth?' Again, by AD 75, it was obvious to the most ardent opponents that Jesus had won over many Jews and many of the Greeks; and it was equally obvious, some 45 years after the crucifixion, that the community of his followers had not disappeared but were claiming, as Josephus reports, that Jesus had appeared to them on the third day, in accordance with the prophecies they quoted.

However, there may be a hint of irony in this statement. The countless prophecies, which Josephus mentions, were in fact not even claimed by Jesus' most committed followers. Josephus alludes to the fact that the first Christians pointed at prophecies – as the risen Jesus himself had done on the road to Emmaus – but he keeps a distance, by using the ploy of exaggerating the actual claims. A Christian forger or 'interpolator' would not have wanted to add such an ironical exaggeration. The only statement which does look odd in a Jewish-Roman historian's account is the one sentence, 'He was the Christ'. Josephus does not say 'he was called the Christ' (as he does in the passage about James), nor does he say, 'he was the Christ for them', or, 'he was their Christ'. Are these words a forger's fingerprints?

It seems that the historical truth behind the unaltered authentic statement, literally 'This one was the Christ', sheds some light on Josephus himself and on his own messianic hopes and expectations. The early decades of the first centuries were vibrant with messianic fervour.

The Essenes (whom Josephus knew well, as he had studied with them) expected the Messiah to come in those days, as did most other Jews, and the vast majority was hoping for the victorious Davidic Messiah, the one who would start the final eschatological battle, destroy both the enemies from outside – the Romans – and those from within – fellow Jews who did not conform to the orthodox line, collaborated with the Romans or did not even believe in the imminence of Messianic times. When Jesus appeared on the scene, there had been several leaders of revolutionary movements, even from Galilee, but none of them had claimed the Messianic title. Suddenly, there was Jesus. He was hailed as the Son of God, he was the Messiah (or, in Greek, the Christ): the closest circle of his followers said so on his behalf, and he never contradicted them. On the contrary, when Caiaphas the High Priest interrogated him, he confirmed the claim in the strongest messianic terms any Jew could have used. But this Messiah was crucified and, from the perspective of Josephus, nothing had changed. The Romans and the corrupt high priests remained in charge, oppression continued, a real armed revolt began in AD 66, Josephus himself was part of it, and it ended in the destruction of the focal point of Jewish observance, the Temple. Desperately disappointed, Josephus changed sides and eventually became a Roman court historian.

In other words, it is a very personal comment. 'This one *was* the Messiah.' The Messiah came, and the Messiah went, destroyed by the Romans who, by God's judgement, were left in charge. All messianic hope had been in vain. Quite literally, the sentence means what it says: this one was the Messiah – full stop. The message of Josephus to his fellow Jews is stark: do not revolt against the Romans and forget about the Jewish Messiah. We had him and he failed.

Needless to say, orthodox Judaism does not share this assessment. To this day, observant Jews still expect the coming of the Messiah. But that is not the point. Josephus is expressing the sadness of his very personal position. If anything, his allegedly spurious sentence in the Testimonium Flavianum is its most authentic part. And historically speaking, it tells us what a Jew like Josephus, who mentioned Jesus not once but twice, knew and believed. As a contemporary voice, he provides the evidence for the controversies about Jesus among first-century Jews, based on the facts which he had ascertained and which confirm the Gospel accounts.

There is even more to be discovered behind the surface of Josephus' statement. The early to mid third-century Christian author Origen, who knew the works of Josephus, stated in two of his own writings that Josephus did not believe in the Messiahship of Jesus.[26] Neither did Eusebius, who a century after Origen quotes the Testimonium Flavianum in his *Church history* (1.11,7–8) and elsewhere, claim that Josephus had become a Christian on the strength of his statement about the Messiah Jesus. In other words, both Origen and Eusebius must have interpreted the statement in the way it was intended. Josephus certainly did not believe in Jesus as the Messiah who was being expected by the vast majority of contemporary Jews: the Davidic one, who would bring military victory over the oppressors – i.e. the Romans (or Kittim, as they are called in the Dead Sea Scrolls). As such, Jesus had failed dismally. He was crucified; the Romans remained in power; and a later uprising, witnessed by Josephus, resulted in the destruction of the Temple. Josephus was spared the sight of the Bar-Kokhba revolt of AD 132–5, which occurred under a leader who was hailed as the military Messiah by no less a charismatic rabbi than Akiba, but which resulted in utter defeat and the annihilation of Judaism in Judaea.

'This one was the Messiah', Josephus writes, and if we follow the Greek to the letter, we may even translate as 'The Messiah this one was'. Apart from the fact that the sentence occurs in all of the surviving manuscripts without even a text-critical hint at later manipulations, we also have the past tense noted above: 'This one *was* the Messiah.' This past tense, which no Christian scribe could have inserted, forces us again to ask why Josephus himself used it. The great historian and philologist (and arch-liberal theologian) Adolf von Harnack noted the point in 1913, quoting a British author in support.[27] Harnack, not yet quite convinced himself, started his own investigation. In the end, he comes to his own positive conclusions,[28] basing them on solid philological and historical arguments, and sums them up as follows (translated from the German original):

The need for sensation – his Jewish history is a history of sensations, and it is full of sensational heroes – plays a major role in the writings of Josephus. The messianic hopes and the Messiah (Christ) had lost their nucleus for Josephus; they had become a dead loss. Now he could play with them so much more easily and could turn them into sensations. Many educated Greeks in Rome and in the Empire had heard the rumours about the Jewish 'Christ'. Now Josephus tells them what it is about: this wise Jesus was the Christ, not just the so-called Christ, but really the Christ. However, one has to add in one's thoughts: there is nothing about this Christ as Christ; that is a religio-political figure, which has been revealed, in our days, and by the downfall of the Jewish state, as a big mistake. Seen like this, Josephus could very well write: 'He was the Christ.' Hardly anyone among his Greek readers would have misunderstood him, and he did not think of Christian readers.

So, one may agree with Harnack (or Burkitt), or prefer to think of Josephus as a tragic character whose statement about the Christ who had come and gone without securing the expected wordly victory over the oppressors reflected a very personal sadness about lost hopes. It is, in any case, difficult to see how anyone but a Jew like Josephus could have written that Jesus *was* the Messiah. In fact, all those who are inclined to think that the whole Testimonium is wholly or partly a Christian invention will have to come up with solid arguments rather than the gut feeling (or ideological prejudice, or, in some conservative circles, unnecessarily apologetic rearguard action) that no-one outside the New Testament and later Christian literature could have spoken about Jesus as the Messiah, the wise man and miracle-worker who was reported by his followers to be alive on the third day. Josephus passed on what he knew, and he added his personal comment. This is what makes the passage so uniquely valuable. One of the problems of modern biblical scholarship is the widespread idea that one has to re-invent the wheel and start from scratch, rather than simply take some notice of the results reached a generation or two ago. The problem of the Testimonium Flavianum was solved in 1913, but one can search in vain for references to, let alone correct evaluations of, Burkitt and Harnack in current publications.

There is, however, another surprising insight to be gained by looking at Josephus. He did proclaim his own Messiah: the Roman Emperor Vespasian. When he realized that the prophecy in Genesis 49.10, about the ruler who will come from Juda, was just wishful thinking by the Jewish revolutionaries in their war against the Romans, he switched sides. The new world domination would indeed come from the land of Juda, but the ruler, the Messiah, would be a Roman rather than a Jew – the one who became Emperor after his victories in the Jewish homeland. Josephus prophesied that the Roman general Vespasian (who had just taken him prisoner) and his son Titus would become emperors.[29] And he interpreted his own prophecy: 'What incited them [the Jewish revolutionaries] more than anything else to wage war, was a double-edged prediction, which could be found in the holy Scriptures – that in those days someone from their country would rule over the inhabited earth. This they related to someone from their own people, and many of the wise men erred in their judgement. The word of God much rather indicated the reign of Vespasian, who was acclaimed Emperor in Judaea.'[30] Tacitus (c.AD 55–120) and Suetonius (c.AD 75–150), the two Roman historians who wrote about the period, agreed: Vespasian was the ruler of the world who came from the land of Juda.[31] Josephus was also free to recall the prophecy in Isaiah 45.1–5, where another non-Jew, the Persian king Cyrus the Great – the Saviour of true Judaism, the man who allowed the Jews to return from Babylonian captivity and even permitted the reconstruction of the First Temple – is hailed by God himself as the Messiah, in Greek 'the Christ'. Josephus was a political animal if ever there was one. Calling Jesus the past Messiah ('he *was*'), and Vespasian the present one, he places his hopes in the future under Roman rule.

Finally, let us look at the question from a different perspective. If Jesus was the Messiah, but not the military, victorious one whom Josephus needed and proclaimed in Vespasian, what kind of Messiah was Jesus for him? Again, we know the answer. Many Jews expected at least two Messiah figures: the other one was not Davidic, but Aaronitic, from the line of the brother of Moses. He would be priestly, rather than military. Some Jews thought that both would come in the last days, some thought that there would have to be a sequence: in any case, Josephus, who had studied the teachings of the Pharisees, the Sadducees and the Essenes in his youth, was fully aware of these multifaceted expectations. The Essenes taught that the Aaronitic Messiah would 'teach justice in the last days'.[32] He would win a decisive victory against the godless enemies, but without military means.[33] Thus, Josephus, a man who knew these texts, a man who never became a Christian, nor an Essene for that matter, rejected the Aaronitic Messiah, but accepted that he did exist: in Jesus, who 'was the Messiah', and who, in accordance with ancient prophecies, performed miracles and even rose from the dead on the third day. After all, who would dare to suggest that Josephus did not know Hosea 6.2 ('After two days, he will revive us, on the third day he will raise us up, that we may live before him') and was unable to link this prophecy with the information he had received from Christians? Or indeed the voice of the greatest of the prophets, Isaiah: 'Your dead shall live, their corpses shall rise' (Isa. 26.19); and, for good measure, Daniel 12.2: 'Many of those who sleep in the dust of the earth shall awake, some to everlasting life, and some to everlasting shame and contempt.'

Josephus, the Pharisaic priest, knew such prophecies by heart. And as someone who had studied with the Essenes for a few years (*Life* 10–11), he also knew that they too expected a bodily resurrection. Among the Dead Sea Scrolls, Qumran fragment 4Q521 is specific enough. After an extensive list of messianic deeds, we read: 'And the Lord shall do glorious things which have never been achieved . . . For He shall heal the pierced, He shall revive the dead, and bring good news to the poor . . . And he will open the tombs.' If that was not emphatic enough, another Essene text, the so-called Thanksgiving Hymn, says it again: 'You [the Lord] have purified man from sin, so that he may be made holy for you, with no abominable uncleanness and no guilty wickedness, so that he may be one with the children of your truth and share in the lot of your holy ones, so that bodies gnawed by worms may be raised from the dust, to the counsel of your truth.'[34]

Josephus, it seems, was willing to accept that there will be a bodily resurrection for the pious people of God. As a Pharisee (albeit by now a Roman citizen and court historian), he never denied the validity of these Jewish prophecies. He, who described the courageous last stand of the Zealots on Masada with an intriguing mixture of fact and fiction, may not have known what archaeologists established when they discovered some scroll fragments underneath the floor of the synagogal library at the fortress: these defenders read Ezekiel 37, the prophecy of the 'dry bones', with its detailed depiction of a physical resurrection in the last days. But he knew of this prophecy, as he knew of all the other prophecies which kept Jewish hopes and expectations alive. Was it impossible to accept that one single Jew, the Messiah, should rise before the others? As the Aaronitic Messiah, Jesus was acceptable even to Josephus, who could report that his followers believed in the bodily reality of his resurrection. But obviously, Jesus was not the Messiah he, Josephus, wanted and needed. Even the well-attested testimony he had received from Christians did not turn him into a follower of the one Messiah who, for him, was the wrong one, a past and spent force, crucified by those he had been expected to defeat. Josephus demanded a military Messiah. Everything else was past history. And if anyone should have persevered and suggested to him that Jesus was the Davidic, military Messiah, he would have rejected this anyway, since as such he had failed. In other words, there was no Jewish Messiah who mattered to him anymore. His choice was the new Cyrus – Emperor Vespasian. It was a political decision, with religious overtones.

Today, we can understand that Jesus was both Aaronitic and Davidic through the ancestry of his mother Mary, and that he was in addition confirmed in his Davidic ancestry through his adoption by Joseph.[35] And we know that Jesus redefined the Davidic Messiahship on the cross, when he prayed with David's Psalm 22, the psalm which leads from forlornness and suffering to the final triumph of the Messiah, the bringer of salvation.[36] Josephus drew his own conclusions; his hopes were not eschatological, but rooted in the here and now: in his own survival, in the acceptance of Roman supremacy, and in his efforts to salvage a Jewish future under the Roman, messianic, emperors. But in the end, there is no way around it: Josephus' statement about Jesus is true to character, it is pure Josephus, and we should continue to use it as an authentic testimony to the Judaeo-Christian world of the first century.

In a way, Josephus did for the study of early Christianity what he did for the study of early anti-semitism: never a Christian, he recorded the earliest reliable information about Jesus and his brother James outside the New Testament and became a reference point for classical historians; never an enemy of his own people, he collected Greek and Roman sources about the hatred of the Jews and thus became the single most important source for students of early anti-Judaism.

One of the most colourful personalities of the first century, Josephus will remain controversial. His statement about Jesus, however, should not be treated as controversial any longer.

Notes

1   *Odyssey* 14.152.166.

2   Aristophanes, *The Knights* 656.

3   *Letters to Atticus* 2.3.1, 13.39.1.

4   *On Sobriety*, 56.

5   See H. Hänlein-Schäfer, *Veneratio Augusti. Eine Studie zu den Tempeln des ersten römischen Kaisers*, Rome 1985, 16.

6   For further details on the historical and literary context of Mark 1.1, see C.P. Thiede, *The Cosmopolitan World of Jesus. New Light from Archaeology*, London 2004, 48–52.

7   See M. Hengel, *Studies in the Gospel of Mark*, London 1985, 81–2; cf. C.P. Thiede and M. d'Ancona, *The Jesus Papyrus*, London 1996, 41–6, 95–7.

8   *Politika* 1282a.

9   Homer, *Iliad* 11.514–15, etc. For Luke as a travelling companion of Paul, see Acts 16.10–40; 20.5–21.18; 27.1–28.16.

10   For a discussion of this verse and further literature, see note 7 of Chapter 3.

11   One even finds the argument that Luke must have known about the destruction of Jerusalem because of the precise language he employs when he has his Jesus prophesy that 'when you see Jerusalem surrounded by armies, then know that its desolation has come near' (21.20), and that 'the days will come upon you when your enemies will set up ramparts around you and surround you, and hem you in on every side' (19.43). Both Jesus and Luke, like any other contemporary, would of course have known how the Romans laid siege to a town or city – the *circumvallatio* was a technique which is as old as any military strategy – and that a conquered place would be 'desolated'. It is not only a Roman procedure (documented since 146 BCE), but is known from the Old Testament as well: 'There is not a single trait of the forecast which cannot be documented directly out of the Old Testament' (C.H. Dodd, *More New Testament Studies*, Manchester 1968, 79). Cf. B. Reicke, 'Synoptic Prophecies on the Destruction of Jerusalem' in D.E. Aune (ed.), *Studies in New Testament and Early Christian Literature*, Leiden 1972, 121–34.

12   Rabbis also interpreted the destruction of Jerusalem and the Temple as divine punishment – references can be found as early as Flavius Josephus. They of course did not understand it as a sign of God's wrath about the denial of his Son as the Jewish Messiah, but, more generally, as further punishment for disobedience to God, as the prophets of old had frequently formulated it.

13 *Jewish Antiquities* 20:200.
14 A. von Harnack, *The Date of the Acts and of the Synoptic Gospels*, London 1911, 90–116.
15 U. Victor, 'Einleitung' in U. Victor, C.P. Thiede and U. Stingelin (eds), *Antike Kultur und Neues Testament*, Basel 2003, 12–29, here at 16–17.
16 Jerome writes: '*licet plerique tradant, Lucam evangelistam ut proselytum hebraeas literas ignorasse*'.
17 Cf. E.E. Ellis, 'The Circumcision Party and the Early Christian Mission' in *id., Prophecy and Hermeneutic in Early Christianity*, Tübingen 1978, 116–28.
18 Some manuscripts and several modern translations put it in again. For the general picture, see also A. von Harnack, *Luke the Physician*, London 1907.
19 Even Pliny the Elder (AD 23–79) shared the conviction that all snakes are poisonous (*Natural History* 8.35, 86). Pliny, who was perhaps the most erudite collector of knowledge in the first century, wrote his *Natural History* in 37 books, which he dedicated to the son of Emperor Vespasian (the future Emperor Titus) in AD 77. He also shared the popular belief that snakes may bite to kill in an act of vengeance (*Natural History* 8.35, 86), and this is what the Maltese apparently thought had happened when Paul was bitten (28.4). Thus, the Maltese may be excused; but it is remarkable how Luke the physician differentiates between Paul's reaction to the bite, his own detached assessment of the situation, and the attitude of the Maltese. On Luke as an expert physician, see also W. Ramsay, *Luke the Physician and Other Studies in the History of Religion*, London 1908 (repr. Grand Rapids 1956), here at 63–5.
20 *Jewish War* 4.11.
21 *Life* 85.
22 Some scholars argue that an original 'Ammathous' was changed later to make it resemble the other two, but it would be odd to assume that later scribes actively contributed to possible confusions – unless, of course, they changed the spelling by mistake. Ammathous can be found in the eleventh/twelfth century codex Pl. 69 No. 19 (Florence, Bibliotheca Laurentiana). Ammaous is the reading in five other codices from the tenth to the twelfth centuries (*Codex Ambrosianus,* Bibliotheca Ambrosiana, Milan; *Codex Vaticanus* Gr. No. 148; *Codex Vaticanus Palatinus* Gr. No. 284; *Codex Vaticanus Urbinas* Gr. No. 84; *Codex* Gr. No. 383, Bibliotheca di San Marco, Venice). Emmaoûs is the spelling in the *Codex Parisinus* Gr. No. 1425 (Bibliothèque Nationale, Paris), of the tenth century. Josephus also mentions this place in his *Jewish Antiquities* (18.36), where we encounter a similar textual situation, with manuscripts offering Ammaous and Am(m)athous. For Emmaus-Nicopolis, the manuscripts have either Ammaoûs, Emmaoûs, or Ammathoûs; in the case of Emmaus-Colonia, all Greek manuscripts read Ammaous. Since the initial 'A' and 'E' are interchangeable, it is obvious enough that all three places are an Emmaus, in our modern transliteration. The rest is a result of guesswork,

scribal errors and such like. It is remarkable, though, that the real Emmaus of Luke's Gospel did not suffer from these variations. In Josephus, it is always Greek Ammaoûs, and the single exception is offered in a Latin translation, by the scribe mentioned previously, and by his followers, who mistook it for Mas(s)ada. Luke obviously did not know Josephus, who wrote some three decades later, and nor did Josephus consult Luke. Thus, Luke's Greek spelling Emmaous, which is equally persistent in all manuscripts (with the odd and meaningless exception of Oulammaous in Codex D, apparently caused by a mistaken identification with Bethel, which is spelt like this in some manuscripts of the Greek Septuagint in Genesis 28.19), serves as an important reminder of the fact that Luke and Josephus are truly two independent sources for the identification of the same site.

23   As to Emmaus-Nicopolis, traces of (once) possibly warm springs were found 4km southwest of the ruins, and cannot be linked to the city which had pleasant, allegedly beneficial springs, but certainly not warm or hot ones. At Emmaus-Colonia, the various springs are not warm or hot either, but the major one, some 150m from the present excavation site, has an agreable warm 'feel' to it (the temperature has been measured to have a maximum of 18° C), which makes it a very popular 'mikveh' (purifying bath) for members of an orthodox group who come to bathe here daily and often regale us with their stories when they walk past our site on their way to the 19th century synagogue.

24   *Jewish Antiquities* 20.200–3.

25   'Brothers, I am a Pharisee, a son of Pharisees' (Acts 23.6; cf. his own letter to the Philippians, 3.5).

26   *Against Celsus* 1.47; Commentary on Matthew 10.17.

27   Francis Crawford Burkitt. He argued for the uncorrupted authenticity of Josephus's statement in his article 'Josephus and Christ', *Theologisch Tijdschrift* 1913, 135–44.

28   A. von Harnack, 'Der jüdische Geschichtsschreiber Josephus und Jesus Christus', *Internationale Monatsschrift für Wissenschaft Kunst und Technik*, 7/9, 1913, 1037–68.

29   *Jewish War* 3.399.

30   *Jewish War* 6.312–15. The prophecy which Josephus interprets in this way is Genesis 49.10. In the New Testament, Hebrews relates the very same prophecy to Jesus (Hebrews 7.14).

31   Tacitus, *Histories* 5.13.1–2; Suetonius, *Vespasian* 4.5. According to Suetonius, astrologers had already predicted that Nero, should he be removed from office in Rome, would become ruler of the Orient, particularly of Jerusalem (*regnum Hierosolymorum*): Suetonius, *Nero* 40.2. Nothing came of this, of course; and thus, the fulfilment of Josephus' prediction is all the more remarkable.

32   Damascus Scroll CD 6.11.

33   Qumran fragment 1Q 28b 5.20–26.

34   4Q521, fr. 2, and IQH 19 [11] 10–14. In his own writings, Josephus never discusses the Jewish-Essene faith in a physical resurrection, although he does not expressly exclude the possibility (cf. *Jewish War* 2.154–5; *Jewish Antiquities* 18.18). Nor did any of the others who wrote about the Essenes and their belief system – Philo of Alexandria and Pliny the Elder more extensively than other of the ancients – attribute a resurrection faith to the Essene movement. The exception was Hippolytus (c.AD 170–236), a Christian presbyter in Rome. In his *Refutation against all Heresies*, he used Josephus, and many of the other Jewish and non-Jewish authors, in an impressive array of philosophical and theological arguments, and he also knew Qumran Essene documents which must have reached Rome but were unknown to scholars until the discovery of the Qumran Caves. In Book 9.27, he wrote: 'The doctrine of the Resurrection has also derived support among them, for they acknowledge both, that the flesh will rise again, and that it will be immortal, in the same manner as the soul is already imperishable.' Until fr. 4Q521 was published, quite a few scholars assumed that Hippolytus was mistaken.

35   The Davidic ancestry of Jesus through his mother Mary is confirmed by Paul in Romans, 1.3; cf. Luke 1.32. The Aarontic lineage is implied by Luke in his Gospel (1.5 with 1.36). Joseph as a descendant of David is mentioned several times, e.g. Luke 2.4; Matthew 1.6 with 1.16.

36   According to Mark 15.34 and Matthew 27.46, Jesus prayed the first verse of Psalm 22. It is the fourth of his seven last words in the chronological order which can be established from the evidence of all four gospels, and it is the only one of the seven which is mentioned in more than one Gospel. There are those who have doubted that Jesus could have spoken more than one last word, but this is far from incredible. Suetonius for example records three last words of Emperor Augustus (*Augustus* 99). Jesus may have prayed the whole psalm, with Mark and Matthew merely recording the beginning: but even if he did not, every Jew knew this psalm, and would have understood that it was not a hopeless cry of utter despair and of separation from God. Verse 1 is the beginning of a spiritual and prophetic journey which ends in the triumph of God and his Messiah.

5

An Emperor Joins the Fray: Vespasian's Emmaus

A Swiss banker's son

Emmaus has been rescued from oblivion thanks to Emperor Vespasian. This, at any rate, is the conclusion if lateral thinking is applied to the surviving sources. After all, if Vespasian, the 'messianic protector' of Josephus, had not built a colony for 800 veterans at Emmaus, Josephus would probably not have mentioned this village, and we would have missed the decisive clue which links the Moza of Joshua 18.26 with the Emmaus of Luke and Josephus, the Colonia of Vespasian, the Queloniya of the Mishna, the Arabic Qaloniyeh and the terraces of Moza in modern Israel: to anyone who did not happen to live there, it was just another village, a leafy suburb of Jerusalem. It owes its place in the history of mankind to two events which both were mentioned by only one contemporary author: first, the resurrection appearance of Jesus in the late afternoon of 9 April 30; and second, 40 years later, the establishment of Vespasian's colony in late AD 70/early AD 71.[1] The contributions of Luke and Josephus to our quest are beyond doubt. But what exactly did Vespasian do to deserve a place in early Christian history? One thing is certain: it is not every day that the son of a Swiss banker helps to preserve a biblical site.

Vespasian was born on 17 November AD 9. His father was Flavius Sabinus, who had earned a certain renown as the imperial tax official of the Roman province of Asia. According to his biographer Suetonius, he was not a corrupt tax collector of the type we find in the pages of the New Testament, but popular and highly respected – amazingly, the citizens even erected statues in his honour, with an inscription which praised him as 'the good tax collector'.[2] Sabinus then moved to the country of the Swiss, *apud Helvetios*, where, again according to Suetonius, he became exceedingly rich as a banker and where he died, leaving a wife, Vespasia Polla, and two sons. The elder son, Sabinus, became a city prefect, and the younger one is our Vespasian.[3] Vespasia Pella was the descendant of an old senatorial family, but her husband was of humbler origins, and thus Vespasian did not deify him after his accession to the emperorship. Unlike Augustus, Tiberius and other emperors, he therefore was not a *Filius divi* (in Greek a *Huios Theou*), no 'Son of God'. This did not deter him from cracking one of his better jokes: in AD 79, when he was on his death-bed, knowing that his son and successor Titus would have him deified by the Senate of Rome, he quipped, 'O dear, I think I will become a God'.[4]

Under Emperor Claudius, Vespasian served in Britain and conquered the Isle of Wight. From 63–4, he was Proconsul of Africa, and in 66, Nero sent him to the province of Palaestina, where he became the political administrator and military commander of the campaign against the revolutionary Jews. Nero's appreciation of Vespasian's abilities was apparently stronger than his dislike of the man's lack of *savoir vivre*: Vespasian had accompanied Nero on his musical tour of Greece, and whenever the Emperor performed, singing and reciting, he quickly fell asleep or left the audience.

In his biography, Suetonius follows this anecdote with a remarkable passage.[5] Confirming the messianic theology of Josephus from his own, slightly more detached vantage point, he writes: 'Throughout the Orient, it was the old and unanimous opinion that, according to a soothsaying, the reign over the world would be taken in possession from Judaea. This had been said about a Roman Emperor, as later events were to show. The Jews however applied this saying to themselves and began an uprising.' Suetonius then briefly mentions some of the things the Jews did in the early stages of the revolt, and explains that Vespasian was chosen to deal with the revolutionaries because he had proved his mettle as an energetic commander and at the same time was no threat to Nero (successful regional commanders were often seen as potential rivals), since he came from humble origins. Vespasian organized his legions and fought in the frontline, was hit in the knee by a stone and received several arrows in his shield.

While all this was going on in Judaea, Nero committed suicide and three unsuccessful pretenders – Galba, Otho, and Vitellius – succeeded each other within a year. Did Vespasian believe or hope he might become the fourth, and more enduring, emperor after Nero? Suetonius apparently thought so, for he offers no less than four paragraphs on ominous signs which allegedly encouraged Vespasian to expect an imperial future for himself, even while Nero was still alive.

Eventually, Vespasian asked 'the oracle of the God of Mount Carmel' in Judaea, and was given several oracular responses that made him 'very optimistic', as they seemed to promise that he would be successful in all his plans.[6] At this stage Suetonius mentions Josephus, calls him 'one of the noble prisoners' of Vespasian and has him say, 'while he was being put in chains, that he would soon be freed by the very same man, who by then would be the emperor'. We do not know if Suetonius had read the *Jewish War*, but in any case, he and Josephus could have met in Rome, where Josephus was living in an imperial villa until his death in or soon after AD 98, at a time when Suetonius, born in c.AD 75, was a public orator and lawyer.

Later, after Josephus' death, Suetonius began a career at court and finally became the cabinet secretary and director of the chancellery (the *vir ab epistulis*) under Emperor Hadrian. In this capacity, he had unlimited access to the imperial archives, and it is certainly plausibile that he consulted the *Jewish War* during his research on the biography of Vespasian. It is of course prudent to remember that Josephus lived his life, and Suetonius started his, during the reign of the Flavian emperors, Vespasian, Titus and Domitian, and that one should not expect too much criticism of the founding father of this dynasty. Thus, to give just one example, when Suetonius tells the anecdote of Vespasian falling asleep during Nero's concert tour in Greece, this is a critique not of the future Emperor's behaviour, but of Nero's artistry. Indeed, later in his biography, Suetonius praises Vespasian as a sponsor of the arts and the sciences: not only did he pay the teachers of Greek and Latin rhetorics an annual salary of 100,000 sestertia from his private funds – this was just political strategy, since he wanted to guarantee an excellent education for the next generation of civil servants – he also showered lavish expenditure on poets, sculptors, artists, actors and musicians. It was Vespasian who ordered the rebuilding of the Theatre of Marcellus, which had been destroyed during the unrests at the end of the reign of Vitellius, and personally invited the great and the good from the guild of performers to appear during the opening festivities.

In other words, Vespasian cannot be dismissed as a semi-educated military man who happened to be promoted after a distinguished army career. Like so many Roman officers, he was well acquainted with the arts, and his speeches, both public and private, often glistened with literary allusions. In fact, one of the archaeological snippets of evidence for the literary education of the Roman officer class at the time of Vespasian was found at the fortress of Masada near the Dead Sea, and is in the form of a papyrus in Latin, with a quote from Virgil's national epic, the *Aeneid* (4.9): *Anna, soror, quae me suspensam insomnia terrent?* – 'Anna, sister, why do these nightmares keep me awake?' A Roman officer wrote the line from memory, unable to sleep after the conquest of the fortress in AD 73/74, when he would have witnessed those countless Jewish defenders who had killed themselves rather than fall into Roman hands (as Josephus was to recount in gory detail). At a time when pastoral counselling and psychoanalysis were not available to soldiers, self-therapy could be attempted by writing down telling quotes from a poet like Virgil.[7] When Vespasian became Emperor in AD 69, his son Titus ended the war; under his command, Jerusalem and the Temple were destroyed in AD 70. But it was the Emperor himself, not his son, who decided to build a veterans' colony at Emmaus. What made him choose this site?

Miracles and fate

The simple and straightforward answer to this question is that we do not know. Josephus does not give an explanation, he merely underlines that it was the only veterans' colony established by Vespasian in Judaea. The advantages of the site are obvious: it was on the main road to the Mediterranean ports, and, above all, it was one of the loveliest spots anywhere near Jerusalem, with a fresh water supply and shady trees, not too warm in the summer, not too cold in the winter, a wadi – the Nahal Sorek – which never dried up (even in the hottest of summers), and the most fertile land in the vicinity of the city. In 68, when he marched past the village to begin the encirclement of Jerusalem, Vespasian must have noticed the spacious houses, built in the Herodian style that incorporated fashionable Roman architectural features, and he probably made a mental note that this would be the ideal area for a colony once the war was over and won.[8] But since Vespasian himself was a great believer in *fatum*, providential fate, let us play his game for a moment and 'find' an element of providence in his choice for the only veterans' colony in Judaea.

Like Jesus, Vespasian was a miracle worker. This may sound odd, but the sources are unequivocal in this respect. No Roman Emperor before him or after him during the first centuries of Imperial Rome was credited with miracles, but Vespasian performed two, some 40 years after the death and resurrection of Jesus, when the gospels had been written and their message was known even in imperial circles, from Nero to Vespasian himself.[9] In Alexandria, on his way back to Rome, Vespasian healed an almost blind man, and another with a paralysed hand.[10] Vespasian did not volunteer his services: he was approached by the two men in public, who claimed the god Serapis had appeared to them in their sleep with the message that the Emperor would heal them. Vespasian hesitated, he even mocked those around him, but so as not to look like a coward, he gave in, consulted doctors who diagnosed both cases as not so severe and advised the Emperor to exercise a healing act which, after all, may be in the interest of the gods whose servant he was. Vespasian put spittle on the eyes of the blind man and trod on the hand of the other, just as they had asked him to do, and they were healed.

There is no apparent reason to doubt these two healings. Tacitus in particular, writing before Suetonius, alerts his readers to the professional quality of his research about the event and, writing in c.AD 105, adds a noteworthy comment: 'Eyewitnesses talk about both events to this day, when it would not profit them to tell a lie.' Both cures, miraculous or not, are known from classical literature; treading on a paralysed hand is even recommended in medical treatises.[11] Even the most hardened admirers of Vespasian will admit that two miracles are not really remarkable, if compared to the 34 performed by Jesus: but in any case, Vespasian was one of only four people seriously credited with having performed healing miracles in the first century.[12] This then, put in Roman terms, is *fatum*: could it be that Vespasian built his veterans' colony at a site where his co-miracle worker Jesus of Nazareth had appeared after the miracle of the resurrection?

Vespasian seems to have met Jewish Christians in Galilee, and later in Judaea – and they posed him with a problem. On the one hand, they were, so to speak, the 'good' Jews, since they had refused to take part in the violent uprising against the Romans and had fled to Pella in Transjordan in order to escape the attacks of the insurgents who were so ruthless that they were prepared to kill non-revolutionary fellow Jews. Soon after the revolt, Vespasian allowed these Jewish Christians to return to Jerusalem, and for a while they were the only Jews in the devastated city. The leader of the Christian community (which returned from voluntary exile in Pella with imperial permission) was none other than Simeon, the son of Cleopas – the son of the man who had met the risen Jesus on the road to Emmaus. But on the other hand, Vespasian had his doubts about these Jews. The leaders of the Jewish-Christians, James and his succesor Simeon Bar Cleopas, had always claimed their descent from David. The family of Jesus proudly presented a family tree which centred on this great king and ancestor of the Messiah. And since the vast majority of Jews expected a militarily victorious Messiah to come from the line of David, it made sense, from a Roman Emperor's perspective at any rate, to eradicate his descendants. This then was Vespasian's dilemma: the Jewish Christians had refused to participate in the revolt, and he had every reason to treat them favourably. But among their leaders there were Davidic men like Simeon Bar Cleopas. Would they remain loyal to the Empire, or at least neutral?

According to the late second-century Christian historian Hegesippus (who may have been a Jewish Christian himself) Vespasian ordered all the descendants of the house of David to be searched out, so that none of the descendants of the royal family should survive among the Jews.[13] But according to Eusebius (the fourth-century church historian who pre-served passages from Hegesippus' *Church History*), Vespasian never planned any actions against the Christians.[14] Although we do not know what Vespasian and his son Titus (who was the man *in situ* while his father was on his way back to Rome via Alexandria) actually did to try to discover if these Jewish Christian descendants were harmless or not, they must have had their ways and means, and one account about a slightly later interrogation has survived: Domitian, the younger son of Vespasian, who succeeded his brother Titus as Emperor from 81–96, had been informed that descendants of David were active among the Christians, and so he decided to question two 'grandsons of Judas who was called, according to the flesh, the brother of the Saviour'.[15] These two appear to have been harmless enough: they were manual workers with callused hands, and Domitian believed them when they explained that the Kingdom of their Messiah Jesus was not an earthly kingdom, but a heavenly one which would come about in the Last Days, at the end of the world, when He would arrive in glory to judge the living and the dead and to award everyone according to their deeds. The Emperor released them and ordered an end to all measures against Christians. Hegesippus adds that these two, because of their unflinching steadfastness and their close family relationship to the Lord, were made leaders in the churches and remained alive until the reign of Trajan. It was not all happiness, however; elsewhere, Hegesippus mentions the martyrdom of Simeon Bar Cleopas (the man who had become the successor of James as 'bishop' of Jerusalem) under Emperor Trajan, at the age of 120.[16]

As for Vespasian, his attitude towards the Jewish Christians, and the descendants of David among them in particular, may have been influenced by Josephus. He, as a newly adopted Flavian and Vespasian's court historian, had not only pronounced Vespasian the Messiah of the Jews, he had also explained to him (as we saw in our discussion of the so-called Testimonium Flavianum) that Jesus was another Messiah, but the wrong one, who had come and gone without endangering anyone's authority: in other words, he was the Aaronitic Messiah, the priestly one. Jesus may of course have been from the line of David too – Josephus takes care not to discuss this point – but his Messiahship was Aaronitic in nature, and harmless: therefore, his followers could be expected to remain equally harmless in their own political activities. It seems that Josephus wrote intending to protect all those Jews who had not taken up arms against the Romans; in fact, Vespasian was the Messiah of the Jews for him precisely because he had rescued true Judaism from the misguided, self-destructive Jewish revolutionaries. And thus for Josephus, too, the Jewish Christians were among the good Jews whom he neither attacked nor condemned.

As a military commander, Vespasian quashed a Jewish uprising, but he did not fight the Jews because they were Jews. None of the Roman historians, nor Josephus for that matter, claimed that he was anti-semitic. There were no collective punishments under his command, and like his son Titus, who later took command in Judaea, he did not intend to destroy the Temple in Jerusalem. To the Roman elite, and particularly to someone who respected all gods, the god of the Jews may have been mysterious – since the Jews venerated only one God instead of many, as other peoples did, and they did not even erect statues of him – but the Temple itself was an architectural wonder of the world, a unique religious monument. Titus, who finally did order its destruction in AD 70, hesitated for a long time. Ironically, his right-hand man was a certain Tiberius Iulius Alexander, the commanding officer of the siege troops at Jerusalem. He was the same Tiberius Iulius Alexander who, as prefect of Egypt, had proclaimed Vespasian Emperor and made his legions take the oath of loyalty to Vespasian on 1 July 69.[17] And this Alexander was not just another Roman prefect: he was a Jew. As a nephew of Philo of Alexandria, the greatest Jewish philosopher (apart from Sha'ul of Tarsus, alias the apostle Paul) during the first half of the first century, he was brought up in an observant Jewish family, was highly learned in Greek and Latin thought, became a Roman civil servant, switched sides completely and was elevated to the office of Procurator of Judaea from 46–8, ten years after Pontius Pilate had been dismissed from the same office.[18] In c.AD 64, he was appointed prefect of Egypt. One cannot escape the ironic twist, which some may want to call tragic. It was this Jewish Roman who was the first to hail Vespasian as the new Emperor, to accept the office of chief of staff (*praefectus praetorio*) towards the end of the Jewish War under Titus, to argue that the Temple must be destroyed, in order to take the centre of their resistance away from the Jews, and to actually command the final assault.[19]

After the uprising, Vespasian struck coins to commemorate the triumph. The inscriptions were in Latin, and they were also issued in the Roman province of Judaea. Since the common languages of the region were Hebrew, Aramaic and Greek, the choice of Latin – and Latin only – underlined the supremacy of the victorious Roman: he did not even bother with any of the languages used by the local Jews. Pontius Pilate, the prefect of Emperor Tiberius, had followed a different strategy. When he gave orders to produce a headboard (titulus) to be put on the cross of Jesus on 7 April 30, he insured that it included three languages: Latin, of course, because it was a Roman judgement, and the official language of the administration had to 'seal' in writing the proclamation of the *causa poenae*, 'the reason for the punishment'. But it also used Hebrew, as the holy language of the crucified man and his people, and Greek, then the lingua franca of the world, so that really everyone, Jews and non-Jews alike, passing the crucifixion site near the western city gate would understand it and – literally – get the message.[20]

The inscriptions on Vespasian's coins read *Iudaea Capta* ('captured Judaea') or *Devicta Judaea* ('vanquished Judaea'), and while the Emperor's head was shown on the obverse, the reverse showed a veiled woman either sitting or kneeling beside a palm tree, the emblem of the Jewish homeland. She represented the subjugated Jewish people, with either a bound Jewish man or a fully armed Roman officer – perhaps Vespasian himself – standing behind her, on the other side of the tree.[21] Another imperial act of Vespasian was the introduction of a tax of the Jupiter Capitolinus, called the *Fiscus Iudaicus*, which replaced the Temple Tax. All Jews everywhere in the Roman Empire had to pay this tax, and we may recall the anecdote repeated above, about the way the tax was collected at the time of Domitian: 'The *Fiscus Iudaicus* was collected with particular harshness. It had to be paid [also] by those who lived like Jews without confessing the faith, or by those who had not paid the tributes imposed on their people, disguising their origins. I remember that I was present as a very young man when a procurator and his numerous entourage inspected a 90-year-old man if he was circumcised.'[22]

On the other hand, however, the same Vespasian guaranteed the survival of native Jewish theology, and eventually of literary Judaism worldwide, after the destruction of the Temple: during the war, he allowed a team of Pharisees, followers of the famous Yohanan Ben Zakkai, to continue with public services outside Jerusalem and to convene a permanent academy (or *Yeshiva*) in the town of Jamnia (Yafneh). Additionally, with imperial permission the Sanhedrin was allowed to relocate to Jamnia soon after AD 70. Under Yohanan, Judaism began to initiate a series of reforms, and it was at this point that Judaism eventually began to cope with the loss of the Temple. Decisions about the canon of the Hebrew Bible, and the first stages towards a literary rather than merely oral tradition of rabbinic teachings, were taken by successive councils. Simply put, important collections like the Mishnah and the Talmud owe their origins and inspiration to the work of the academy at Jamnia after the destruction of the Temple in AD 70. Without Vespasian's express permission, and the consent of his successors Titus and Domitian, this would not have been possible.[23] In other words, Vespasian cannot be portrayed in black and white. He was an efficient military commander; a circumspect emperor who unified the empire after years of internecine strife under Galba, Otho and Vitellius; who consolidated the finances; and who had time to erect magnificent buildings like the Forum of Peace and the Colosseum, the Amphitheatrum Flavium in Rome, which remains a lasting monument to his grandeur (although recent research may have shown that at least some of the money used to build the third and fourth storeys of the Colosseum under Titus came from the vanquished Jews and the spoils of the Temple).

Seen in this light, Vespasian's decision to build only one colony in Judaea, for 800 veterans (and, one assumes, their families), was characteristic of the man. On the one hand, he did not plaster the land with new imperial cities and colonies; on the other, he honoured a sizeable number of legionaries who had distinguished themselves in the conquest and destruction of Jerusalem by giving them Emmaus, a pleasant suburban village inhabited by wealthy Jews.

Evidence found and lost: digging up Vespasian's colony

The film *Indiana Jones and the Last Crusade* may have influenced the image of 'archaeology' more lastingly than Howard Carter and the discovery of Tutankhamen's tomb, or the legendary Bedouin shepherd who found the first Dead Sea Scrolls in the caves at Qumran. There are amateur diggers who model themselves on the man with the big floppy hat and the whip: even in Israel, a certain Vendyl 'Texas' Jones created sensational stories all of his own, claiming to have found the lost site of the Arch of the Covenant in Gilgal, or some of the implements needed for the establishment of a Third Temple in Cave 3 at Qumran. Supplied with seemingly limitless funds, he employed the latest gadgets of field archaeology and made many a mountain out of molehills. Tolerated for a long time by the Israel Antiquities Authority, he was finally banned from digging at Qumran but has continued to claim that George Lucas and Steven Spielberg were inspired by his persona and his allegedly heroic deeds when they produced *Indiana Jones and the Raiders of the Lost Ark*. Vendyl 'Texas' Jones may be a particularly irritating example of the species, but the wider problem is known to psychiatrists in Israel and is called the 'Jerusalem Syndrome'. Technically, it is a temporary state of sudden and intense religious delusion brought on while living in or visiting Jerusalem. The patient often adopts so-called biblical or otherwise eccentric clothing, sometimes merging their identity with that of a character of the Bible or having a strong feeling of mission and attaching an unusual significance to religious relics.[24] Real-life archaeology operates on a different level. Apart from the not infrequent cases where discoveries are made 'accidentally', the actual digging is the last stage after months, or sometimes years, of painstakingly circumspect preparation.

The Qumran Caves are perhaps the most famous example of an accidental discovery. In about 1947 (the exact year is shrouded in legend), three Bedouin shepherds in their early thirties, Muhammad ed-Dibh, Juma Muhammad and Khalik Musa, were looking for safe places to hide contraband. The Ta'amireh Bedouins had been selling ancient coins and other artefacts to workers at the budding Dead Sea industrial plants since the 1930s. They had been smugglers for generations, and in the politically uncertain final years of the British Mandate, they became involved in arms trading, gun-running and similiar lucrative activities. The first of the caves with scrolls was not discovered because anyone – least of all professional archaeologists – had been looking for them, but because the Bedouins needed new hiding places for arms. Thus, the discovery of the scrolls was accidental, but it still was the result of an active search for something.[25] More frequently these days in Israel, archaeologists are called in when a bulldozer hits upon an ancient wall or a mosaic during road works. Salvage excavations, also called rescue digs, will then be carried out under difficult conditions and with limited time, and it is not always possible to preserve the site. Occasionally, the Israel Antiquities Authority will step in even before building work has begun. This has been the case at Moza, just above Vespasian's Colonia.

It was known that the terraces of Moza and Mevasseret Zion were in an archaeologically sensitive region, as it had been a settlement area since the early times of the Benjaminites in the thirteenth century BCE (Joshua 18.26), and probably before. Thus, when a new motorway between Jerusalem and Tel Aviv was being planned, to replace the old highway with its dangerous curves – and we know how dangerous they are, as we are aware of the frequent accidents which happen in the curve near our excavation site below the terraces – the Antiquities Authority began several rescue digs in the areas where supporting pillars for the road had been planned by the civil engineers. The digging had to end in the summer of 2003, and the results were breathtaking. As we will see in the next chapter, some of them have considerably added to our knowledge of biblical history. In one case, the finds were so important that the roads department decided to relocate one of the planned pillars. In other cases, the excavated areas will be protected by a solid but removable cover and may be reopened by future generations, if the new motorway – yet to be built – should ever disappear.

If these are examples of accidental finds or discoveries, the ideal scenario is a different one. Archaeologists will study the sources – and then excavate. The sources may be ancient documents, historical accounts and descriptions, maps, or reports by medieval tourists who saw things which are long since lost. The primary source, in other words, is the text, and archaeologists have learned to trust ancient documents as their starting point. Everyone has heard of Heinrich Schliemann and his discovery of Troy, and although modern archaeologists and classical historians tend to smile benignly when they hear his name, he was one of the first to trust a text which was regarded by practically everyone at the time as ancient Greek folk legend – Homer's *Iliad*. Having studied this, he calculated where the place could be, and found the remnants of a city in an area where no one had dug before him. Was it Troy? And if so, was it *Ilion*, Homer's Troy? Since 1870, when Schliemann first started it all off, a succession of professional archaeologists has been active in the region, more than 46 building phases have been established, and scholars are still engaged in sometimes quite polemical debates about the correct attributions. Schliemann made mistakes; others have made mistakes after him; but no one can dispute the fact that he spotted the correct area because he did what others have done ever since: he trusted the historical nucleus of ancient texts even if they are overshadowed by the prejudice of myth and legend. Obviously, the art of textual interpretation has advanced since 1870, not because scholars have suddenly become more intelligent, but because more and more ancient sources have been recovered and can be studied, compared and, hopefully, understood. There is no guarantee that a modern interpretation of an ancient document is superior to a medieval one (in fact, as far as Troy is concerned, the right site was still known in the fifteenth century), but the sheer amount of material should enable us to reach conclusions about the reliability or otherwise of a textual source.

As for Vespasian's Colonia, the starting point was refreshingly clear: the ancient Roman name had survived in its Aramaic and Arabic forms, and a village called Qaloniyeh, or Qalunya in modern Arabic, existed on the site until 1948.[26] On 11 April 1948, the village was conquered by Israeli forces during the fierce fighting for access to Jerusalem after the assault by the Arab forces on the fledgling Jewish state. There had been a mixed population; 350 Jews, 10 (Arab) Christians and 900 Muslims were counted in 1945. But when the War of Independence began, the Arabs at the Crusaders' Emmaus of Abu Gosh remained loyal to the State of Israel – as they still are today – whereas those at Qaloniyeh turned against the Jews. The fighting resulted in the destruction of most of the houses and villas, among them the country residence of the Mufti of Jerusalem, who had been a fervent supporter of Adolf Hitler and his anti-Jewish politics. The ruins of his estate can be seen just north of our current excavation. Among the objects found when we began our first digging campaign in 2001 was Russian ammunition dated 1948: in those days, the Russians supported Israel.

The location and its names defined the site of Vespasian's colony, although names often 'travel'. A good example is the name of Mount Zion, which in the course of two millennia moved from Temple Mount to the Ofel (the City of David in Jerusalem's suburban village of Silwan) and, finally, to the southwestern hill of Jerusalem. But the wider area of the Colonia was beyond dispute. Good as this sounds, it goes only so far: one cannot excavate a whole region all at once. Instead, one has to reduce a likely area down to a few square metres, in the attempt to find a 'corner' of the site, or even its centre. Only then does one know where and how to continue. A further indication for narrowing down the possible area came from the Mishna (as we saw above). In this collection of sayings and teachings, which was compiled in the 2nd/3rd centuries, we read that the Jews from Jerusalem descended to Moza and Qaloniyeh to collect the branches for their sukkot, the huts to be built at the Feast of the Tabernacles.[27] The description here indicates that Moza was below the hills of Jerusalem, and that Qaloniyeh was below both Jerusalem and Moza. Topographically, this makes sense and implies that the centre of the Roman colony should be in the valley below the terraces. This in turn means that traces of pre-Roman, early Jewish habitation could be expected in those terraces and in the hill-country above them.

Another question could also be answered quickly, that of where the spring was. If they could help it, Romans never built far away from a natural water supply. And indeed, the main source of lower Moza, the perennial spring of En Moza, had never been forgotten. When construction work on the A1 highway between Jerusalem and Tel Aviv cut through an area where archaeological finds could be assumed, a salvage excavation was arranged. From 21 August to 5 October 1973, a team led by Emanuel Eisenberg set to work, was interrupted by the Yom Kippur War and, when they returned, found that the Public Works Department had covered the site without authorization. An open excavation site was not what the authorities wanted if they needed the road ready for defensive action against the Syrian or Jordanian tanks which were threatening to roll towards Jerusalem; and thus, Eisenberg's dig was never finished. But what he found was surprising enough.

Roman remains were recovered, among them a Vespasian coin, dated AD 72. The Romans had been here, and they had left a coin which belonged to the founding period of the colony.[28] The Romans stayed here for a long time, even during and after the Bar Kokhba revolt of AD 132–5, and they did not move, although Emperor Hadrian turned the whole of Jerusalem into the military colony of Aelia Capitolina in AD 135. Living at Emmaus/Colonia was just too pleasant and comfortable, and certainly the climate there was far preferable to that of Jerusalem up the hill.

In March 2002, Eisenberg dug east of the covered area, near the highway bridge, and found a few remnants of Roman walls which could be dated to the early/mid second century. When we began our own excavations (some 100 metres west of Eisenberg's interrupted dig of 1973), we found several Roman coins that helped to establish the continuity of a Roman presence. Apart from Vespasian's coin of a veiled, kneeling woman representing *Judaea capta* (found in September 2004 and mentioned above), there were coins of Marcus Aurelius (161–80) and Commodus (180–92). One would not expect to find many coins in such an area. After all, the Romans lived here peacefully, and never fled in haste, which might have led them to leave coins or hidden hoards in 'safe' places, as they did in quite a few places in Roman Britain, where the treasure troves of Water Newton, Mildenhall or Hoxne document such sudden departures. So every single coin is a particularly valuable source of information about periods of settlement. If nothing has been found after the period of Commodus, this may mean nothing more than that nothing has been found. To put it differently: the absence of evidence does not automatically imply the evidence of absence.

Among the Qumran scrolls, for example, no fragments of 2 Chronicles, Nehemia and Esther have been found. Yet it should be argued that these texts once all existed in the libraries of the twelve caves, 2 Chronicles as the continuation of 1 Chronicles, Nehemiah as a book closely linked to Esra (in later centuries, they were combined in one scroll), and Esther as one of the five Megillot, a closed collection which included Shir ha-Shirim (the Song of Songs), Ruth, Ekha (the Lamentations of Jeremiah) and Quohelet (Ecclesiastes) which apart from Esther were all found at Qumran, in more than one fragment. At Emmaus-Colonia, the lack of coins minted by Titus, Domitian, Nerva, Trajan, Hadrian and Antoninus Pius (who together reigned from 79 to 161) may simply mean that such coins have not yet been found, or that they were not dropped unnoticed in the first place. It certainly does not mean that no Romans lived there between Vespasian and Marcus Aurelius. As we shall see, other finds, discovered in our own areas since 2001, particularly some datable pottery, establish an unbroken continuity until the late second century. No later Roman coins have been found. We do not know when the colony was abandoned by the Romans, but 'missing' coins and later Roman pottery may still turn up. It seems, however, that it must have happened towards the end of the second century, for this apparently is the period presupposed by the Mishna and the Talmuds, when Jews came to collect the branches for the Sukkot huts.

Emperor Commodus may not be a household name anymore, although he earned the name Britannicus for a victory won by his regional commander, Ulpius Marcellus, in the province of Britannia, after the northern border at the Antonine Wall had been overrun in AD 184. But with him, the glorious days of the reign of his father, the philosopher-emperor Marcus Aurelius, came to an ignominious end. Commodus was incompetence personified. He killed everyone who stood in his way – nothing unusual here for the time, to be sure – and became a fervent adherent of religious mysticism who combined a 'holier than thou' attitude with an attempt to be popular with the masses. Games and gladiatorial combats, more sumptuous and extravagnt than ever, emptied the public coffers. He renamed Rome 'Colonia Commodiana', fought as a gladiator and was on the way to complete madness when some members of his closer circle agreed that enough was enough. He was murdered in a conspiracy involving his concubine Marcia and the pretorian prefect Aemilius Laetus. Thanks to Ridley Scott's film *Gladiator*, Commodus has become famous among cinema goers. Russell Crowe's Maximus fighting Joaquin Phoenix as Emperor Commodus in the amphitheatre is one of the lasting impressions of early twenty-first-century cinema, and Commodus as reckless gladiator certainly is from a leaf of the pages of history.

After his death, the succession was violently disputed by several rivals. Septimius Severus gained the throne in 193 and remained in power until his death in York (Roman Eboracum) in 211. By then, however, the wealth of the Empire was in terminal decline. The silver value of the denarius decreased by 50 per cent from Augustus to Septimius Severus, and by the end of his reign it was only worth five per cent of its original value. Inflation was rampant, and currency depreciation and price increases spiralled so fast that fortunes disappeared within months. In the Roman province of Palestine, the Jewish population suffered badly; a new tax, the *annona militaris*, was levied to pay for the feeding of Roman troops marching through the provinces, and as they tended to march through Palestine with gusto, the Jewish rural population, which had to pay all sorts of traditional taxes as well, was increasingly driven into poverty. Soon, the domino effect on the economy reached the Roman occupiers and settlers themselves, and a luxurious colony like that at Emmaus simply could not keep up standards any longer. The Jews left the countryside – a development for which there is even a technical term in the records, *anachoresis* – and spoilt Roman descendants of the AD 70 campaign veterans found themselves without any suppliers around them.

Emmaus-Colonia was, it seems, abandoned at that time, and the Jews from Jerusalem came to collect willow branches.

Emanuel Eisenberg's brief excavation of 2002 helped to establish another point. When the Roman colony was enlarged, it moved eastwards, towards Jerusalem. This was a characteristic of Roman colony building: as a rule, they did not only build close to an existing spring or water source, they also preferred to build towards the next big city, rather than away from it. For us, this meant that the centre of the Jewish village of Emmaus – or, to put it differently, anything still identifiable as typically Jewish rather than Hellenistic or Roman in such a village – would be found west of the Roman traces.

However, there was a minor local difficulty. Some of the building remains that Eisenberg had found in 1973 were not Roman, but Herodian, which means they were built in the typical style of the late first century BCE/early first century AD and imported from Rome, but were built by and for Jews. Parts of a whole quarter of Jerusalem, the so-called Herodian Quarter, were built in the same style.[29] The wealthy among the Jews were able to afford this affluent architecture, with its mosaics, *opus reticulatum* walls, beautiful pottery, and so forth. How could one possibly tell if it was a pagan Roman or a practising Jew who had owned such a house? Again, there is a yardstick: if the mosaics and frescoes contain depictions of human beings or animals, they are Roman; if they are 'neutral', with meandering designs and other, sometimes quite elaborate artwork which does not portray anything created, then as a rule they are Jewish, because until the fourth/fifth centuries Jewish designers honoured the Second Commandment. Only at this late stage did the mosaics of Hammat-Tiberias, the Bet-Alpha Synagogue and other places begin to commit themselves to a less literal interpretation of the Decalogue.

This can of course only be employed as a first indicator, since there are examples of non-Jewish Roman houses and rooms without human or animal forms (in Britain, one is reminded of the lower walls of the 'Painted House' in Dover. If these alone had been excavated, none of the images on the upper portion would be visible to visitors today. Beautiful wall surrounds were painted to imitate marble veneers; only above have broken-off parts of human figures been preserved). But Eisenberg saw the neutral designs on the frescoes he found at Colonia, he saw what he identified as 'Israelite sherds' which reinforced the mortar of the buildings, and he concluded that they were Jewish-Herodian. The problem with this conclusion is evident: he found the painted material, but the potsherds could have been in secondary use, and he did not find any Jewish objects nearby, 'only' a coin of Vespasian which provided a benchmark year of AD 70, when Jewish habitation had come to an end. To the sceptics, the question as to whether this part of Qaloniyeh was Jewish before AD 70 remains open, although the striking resemblance of these murals with those in the Jewish Herodian quarter of Jerusalem strongly suggests the same period – from about 37 BCE to 70 AD – and emphasizes an important observation: whoever these people may have been, they were wealthy and able to afford a high standard of living.

The uncertainty about the users of these buildings is not really a problem, however. When Vespasian first saw Emmaus on his way to Jerusalem, and earmarked the village for later use, he was probably attracted by such luxurious architecture in a beautiful part of the country, close to Jerusalem, and would have given orders not to destroy the site during the occupation of the city. Thus, after the war, his veteran officers were given those villas, with their Jewish-Herodian murals still intact, and made their own use of them, adding a few elements of Roman interior architecture here or there. A modern parallel can be found in Berlin, the capital of Nazi Germany: when Allied bombing raids destroyed the city, particular care was taken not to damage the more exclusive residential areas of Dahlem, Kladow, Gatow, etc. where the victors intended to reside. When these buildings were given back to the Berliners after German reunification in AD 1990, hardly anything had changed: they were still the same early twentieth/late nineteenth-century houses, built in the German style, and did not show any signs of American or British architectural design. In brief, the Colonia of Vespasian, Josephus, the Mishna and the Talmuds was identified, and a probable end of Roman habitation could be established; but as for the rest, much remained to be done.

Notes

1   The appearance of Jesus at Emmaus is mentioned in a second source (as we saw above), in the later, longer ending of Mark's Gospel (16.12), but here, neither the name of Cleopas nor that of the place itself are mentioned, only its location 'in the countryside' since the two disciples walk *eis agron* (literally 'into the countryside'). This detail underlines the fact that by c.AD 120–40, when the longer ending was published, the local Christians were adamant that Emmaus had been a village in the rural area near Jerusalem, not a distant city.

2   *Kalôs telônêsanti.* Suetonius adds that these statues could still be see in his time, in the early second century: Suetonius, *Vespasian* 1.2.

3   *Vespasian* 1.3.

4   *Vespasian* 23.4. On the title Son of God and its politico-religious context, see C.P. Thiede, *The Cosmopolitan World of Jesus*, London 2004, 33–6.

5   *Vespasian* 4.5.

6   *Vespasian* 5.6; cf. Tacitus, *Historia* 1.78.3.

7   Papyrus Masada 721a; see H.M. Cotton and J. Geiger (eds), *Masada II. The Latin and Greek Documents*, Jerusalem 1989, 31–5. Josephus tells the story of the fall of Masada, with many legendary additions, in his *Jewish War* 7. The Virgil papyrus on Masada is not the only example of a quote from this poet in a military context, written down from memory after the horrors of battle. Not much later, between AD 95 and 105, the First Tungrian and Ninth Batavian Cohorts, stationed at Vindolanda south of Hadrian's Wall in northern England, left thousands of slivers of wood, used for all sorts of communications – shopping lists, invitations to weddings, etc. – and among them is another quote from the *Aeneid*, 9.473: see A. Bowman and J.D. Thomas, *Vindolanda: The Latin Writing Tablets (Tabulae Vindolandenses II)*, London 1994, 65–7 (with a list of further Virgil quotes found in military contexts), and Plate 1, 118.

8   On the architecture of Herodian and Roman Emmanus/Colonia, see below, Chapter 6.

9   On the dates of the gospels, see above, and also J.A.T. Robinson, *Redating the New Testament*, London 1976, who dates all 27 writings of the New Testament before AD 70; in spite of manifold attempts, his arguments have never been refuted. Cf. also the detailed analysis of the pros and cons in D. Guthrie, *New Testament Introduction*, 4th edn, Leicester 1990.

10   Tacitus, *Historia* 4.81, 1–3; Suetonius, *Vespasian* 7.2–3; Cassius Dio, *Roman History* 65.8, 1–2.

11   For spittle as a recipe against eye diseases, see the miracle performed by Jesus in John 9.1–12, and Pliny the Elder, *Natural History* 28.37; 28.67. Pliny wrote his unfinished *Natural History* between AD 77 and his death in AD 79, i.e. after

the spreading of the written and oral Gospel message. For the treading on hands, cf. B. Kollmann, *Jesus und die Christen als Wundertaeter*, Göttingen 1996, particularly note 122 (with sources and references).

12   The others are Jesus, Apollonius of Tyana and Hanina ben Dosa. Cf. C.P. Thiede, *The Cosmopolitan World of Jesus*, London 2004, 37–42.

13   Quoted in Eusebius, *Church History*, 3.11–12.

14   Eusebius, *Church History* 3.17.

15   Hegesippus in Eusebius, *Church History* 3.19–20.

16   Eusebius, *Church History* 3.32, 1–4. Trajan, who was not a Flavian, reigned from 98 to 117. In his *Chronikon*, Eusebius dates the martyrdom of Simeon to AD 106/7. As we saw above, this may be a partly legendary account, but its historical nucleus contains the message that the Flavian emperors (Vespasian, Titus and Domitian) did not persecute the Davidic Jewish Christians. For a discussion of the broader historical context, see (among others) M. Sordi, *The Christians and the Roman Empire*, London/New York 1994, 38–54.

17   Ten days later, Vespasian's own troops in Judea followed suit. Suetonius, *Vespasian* 6.3.

18   Pilate was 'prefect'; under Emperor Claudius, the office was changed from a military to a civilian status, and the prefects became procurators. By mistake, Tacitus called Pontius Pilate a procurator, but the famous inscription found at Caesarea Maritima proves that Pilate was a (military) prefect of Judaea. For further details, see C.P. Thiede, *Jesus und Tiberius. Zwei Söhne Gottes*, Munich 2004, 239–51.

19   Josephus, *Jewish War* 6.236–43. Cf. Sulpicius Severus, *Chronica* 2.30

20   John 19.19; for the details, see C.P. Thiede and M. d'Ancona, *The Quest for the True Cross*, London 2000, 78–122.

21   In September 2004, we found one of these coins, minted in Rome in AD 71, at our Emmaus excavation site. Both Titus and Domitian continued to mint *Judaea capta* coins. Such coinage was produced after victories over other peoples and by other emperors, too; there are, for example, numerous *Germania capta* coins.

22   Suetonius, *Domitian* 12.2.

23   In the Mishna, a collection of teachings which was assembled between the second and third centuries, Yohanan Ben Zakkai is seen as the guarantor of continuity and new beginnings; here one finds the almost proverbial expression, 'After the destruction of the Temple, Rabbi Yohanan Ben Zakkai enacted' (Succa 3.13; Menahot 10.5; Eduyot 8.3, etc.). In later centuries, other rabbinic schools, such as those in Tiberias, became rival centres of learning. See also, on the consequences for Jewish-Christian relations, F. Manns, *John and Jamnia: How the break occurred between Jews and Christians c. 80–100 AD*, Jerusalem 1988, 9–26.

24   See Y. Bar-El, R. Durst, G. Katz, J. Zislin and H.Y. Knobler, 'The Jerusalem Syndrome', *British Journal of Psychiatry* 176 (2000), 86–90.

25   See C.P. Thiede, *The Dead Sea Scrolls and the Jewish Origins of Christianity*, Oxford 2000, 61–73.

26   Transliterations from Aramaic and Arabic into English are notoriously difficult, and there will always be variant readings: so we have Moza/Motza/Motsa, and Massada/Masada/Metzeda, Emmaous/Ammaous/Amwas/Imwas, etc. In any case, no one doubts that the different spellings, from Qaloniyeh to Qalunya, all reflect the Latin *colonia*.

27   Mishna Sukka 4.5; cf. Babylonian Talmud Sukka 45a; Jerusalem Talmud Sukka 54b.

28   The coin has not yet been published; I am grateful to my colleage Emanuel Eisenberg for discussing this important find with me. Two preliminary reports on the pre-Roman discoveries have been published: E. Eisenberg, 'A Settlement from the Beginning of the Early Bronze Age I at Moza', *Atiquot* 22 (1993), 41–8; and *id.*, 'Motsa', *Revue Biblique* 82 (1975), 587.

29   Cf. N. Avigad, *The Herodian Quarter in Jerusalem*, Wohl Archaeological Museum, Jerusalem 1989.

6

Archaeologists at Work: The Finds of Emmaus

The standard-bearer and the sceptre head

Leave Jerusalem on the Shderot Ben Gurion road which turns into the A1 motorway and follow it until you reach the Moza Interchange. Do not turn off towards Emek Arazim, Shkuna Tet and Mevasseret Zion East, but continue for a few hundred metres until the road bends sharply to the right. The first thing you see in the bend is a medieval wall, partly rebuilt as a retaining wall for a modern house. This once was the Qasr Malik el-Yahud or Qasr Bint el-Malik, a structure erected immediately after the last Crusaders had left the region. The ruins of the Crusaders' watchtower, with the typical voussoir stones and ashlars, can be seen from the road, immediately after the bend.

Here, between Qasr Malik el-Yahud and the tower, Emanuel Eisenberg dug in 1973. The Roman and Romano-Jewish remains did not really come as a surprise – after all, although situated just to the east, this still was the wider area of Colonia/Qaloniyeh. What was unexpected was the presence of a settlement of the fourth millennium BCE, from the Early Bronze Age I. Because of the nature of the rescue excavation, only parts of it were found, under a building from the Herodian period, in an area covering about 40 square metres.[1] The archaeological evidence was unmistakable: fragments of bowls, holemouth vessels, jars and blades were all typical of the Canaanite era. The ceramic finds had not been imported; they were made from a local type of clay known as Moza huwwar. The flint tools, of a type found in quite a few other sites all over Israel, were characteristic of mass production, of the Canaanite 'blade industry' in the fourth millennium BCE. All in all, these finds have fuelled an intense debate about the people of that culture and how widespread their architecture was. For while most of the pottery was local and simple, other objects (with thumb-indented ledge handles and rope-decorated rims, for example) closely resemble finds from a site called Palmahim in the coastal plain and other sites in the north west. In the south, Lachish produced similar ware. Curvilinear houses were more popular in the north, but Moza appears to be in the area of the overlap, where northern and southern influences met and merged.

In other words, the Canaanite culture which used such refined ceramics and lived in such houses spread all the way from the southern coastal plain to the northern Negev, and touched the Judaean hills with Moza, Gezer and other places. A thriving, creative culture, one and a half millennia before the Israelites arrived and decided that this was to become a part of the territory of the tribe of Benjamin (Josh. 18.26): if anything, this goes to show that the Romans with their Colonia and the Jews with Moza and Emmaus were not the first to discover the attractions of the region, but rather continued and developed a vibrant tradition. Moreover, their settlement at Moza was not an isolated exception. The next rescue dig produced further surprising finds, not in the valley of the motorway this time, but to the north, in the terraces.

Between August and December 1993, the Israel Antiquities Authorities, alerted by the Public Works Department (which had given planning permission for a new trajectory of the motorway between Jerusalem and Mevasseret Zion), asked two of their archaeologists, Zvi Greenhut and Alon De-Groot, to direct the first of what was to become two salvage excavations.

The first site was located on a slight spur at the junction of two stream beds, the Nahal Soreq and the Nahal Moza.[2] The archaeologists discovered two building phases from the Middle Bronze Age II, beginning roughly 2000 BCE or, in other words, in the millennium after the Bronze Age finds in the valley below. This was followed by early Iron Age structures (eleventh–tenth centuries BCE), and a kiln of the (early) Hellenistic period, somewhere in the last quarter of the fourth century BCE.

So far, the general impression was one of continuity, setting in after the valley was inhabited and lasting until at least the period of Alexander the Great and his successors. That this assessment was too limited was soon proven by finds in the third of the areas excavated in 1993, where Neolithic flint tools and an arrowhead were found: apparently, people had lived and fought here as early as the late ninth millennium BCE, the time when Jericho was built at the perennial spring which today is called En es-Sultan. Two discoveries stood out. First, 36 silos for grain storage from the late Iron Age; and second, a sceptre head in the shape of a pomegranate surmounting three rows of drooping leaves. Made in Egyptian blue, it was dated to the central period of the kingdom of Judah, in the eighth/seventh centuries BCE.

This sceptre head was found *in situ*, in a building of the late Iron Age with a massive north wall, two metres deep, with several steps leading to its east-facing entrance. Stone column bases were uncovered on the floor, and it was near those columns that the sceptre head was discovered. What exactly was its purpose? The jury is still out. Only one thing is certain: it predates the Babylonian Exile of 597–538 BCE, and this means that it belongs to the period of the First Temple. Was it a sceptre head used in Temple services on high holidays and kept at the home of the high priests' standard-bearer in Moza? Was it part of a royal sceptre, ready for use at one of the residences of a king of Judah – of Josiah perhaps, who ruled from 639–609 BCE, and who destroyed pagan shrines and reformed the orthodoxy of the Temple cult? The building structure itself goes back to the earlier period of King Rehobeam and the Egyptian conquest under Pharao Shishak in the tenth century.[3]

These are intriguing questions – and they are all the more tantalizing because the debate about the authenticity of some objects dated to the period before the first Babylonian Captivity has become quite heated in recent months. The most famous sceptre head ever 'found', an ivory pomegranate dated to the eighth century BCE, with the Paleo-Hebrew inscription 'Belonging to the Temple of YHWH, holy to the Priests' and on prominent display in the Israel Museum Jerusalem, probably is a forgery from the same workshop which produced two other faked objects in 2002, the 'Joash' inscription allegedly from the First Temple Period and the 'James Son of Joseph Brother of Jesus' ossuary, purporting to provide archaeological proof of the existence of Jesus, his adoptive father Joseph and his brother James. Bought for millions of dollars, the ivory pomegranate had not been discovered by archaeologists during a documented dig, and the Israel Antiquities Authority is currently examining every single object acquired from murky sources in earlier years of optimistic trust in the reliability of dealers and well-known epigraphers. Late, but not too late – and anyone wanting to see that ivory pomegranate should go to the Israel Museum soon, before it is relegated to the archives, only perhaps to reappear one day in a special exhibition of forgeries. By contrast, the Egyptian blue sceptre head from Moza is authentic, it being found during an official, documented excavation.

If Moza was a place of royal and cultic importance between the tenth and seventh centuries BCE, it also was an agricultural centre. Those 36 silos for the storage of grain are a unique find in the vicinity of Jerusalem. During the late Iron Age, this was the place which supplied the capital of Judah and the surrounding villages with grain, up until the time of the Babylonian Captivity, when the silos became refuse dumps. This was the state of affairs until April 2002, when the construction of the new motorway appeared at last to be imminent (in fact, three years later, is still has not begun in earnest), and a second rescue dig was carried out by the same team under Zvi Greenhut and Alon De-Groot.[4] This time, missing links were found, connecting the neolithic or late Stone Age period with the Early and Middle Bronze Age. This showed that people had been living in the terraces and in the valley simultaneously at least since the Bronze Age. The whole region of Moza-Emmaus had been inhabited since the ninth millennium BCE, without noticeable interruptions. There was a gap, however, and it began at the end of Iron Age II (or, in different terminology, with the first Babylonian Exile), when most of the Jewish population, especially the elite, were marched to Babylon in 597 BCE. If Moza had been one of the centres of Jewish administration and agriculture until then, it made sense that it was abandoned when Nebuchadnezzar, King of Babylon, conquered the kingdom and the capital city of Jerusalem, and destroyed the Temple on 16 March 597. Returning from exile in 538, the Jewish elite focused on Jerusalem and the reconstruction of the Temple, which was consecrated on 1 April 515 BCE. Moza, it seems, had no role to play in the renewed kingdom of Judah. And while the fertile region of the valley was never completely abandoned, the settlement in the terraces was left in ruins until the late fourth century AD, when Byzantine Christians arrived, enjoyed the view over the lush, hilly countryside, and built a couple of houses. One of them was excavated, and it seems it was not really part of a settlement.

As we shall see, Byzantine Christians preferred to live in the valley below, under the motorway, as it were: most of their buildings, including a fifth-century monastery, were covered, damaged, or destroyed when

From left to right: Rafi Lewis, Inspector at the Israel Antiquities Authority Jerusalem; Egon Lass, Field Archaeologist and co-director of the dig, Wheaton College, Illinois; Pnina Shor, Head of the Department of Artefacts Conservation and Restoration at the Israel Antiquities Authority Jerusalem; Avital Rabin, a student volunteer; and Carsten Thiede.

Beginning the excavation, Summer 2001: Carsten Thiede and Egon Lass, with student volunteers.

Egon Lass, sorting pottery in the afternoon, the results of the previous day's digging.

Egon Lass – Square B.

A 'general view' of two of the squares, September 2004, where all sections can be seen together: the southern wall of the medieval (Crusader) village, and at the top of the photo, just a bit of the modern A1 motorway linking Jerusalem and Tel Aviv; in front of the wall, the 12th century floor; on a lower level, the Byzantine floor (4th–6th centuries); and in front of that, slightly higher again, the Mameluk floor (7th–11th centuries), and to the left (dark lower area towards the bottom left), a section of the 1st century Emmaus floor, prior to AD 70.

A part of the aqueduct which leads from the Iron Age source to the Crusaders'
cistern.

Aqueduct.

Dirk Heinze on the second excavation.

Partial Roman vault, found next to the Moza excavations on the north side of an old synagogue, still in use.

Corner of various architectural phases, found behind same synagogue.

Egon Lass – Area B.

the present highway was built in the late 1960s. The houses in the terraces may have been outposts or lookouts. Whatever the Byzantine Christians may have done up here (apart from looking longingly towards Jerusalem and watching the road), they were the first after the Babylonian Captivity to settle permanently in the terraces. During the Late Second Temple Period (the Herodian Era, and thus the years of the Emmaus disciples), no Jews seem to have built and lived up there, in this part of the wider area above the Sorek Valley. But those who had inhabited this land before did leave impressive traces, including late Stone Age bracelets, stone and shell beads and a small stone figurine representing a woman. A pyxis and a cooking crater from the neotholic period were also found, confirming the previous suspicion that Stone Age people had lived here – and had been living well, with 'jewellery', and artwork in their houses. Something or someone must have destroyed these buildings in the tenth century: a thick burnt stratum 'sealed' the floors. Rebuilding activities were taken up soon afterwards, and traces of stone installations, one of them coated in yellow plaster, prove that the site remained important throughout the ninth and eight centuries BCE. Even here, however, the pottery and the large quantity of stone debris show that the building was abandoned at an unknown stage after c.700 BCE. Could this again point towards the conquest under Nebuchadnezzar, or had there been an earlier catastrophe?

Was it perhaps the result of an inner-Jewish measure under King Hezekiah (724–695 BCE), who had begun to fight pagan cults and to destroy their shrines? If a building with steps leading up to what looks like a *bema* (a podium for an altar), could be interpreted as a destroyed shrine of the popular goddess Ashera, then this might make sense. Hezekiah's people had come and destroyed a cultic place not far from the city of the Temple. A hundred years after Hezekiah, King Josiah again began to demolish pagan shrines and temples, beginning in the north and moving towards Jerusalem. He never finished the job, as he was killed in battle by the Egyptian Pharaoh Necho at Megiddo in 609, and his son Jehoiakim returned to the pagan cults. The remnants of the *bema* at Moza, 8.5 kilometres west of Jerusalem, may document the turning point, where Josiah's religious cleansing attempts came to an abrupt end in 609.

However, the dates and actions of pre-exile kings are hotly disputed among scholars, particularly among those who are not prepared to trust the accounts in the Bible.[5] Thus, for the time being certainty remains elusive. But among the debris were the fragments of pottery vessels which could be dated to the end of the Iron Age, and two of these fragments tied in with the discovery of the sceptre head in 1993. I remember the day when Zvi Greenhut first showed them to me in 2002: his finder's joy and pride were infectious. Two unique Hebrew inscriptions could be deciphered. The first one, on a holemouth jar rim, reads *lzfn bn nss*, the other one, on the handle of a vessel, damaged at the beginning and the end, *[ln]ss lsmkhyh[u]*. It is not easy to vocalize, transliterate and translate these inscriptions, since some of the words or combinations of words are rare and have never before been found in this context. Those who have seen the inscriptions agree, however, that 'NSS' should be read 'Nasas' and means sceptre-bearer or standard-bearer. Zvi Greenhut suggests the following rendering: for fragment 1, 'LeZafan Son of Nasas', that is, 'Zafan, the son of the Standard-Bearer', and for fragment 2, '(LeNa)sas LeSmachia(hu)', that is '(To the Standard) Bearer, to Semachia(hu).'[6] A man of this position, and his son, apparently had a house at Moza, within easy walking distance of Jerusalem. Was this his home, or his secondary residence in the country?

The connection with the sceptre head is too obvious to be missed. The man who officiated as standard/sceptre bearer had the sceptre head near him – but was he on duty or off duty? Was he the High Priests' sceptre-bearer, and would this then be the authentic counter balance to the forged ivory pomegranate belonging to the period of the First Temple? Since there is no inscription on the pomegranate sceptre head from Moza, we cannot be sure. If Moza was a royal residence at the time of the Kingdom of Judah, the bearer could well have been resident, officiating whenever the King needed his services, with a royal rather than priestly standard. And then, of course, there is a third option: if this was a place of idolatrous worship at the time of Hezekiah and/or Josiah, and if it was destroyed at that time, the sceptre head could well have been part of Ashera rites, and the sceptre-bearer a Jew who worshipped Ashera. Since the pomegranate-shaped sceptre head was found quite close to what may have been the *bema* of an Ashera altar, this would also explain why it was found at all: it was thrown away, into the debris of the destroyed shrine. The two inscriptions, incised on broken vessels, were also found in the rubble of a collapsed building – potentially an indication of destruction. We shall have to wait in suspense for further insights from the continuous debate of the experts.

A skeleton and a Jewish-Christian tomb

An altar, a royal residence, a Byzantine house serving as a lookout, agricultural silos: they made sense in the terraces, just below the hillock of today's Mevasseret Zion. For a village, however, the green valley below was the site to be preferred. Profiting from the natural wealth of springs, olive groves, vines, and the closeness to the main road between Jerusalem and the Mediterranean, people settled here at least since the Early Bronze Age, as Emanuel Eisenberg's excavation had shown. Eisenberg found only a handful of Iron Age implements, which means that the Iron Age settlement was not on top of the Bronze Age houses, but somewhere in the immediate vicinity. When we started our own excavation to the west of Eisenberg's dig, looking for the Jewish village of the 'Emmaus period', we found late Stone Age (Chalcolithic), Bronze Age, and Iron Age pottery fragments, confirming the unbroken habitation in the valley. Pleasing as this was, the original purpose of our dig was the search for archaeological evidence supporting a conclusion we had reached after almost two years of research in ancient records, medieval accounts, British Mandate maps, and after a number of surveys: that this was as close to the centre of the Emmaus mentioned by Luke and Josephus as we could get, in spite of the motorway which dissected the whole valley.

We knew that there had been excavations in the centre of the valley 60 years before, and another, final rescue dig, just before the old road was converted into a motorway. No Jewish settlement remains were found, although the discoveries were exceptional in their own right: in 1946, still during the British Mandate, a mosaic floor with Byzantine Greek inscriptions; three other mosaics, one of them in beautifully arranged red, white and black tesserae; a wine press; lamps; bowls; tiles; and even pieces of window glass were found in four rooms with a chapel near the ruins of a small church with three aisles and a narthex. Under the main mosaic, some traces of a Roman building and several *ostraca* (inscribed potsherds) were discovered – but to this day, no report has been published. I have seen the unpublished notes in the archive of the Israel Antiquities Authority, as far as they still exist, and they are incomplete and not very conclusive. All one can gather from the files is the typical structure of a fifth-century Byzantine monastery.

Five years later, by now on the territory of the young State of Israel, the same area was investigated once more, and this time a very brief preliminary report was published.[7] The existence of a fifth-century Byzantine monastery and of Roman buildings 'underneath' it were confirmed, but nothing older or younger was discovered. So far, then, it was apparent that the Romans had extended their Colonia not only eastwards, but southwards, too, which was a sensible step if they wanted to stay more or less on the same fertile level, rather than building upwards into the terraces. By doing this, they moved beyond the confines of the Jewish village of Emmaus mentioned by Luke and Josephus: the 1951 dig, like that of 1946, did not produce any Jewish finds. To the excavators, the discovery of a Byzantine monastery was much more interesting, not least because it was unexpected: no surviving literary record referred to it. Even Cyril of Scythopolis (Scythopolis = Bet Shean) had not mentioned it, although there is a reference to 'the source of Colonia' in his biography of St Saba (*Mar Saba*), written in c.525.[8] What had been going on? Either Cyril ignored its existence on purpose, because he did not want to draw attention to a Christian presence near a site called Emmaus by Josephus and Luke, and so a rival to the 'official' Byzantine Emmaus at Nicopolis, or the monastery simply had not been built by 525. Since we do not know if Cyril was aware of the *Jewish Antiquities* of Josephus and put one and one together, and since there is indeed no extant literary reference to the monastery and to the reasons why it was built, we simply do not have the answer. However, the archaeological evidence strongly suggests that the monastery had been built some 30 to 40 years before Cyril wrote his *Life of St Saba*, and thus his silence is strange, if not suspicious.

A final salvage excavation was carried out in 1964–5. This again confirmed the conclusion of the previous digs, adding additional pieces of evidence.[9] Then the motorway was built, and the ruins of the monastery disappeared under the tarmac. It seems however that remains had been seen in the open by nineteenth-century travellers. The famous German architect and explorer Conrad Schick saw some of them on a visit in August 1886, to the southeast of the bridge and in a vineyard, and described a tomb with a female skeleton, two Greek inscriptions and a coloured fresco showing two cherubim surrounded by garlands with green leaves and red flowers. 'The western and southern sides were preserved when the cave was opened,' Schick writes in his account, 'but a few days after the plaster fell off. As I came soon enough I could copy them.' Intriguingly, Schick adds that 'the Russian Archimandrite told me that the figures and the inscriptions belong to the third century, and that the inscription on the wall is the words of the malefactor on the Cross, "Lord, remember me". The one on the ceiling to be read: "God and His anointed".'[10] Unfortunately, Schick's Greek was worse than his English, and his rendering of the inscriptions is faulty (unless, of course, the inscriptions themselves were riddled with mistakes). The first one is indeed dedicated to 'God and His Christ' (in Greek, *Eis Theos kaì ho Christós autoù*, with the 't' of 'Christos' missing); the second one is a fragmentary, bowdlerized rendering of Luke 23.42.

Schick observed that the tomb could be closed by a stone slab that he found, although later a wooden door was made, and he suggested that it was originally a Jewish tomb, 'then afterwards used by Christians, or (and this is more likely the case) the tomb was for a certain time used as a kind of chapel, or an anchorite lived there for a time'. The tomb, the wall paintings, the inscriptions and the skeleton which today could be dated with the appropriate methods have all gone, and Schick's drawings are ageless, so to speak – if the murals were Byzantine, or earlier, or later, is impossible to judge. Thus, there is the intriguing possibility that the Russian Archimandrite was right when he dated the figures and inscriptions to the third century, unlikely as this sounds and looks. Could this have been a Judeo-Christian burial site, with a kind of anchorite living near a female martyr's tomb, even before the Byzantine Age, and before Christianity was protected by the Emperors? As we suggested above, the site of Emmaus-Colonia was probably abandoned by the Romans in the late second century. No one would have prevented Christians from returning to what once was Emmaus immediately afterwards. And who knows: one day, when that new motorway will be built, and when the present highway will be reduced to the status of a regional road, the search for the traces once seen by Schick, Leibovitz, Baki and Eisenberg may well begin.

How green was my valley – Emmaus rediscovered

We had pinpointed the first squares of our excavation, and we knew from our research that there was – in theory, at any rate – no alternative. The Jewish village of Emmaus had to be north of the 'Byzantine' structures under the motorway, and just west of the Bronze Age and Roman finds.[11] Supplied with a licence by the Israel Archaeological Authority, supported by old friends and colleagues like Pnina Shor and Zvi Greenhut at the Authority, and prodded by friends like the anthropologist Joe Zias and the archaeologist Shimon Gibson, I chose my team, and invited one of the leading field archaeologists in Israel, Egon H. E. Lass, to be my co-director. Six of my students from Basel were adventurous enough to volunteer as assistants.[12]

Work began on 10 August 2001. Archaeology is team work, and you have to rely on each other if you want to get on. My students had no previous field experience, although they had all been introduced to the intricacies of Roman archaeology at the most important site in Switzerland, Kaiseraugst (the Roman Colonia Augusta Rauricorum). A few minutes by tram from Basel, this was where Emperor Augustus had established a colony in c.13 BCE, later abandoned during the central European turmoils at the end of the third century, but then rebuilt at the beginning of the fourth century, destroyed by an Alemannic uprising after AD 350, and rebuilt once more around 370. The famous silver treasure of Kaiseraugst (from the mid-fourth century), and the remains of an early Christian church – erected probably during the reign of Constantius I, the son and successor of Constantine the Great – attract scholars from all over the world. Not a bad place to learn about Roman and early Christian archaeology, but no subsitute for real experience: the students had to acquire the basic techniques *in situ*, and were trained in the time-honoured process of learning by doing.

It was a challenge tackled with efficiency, patience and a caustic sense of humour by Egon Lass, so successfully in fact that the students found coins, flint stones, ostraca and other small objects, instead of overlooking them or throwing them away literally by the bucketful (as legends have it about many another excavation site). To know what to expect, the students had been asked to get physically as well as mentally fit. Getting up at 5 a.m. six days a week – we took only the Sabbath off, honouring Jewish custom – to begin work just before sunrise; to keep digging in the increasing heat until lunchtime, moving earth, carrying heavy buckets and heaving stones; and to spend two hours each afternoon cleaning and cataloguing the daily finds is not everyone's idea of a holiday in Israel, and requires the stamina one does not normally acquire in term time. Fortunately, a few driving minutes from the site is Kibbutz Tzuba, where we stayed every summer since 2001, a veritable oasis of recuperation, offering hotel-like rooms, a swimming pool and excellent food which helped us all to start every new day with batteries recharged. Reuven Kalifon, a teacher and the Kibbutz archaeologist, introduced the students to Kibbutz life and the art of seeing things simply by walking attentively through the countryside, and thus opened their eyes in more senses than one.

For mental fitness, the students read the sources, and so they knew that we were not alone in our conviction that Qaloniyeh was the true site of Emmaus, where Jewish finds of the Late Second Temple Period should be expected. Only a few months before we started our first season, the New Testament scholar Anna Maria Schwemer had published an article on 'The Risen One and the Emmaus Disciples' where she argued lucidly and concisely that Moza/Qaloniyeh was undoubtedly the right site.[13] She enlisted support from the arguments of other scholars like Martin Hengel, who had previously excluded the possibility that Luke could have meant the remote city of Emmaus.[14] For Schwemer, it is Luke's remarkable insistence on detail which must not be overlooked. Calling Emmaus not once, but twice, a village, was the author's emphatic way of pointing out that he does not mean the distant Emmaus which had enjoyed the status of an administrative capital city of a district since 47 BCE, and which was quickly rebuilt and reestablished after its destruction by Quinctilius Varus in 4 BCE. As we saw above, when we discussed the arguments for and against the different sites of Emmaus, this is indeed one of the most persuasive arguments against Emmaus-Nicopolis: Luke knew that there were two places of the same name at his time, and he did everything he could to make sure his readers understood which of them he meant. Status and distance are unmistakable pieces of information. The students also consulted the standard work by Fischer, Isaac and Roll on Roman roads in Judaea, and found the decisive summing up: 'It may be concluded that the ancient Motzah/Motza, Colonia, Josephus' Ammaus, and the Emmaus of Luke are all to be sought near the Arab village of Qaluniya, modern Motza.'[15] They read commentaries on Luke 24.13–35 and other theological studies, and were well prepared when our trowels and pickaxes hit the unexcavated soil.[16] What happened next?

Archaeology is destruction. Every cut of the spade changes the landscape, every stratum dug up and investigated will never be the same. This may sound somewhat overdramatized. Diggers know, however, that the first evidence may lurk only a few centimetres below the surface. This is where we had found the first roof tiles, Herodian *tegulae*, during the survey of 2000. Was there a building so close to the surface, or were these the sad remains of an act of destruction which muddled the strata? Had it been done by human hands, or by an earthquake? If it was the latter, a careful analyis of the collapse might tell us about the history of the site and its buildings. We decided to shun heavy machinery – no bulldozers, no excavators, no mechanical equipment of any sort. Everything was to be done according to the dictum Egon Lass has told every new group of volunteers since 2001: 'The pickaxe is the extension of my fingertips.' We knew it would take us more than one season to reach the first-century stratum, but we also knew patience and care would be rewarded eventually. To our surprise, some conclusive results quite literally came up during the first few weeks.

On the second day of work, having cleared the undergrowth from our two initial areas of five by five metres each, we immediately found tesserae and pottery fragments, among them the handle of a jug, which belonged to the Late Hellenistic period – in other words, dated to the period before the arrival of the Romans in Judaea in 63 BCE, when Pompeius had conquered the territory and occupied Jerusalem.[17] From then on, the Jewish inhabitants had to pay a tribute to contribute to the salary of the Roman legionaries, a *stipendium* which documented that they had become subject to Rome. The Romans had not made Judea, including Jerusalem, a Roman province – not yet, at any rate, but it would be fair to say that the romanization of this part of the world began in 63 BCE, 26 years before the reign of Herod the Great. Any finds from those years between the Maccabean re-consecration of the Temple (14 December 164 BCE) and the arrival of the first Roman conquerers were welcome indicators: they showed us that people lived here during a period of Jewish rule and inner-Jewish conflicts. And although the first objects we found were not identifiably Jewish, as they were not implements of ritual practice or inscribed with Jewish names, the only people who lived in the area around Jerusalem at that time were Jews. It was a small but helpful step: now we knew that Jews had lived at this site after the late Iron Age and even before Roman colonization.

Pleasing as this was, the first 50 centimetres below the twenty-first century soil were in a complete mess. Something must have happened to throw such Late Hellenistic objects together with Neolithic, Chalcolithic, Bronze Age, Iron Age, Roman fragments, an Eastern Terra Sigillata rim of the early–mid first century (thus, contemporarry to the Emmaus incident), Byzantine, Omayyad, Abbasid and even Ottoman pottery. It was quite a harvest for a few days. Acquainted with Emanuel Eisenberg's results further east, we had expected Bronze and Iron Age objects, and of course evidence of the Romans. Late Stone Age pottery confirmed that the settlement in the terraces was not the only Canaanite presence in the region. The Byzantine jar fragments did not come as a surprise, either: only 30 metres south of our site began the area of the Byzantine monastery found by Leibovitz and Baki. Nor were the Abbasids unexpected strangers here: the Abbasid dynasty, named after Abbas, an uncle of Mohammed, ruled over these lands from 750 until the conquests of the First Crusade in 1099. Haroun al-Rashid (786–809) was their most famous caliph; in 797, he acknowledged Emperor Charlemagne as protector of the Holy Sites in Jerusalem. An Abbasid presence in the lush surroundings of Colonia-Emmaus is as unsurprising as that of the Omayyads, the caliphs who preceded the Abbasid Dynasty after the first Muslim victory over the Byzantine Army in 636. But what about the Ottomans?

They are, frankly, a problem. The term is used to describe the Turkish Empire, which lasted from the late thirteenth century until the end of the First World War. 'Ottoman' comes from the Arabic *Othmani* meaning 'Turkish', and was derived from Othman/Osman I (1259–1326), a Turkish sultan whose military victories and political astuteness established the Empire. Unfortunately, from an archaeological perspective their architecture and pottery hardly changed during the six and a half centuries of their rule (although the later, eighteenth to early twentieth century products are less carefully executed than those of the great days of their much admired, supposedly benign and tolerant reign in the Middle East). It takes the eye of a true expert in ceramics to distinguish the different Ottoman centuries. But then again, athough we enjoyed the frequent visits of Shimon Gibson, the leading pottery expert in Israel, the nuances did not really matter for our purposes. We recorded every single Ottoman object, with the stratum and locus where we found it, we analysed and dated it, but left the deliberations on the archaeology of the Ottoman Empire to others: our main focus was rather on the Late Second Temple period, the time of Emmaus. On the other hand, we were curious enough to note that the Ottomans, too, cherished the pleasures of the green valley of Emmaus, and we looked for evidence of the beginning and end of their presence. Did they stay until the beginning of the British Mandate? Who, if anyone, followed them, and when? We were to find an answer during our second season.

Meanwhile, we celebrated the unexpectedly early success with a few bottles of red wine from the Shefela (literally, the 'low lands'), the region which begins near Moza and is defined by three water courses – the Nahal Kesalon, the Nahal Refaim, and the Nahal Sorek – between Jerusalem and the Yavne/Tel Aviv area. Anyone adventurous enough to follow the course of the Nahal Sorek from our site would be led first to an ancient village called Sataf. Opposite Sataf and its springs, overlooking the Sorek Valley, there is the Monastery of St John in the Wilderness, called *Ein el-Habis* in Arabic (the 'Spring of the Hermitage'). Originally a cave rather than a proper monastery, it was reconstructed and extended by the Franciscans, who are currently the custodians of the site. According to legend, John the Baptist stayed here – his traditional birthplace (not mentioned in the New Testament), Ein Karem, is just three kilometres to the east.[18] The course of the Sorek then takes us to Beit Shemesh (the 'House of the Sun'), a leading Old Testament city with important archaeological remains which is not mentioned in the New Testament but was settled by Byzantine monks, who built the Monastery of St Samson in the fifth century.[19] Timna (Tel Batash) is next, where Samson married an unnamed Philistine woman (Judges 14.15–15.8) before he got involved with Delilah, 'a woman in the Vale of Sorek' (Judges 16.4).

And finally we reach Yavne/Jamnia, the last western city on the territory of the tribe of Judah (Josh. 15.11), but pagan by Hellenistic times (2 Macc. 12.40), the retreat centre of the Seleucid general Gorgias after his defeat by the Maccabean forces at Emmaus (the city, not the village of Luke) in 165 BCE and destroyed by Judas Maccabaeus (2 Macc. 12.1–9; see also 1 Macc. 10.67–73 for a later battle at Jamnia). The Romans did not destroy Yavne during the First Jewish Revolt of AD 66–73, perhaps because of its mixed Gentile-Jewish population: as we saw in a previous chapter, it became the seat of the Rabbinical Academy of AD 70 with Roman permission. Nothing much has been excavated here as yet, but the area deserves a visit.

It was here, too, that Rabban Gamaliel II introduced an additional text into the 'Eighteen Benedictions' in the 80s of the first century: the curse on the Nozrim (the followers of Yeshua ha-Nozri, Jesus of Nazareth) and on the Minim (all those who followed divisive teachings): 'May apostates have no hope and the kingdom of impertinence be uprooted in our day. May the Nozrim and Minim disappear in the twinkling of an eye. May they be removed from the book of the living and not inscribed among the just. Blessed be you, O Lord, who casts down the proud.'[20] Thus, following the Nahal Sorek from Moza-Emmaus to Yavne, one walks through biblical and post-biblical times, through Jewish, Roman and Christian history. Such were the thoughts and experiences we mused upon, surrounded by ceramic fragments from all these periods, stimulated by the delightful wine from the northern Shefala. And then, a couple of days later, there was another breakthrough.

We found a section from the base of a bowl, made from the best reddish brown clay-like earth called *terra sigillata* (Latin for 'sealed earth'), from which valuable earthenware pottery is produced. It was not just any odd piece of pottery, however, for here the craftsman had left his 'seal', a circle surrounded by a square, and to the right of this there was a Hebrew name in the characteristic style of the Late Second Temple Period. It was a fragment, and since Hebrew is written from right to left, we had the end, but the first letters were missing. Experts in Herodian scripts came to look at it, and after much debate and comparative study we decided that the visible letters – a complete Mem and an Ayin, with the tiny rest of the preceding letter, a Shin – probably ended the Jewish personal name Sh'ma. It occurs several times in the Old Testament, and in 1 Chronicles 8.13 it is mentioned as the name of a man from the tribe of Benjamin who was settled in the region of Moza (Josh. 18.26). The Benjaminites had a motley history in the Old Testament, but one eminent New Testament figure, the apostle Paul, proudly introduced himself as a Benjaminite (Rom. 11.1; Phil. 3.5). In any case, even if the reconstruction of the name must remain provisional, the inscription belongs to the decades before AD 70, before the destruction of the Temple and Vespasian's colony. If we had needed proof positive of the existence of a Jewish settlement at this site during the period leading up to Luke's Emmaus account, we had found it. And in a way, it meant that the main purpose of the dig had been achieved on the eleventh day of the first season, 21 August 2001: seen from the perspective of Luke's historical credibility, Jews had been living here at the right time. Our work on paper, all the research put into the selection of two areas which we assumed to be parts of central Emmaus in the first seven decades of the first century, had come to fruition.

On the same day, we made two further discoveries which immediately caught the attention of other experts. First, we established the upper part of a vault in the northern dig area; and then in the southern area, we found a wall tile with an eight-pointed cross. Such crosses are familar to anyone who has visited the Church of the Holy Sepulchre in Jerusalem: to the left and right of the steps which go down to the Chapels of St Vartan and St Helena, Crusader Knights left them as pilgrim marks, incised into the walls. But here, in Emmaus, it was definitely not a Christian pilgrim's graffito. The cross had been incised prior to the firing of the clay. It was a commissioned work, meant to indicate a Christian building, perhaps a chapel. Not just any Christian building, of course: just after 1125, Frà Raymond du Puy, the Master of the Order of the Hospital of St John of Jerusalem – more generally known then as the Hospitallers or Knights Hospitaller, and today as the Order of St John, with its St John Ambulance (and the Roman Catholic branch as the Maltese Knights) – had published a rule of the order. In its wake, the knights began to use the eight-pointed cross instead of the traditional Latin Cross.[21]

The 'new' cross shape was in fact 'inherited' from the merchants from the South Italian Sea Republic of Amalfi, who had owned the area of the Muristan quarter in Jerusalem with its hospital, which had stood there since at least the days of Charlemagne in the early ninth century. Amalfi's municipal coat of arms was the eight-pointed cross. The design of the cross on Amalfi coins from 1088, ten years before the First Crusade, is similar to most of the crosses on the walls going down to the Chapel of St Vartan in the Holy Sepulchre, and to the wall tile at Moza-Colonia.[22] One of the reasons for this change of design may well have been the increasing rivalry between them and the Templars, the Knights of the Temple of Solomon, who had come into being by about 1118 and who also wore a traditional Latin Cross on their cloaks. By 1489 at the latest, when the Hospitallers' under Grand Master Pierre d'Aubusson debated new statutes during the General Chapter on Rhodes, the Order found a symbolic interpretation of the eight points, meant to symbolize the Eight Benedictions from the Sermon on the Mount (Matthew 5:3–10).

Since we found the wall tile in a stratum which, in spite of all the disturbances, was no 'younger' than about 1150, the tile with its cross could be dated roughly to within a quarter of a century of that time. This made it the earliest Maltese Cross ever discovered, preceding the pilgrims' marks in Jerusalem and the eight-pointed cross found on a keystone in the Crusader Church of Akko. We suddenly found ourselves standing in the remains of a Crusader establishment no one had expected at this site: and since the vaulting in the northern square looked suspiciously like the vault we had seen and measured just west of the ruins of the Crusader watchtower near our dig, we knew we were on to something. Little did we know then that we were about to rewrite the history of the Hospitallers near Jerusalem.[23] From that day on, we continued to record every detail of Crusader evidence, comparing it with other establishments of the Hospitallers in Judaea, from Jerusalem to Abu Gosh/Fontenoid/Castellum Emmaus, Aqua Bella and Latrun, without losing site of our principal focus – Emmaus in the Late Second Temple Period. And as exciting as the discovery of the Hospitallers' Cross and the upper vault of one of their buildings certainly was, we realized that we needed to establish a few facts about them.

Although the nearest Hospitallers' buildings where vaulted rooms had survived – Aqua Bella (called Ein Hemed in modern Israel) opposite Abu Gosh, and Belmont Castle near our Kibbutz Tzuba – were later than our structure, perhaps by 20 years, they had one thing in common. These rooms were up to five metres high. It dawned on us that if this was the case at our site, too, we would have quite a way to go before reaching the surface of the first century, somewhere below the Crusader structure, and below the traces of the Abassid (early Muslim), Byzantine and possibly Roman buildings which must have preceded the Hospitallers' establishment. Some of us were overheard muttering the short but desperate prayer: Lord, give us patience – now!

Reassembling the jigsaw

By the end of the first season, we had found two large walls, apparently from the same building. The southern wall was a remarkable 1.5 metres wide, and we exposed it to a height of more than 2 metres. At that stage, we were uncertain if the upper part should be interpreted as the beginning of a vaulted ceiling which was no longer extant. The opposite northern wall, 7.1 metres away, did end in a vault of which the lower 65 remained. We quickly established that this was typical for an entrance arcade of Crusader buildings – even the width conformed to the type of rooms at Aqua Bella. One of the rooms we measured there was 7.00 metres wide, another one, on the other side of the courtyard, 6.73 metres. Both walls were made of rough boulders and smaller stones. Close to the northern wall, in locus 7 – the loose soil on top of the stone collapse of the vault – we had found the wall tile with the eight-pointed Hospitallers' cross stamped or incised before its firing. Was this the porch or portico, the vaulted entrance hall to a chapel? We had to dig deeper to confirm our suspicions, and we decided to analyse Hospitaller Chapels in Judaea, Galilee, the neighbouring countries, and in the European homelands of the knights during our second season.

A couple of months after our first season, the report on the coins arrived from the Israel Antiquities Authority. They had been encrusted by soil and dirt, and we had been able to identify only one of them, a Byzantine coin from the reign of Emperor Justininan. Now, cleaned and analysed, they turned out to be a bronze coin of Emperor Hadrian (AD 161–180) from Aelia Capitolina (the name Hadrian had given to Jerusalem after the Bar Kochba revolt of 132–5), and a *follis* of Justinian I (527–37) from Constantinople.[24] The first of these was useful evidence of the continuous Roman presence at Emmaus-Colonia, and the second confirmed what we knew from earlier excavations in the valley and from our own pottery finds – that the Byzantine Christians had been here at least until the mid sixth century. What puzzled us was the third coin. Badly damaged, it was described as 'unidentifiable'. But when Emanuel Eisenberg, an acknowledged expert in pre-Roman archaeology, visited us on the 22 August, he weighed and measured it and thought that the specifications hinted at a Jewish coin, minted before the Romans disallowed Jewish coinage with Hebrew or Aramaic inscriptions (after the end of the Hasmonean rule in AD 37). A bronze coin of Mattathias Antigonos perhaps, the last of the Hasmoneans, with a diameter of 2.3 millimetres, a Hebrew inscription on the obverse ('Mattatayah, the High Priest, and the community of the Jews'), and two cornucopias, and, on the reverse, the Greek line 'Belonging to King Antigonos' and a laurel wreath?[25] It remains a possibility, but in spite of Eisenberg's hunch, we will probably never know for certain. The challenge of unanswered questions is part and parcel of archaeological endeavours.

Our first season gave us all the results we could possibly have hoped for, and we could have concluded the whole project in the autumn of 2001. But those tantalizing aspects pointing to a Crusader chapel, and the search for the floor of the Jewish, early to mid first-century Emmaus were too much of an incentive to be resisted. We all wanted to reassemble the jigsaw. Jon Seligman and Gideon Avni, the two men in charge of supervising and facilitating excavations in the wider Jerusalem District at the Israel Antiquities Authority, who had become supporters, gladly agreed. Shuka Dorfman, the Director of the Authority, whom I have known since the True Confocal Laser Scanning Microscope with its analytical software (which I helped to develop with my colleague Georg Masuch for the analysis of the Dead Sea Scrolls) was presented to the IAA in Jerusalem, did not object.[26] From the perspective of Israeli archaeology, after all, this was not just the excavation of a site mentioned in the New Testament. Whatever happened there on that portentous 9 April 30, Emmaus was a Jewish village, one of the few places west of Jerusalem where, according to Josephus, Jews had definitely lived before and until AD 70.[27] Beyond the shadow of a doubt, Cleopas, his unnamed companion, and, needless to say, Jesus himself, were Jews. Establishing the existence of Josephus' Emmaus, and profiling the way of life at this site in the Late Second Temple Period would be a valuable contribution to the topographical, sociological and even religious aspects of Jewish life west of Jerusalem. Would we be able to find further evidence of the habits and practices of the Jewish inhabitants before, during and after the Emmaus episode? We applied for a renewal of our licence and began to plan for a second season in 2002. After months of drawing-board preparations, practical work resumed on 7 September 2002.

We opened a new Area C to the east and deepened the probes in the existing areas. In one sense, we happened upon further riddles; in another, we got answers. Mameluke pottery appeared, including a beautifully decorated lamp fragment, establishing a Muslim presence after the final defeat and retreat of the Crusaders in 1291. The very distinctive Ottoman pottery fragments which we found in the new Area C had a high sand content and were probably made at the coast – rare finds contributing to our knowledge of the distribution of Ottoman ceramics. Appropriately, we also found sea shells. The usual pieces to be expected all appeared: early Roman-Herodian tiles and jar handles from the period before AD 70, tesserae, Byzantine and Omayyad bowl and jar fragments.

This was satisfactory enough until we opened locus 10 of the new Square C, and found an object which signalled one of those breakthroughs archaeologists always hope for: a fragment of a stone vessel, called a 'Klal' in Hebrew. Looking innocent enough in our hands, it was the bearer of important news. In the third season, 2003, we were to find another, even more elaborate 'Klal' fragment. But even if we had only found this first one, the conclusions were inescapable. The clue to its identification appears in the Gospel of John (2.6), where Jesus performs the miracle of changing water into wine at the Wedding of Cana: 'Now standing there were 6 stone water-jars for the Jewish rites of purification, each holding 20 or 30 gallons.' The ritual cleansing of hands before a meal, and the washing of vessels before and after a meal required ritually clean water, and this had to come from stone jars, since only stone vessels were kosher, and deemed to be uncontaminated.[28] And although many complete or fragmentary stone jars have been found all over Judaea and Galilee, at Qumran and in the Jewish Quarter of Jerusalem, John 2.6 is the only known literary-historical reference to them from the Late Second Temple Period.[29] Therefore, Israeli archaeologists know this reference in John's Gospel and treat it as an historically reliable, trustworthy and con- temporary piece of information, whereas a large number of Christian New Testament scholars still prefer to regard the whole wedding at Cana as a symbolic story invented by John. The Evangelist offers a theological punchline, of course: for such a miracle, the water had to be kosher, and the vessels had to be filled to the brim, to exclude the possibility of any unclean interference. But as historians know, a symbolic message does not negate the historicity of the story behind it, nor does a straightforward historical account force its readers to deny any possibility of a symbolical understanding. The controversies between event and symbolism, myth and fact, history and legend are entirely artificial. The Wedding at Cana may mean all sorts of different things to believing Christians, agnostic scholars and professional historians, but even the most elaborate theo- logical interpretations do not 'prove' that the wedding and the miracle performed by Jesus never happened. Today, the enlightened attitude towards the New Testament accounts is not the one which doubts them, but the one which places them within the realistic context of the first century.[30] And if we should assume, for the sake of argument, that Jesus did not do anything in Cana, and that the wedding never happened, we would still have to admit that John, the Gospel author, knew what he was talking about and was describing a type of jar, and the ritual practice that went with it, which no other author of the 1st centuries BCE/AD recorded.

Our discovery was not sensational in statistical terms, since such fragmentary and broken stone vessels have been a common archaeological feature, and anyone who visits the Israel Museum in Jerusalem can see some of the best-preserved vessels on display, large ones of the size presupposed by John's Gospel, and small ones, for use at table. What mattered, though, was the *consequence* of the find at this particular site: since the manufacture of this type of vessel ended with the destruction of the Temple in AD 70, and since the Romans took over at Emmaus in AD 70/71 anyway, we now possessed further firm archaeological evidence for a habitation of Jews before the arrival of Vespasian's veterans.[31] We had known this, of course, since the discovery of the Sh'ma potsherd, and of some other, smaller objects described above, like the valuable Eastern Terra Sigillata pottery – but this time, the conclusions took us one step further: As a *klal* was used for ritual purposes, the people at Emmaus appear to have been observant, practising Jews. And this sheds some light on the community who lived in Emmaus: for although stone vessels were far more expensive than ceramic vessels anyway, both pieces found by us were of a remarkably beautiful design, with concave and convex forms and elaborate lines, works of art and not just of ritual. The families at Emmaus who had ordered these stone jars were both pious and rich.

This ties in with Emanuel Eisenberg's discovery of a house with murals and mosaics in the Roman part of Emmaus-Colonia, which he had found in 1973. As we have seen, it may be assumed that the Roman veterans on the eastern outskirts of Emmaus could have occupied such a house without changing too much of the exquisite Jewish-Herodian interior design. The cumulative evidence now suggests that the Jews at Emmaus were no ordinary villagers. For them, both wealthy and observant, Emmaus was a leafy suburb, where they could live close enough to the city of the Temple to reach it at leisure for the obligatory services, but just far enough away to offer a luxurious escape from the crowded streets of Jerusalem. The city had a population of up to 100,000 at the time of Jesus, and around one million pilgrims came every year from all over the Roman Empire for the three major pilgrimage festivals of Passover, Shavuot (Pentecost) and Sukkot (Tabernacles), and there would have been a constant stream of people visiting the Temple throughout the year.[32] Not everyone, not even all of the rich, could own one of the spacious villas in the Herodian Quarter of the city, on the eastern slopes of the western hill and facing the southwestern part of Temple Mount, to which they could have withdrawn.[33] Emmaus was the alternative place to be, and it had one advantage compared with Jerusalem: the air was much fresher in the Sorek Valley, and the water was cleaner near the springs of Moza.

Aqua Bella – the 'Beautiful Spring'

Our second season at Emmaus produced another result: the roof of the Crusader building had collapsed, but this had taken place at a surprisingly late date. We found medieval soil in the core of its walls and collapsed ceilings which had got mixed with soil from the Mameluke occupation after 1291. We gathered that the Mamelukes had not destroyed the building but instead used it for their own purposes, as they did at Abu Gosh/Fontenoid, the Emmaus of the Crusaders, where the church was turned into a cowshed. The building at Moza-Emmaus, which we tentatively identified as a Hospitallers' chapel, would have been too small for more than a few animals, but it could have been used as a storage centre or a kitchen: in Area C, we found what may have been a small oven of the Ottoman period, and later, in the third season, we discovered an Ottoman clay pipe, the first of its kind ever found in the Holy Land. Clearly, then, these rooms had continued to be used. Whether the inhabitants of the Ottoman period were peasants, cultivating the arable land around Emmaus, or merely squatters enjoying the occasional pipe after a warm meal, is not clear from the evidence. One thing did become clear, though, while we were studying the collapse: in Area C, all the evidence pointed to an earthquake. When Alla Nagorski, an old hand in field archaeology, visited us, she immediately agreed that there must have been an earthquake, probably in the late seventeenth century.

We decided to invite an expert in earthquake dating: over the past few decades, dating earthquakes (and also volcanic eruptions) has provided some fine-tuning to the dating of archaeological strata. The collapse was higher than in the western Areas A and B, and we concluded that the part of the building which was destroyed in Area C had been of two storeys. This made sense: Hospitaller establishments with chapels were frequently constructed as two-storey buildings. The chapel was on one floor, and the other was used as a hospital or infirmary. Covered holes in the ceiling were opened during services, so the bedridden could hear the services taking place below or above them, pronounce the Confession of Sins and receive the Absolution.

I have seen this type of Hospitallers' architecture in several central European towns. San Giovanni di Prè in Genua, built between 1150 and

1180, had the chapel on the ground floor and the hospital on the first floor, with an additional altar so that the sick could receive Holy Communion. The opening in the ceiling (or in the floor, depending on your perspective) was near the upstairs altar. In Scotland is the hospital church of Torphichen near Linlithgow. Torphichen, the seat of the priory of the Order of St John in Scotland until 1560, was built around 1140. The infirmary was on the first floor of the transept.[34] In Germany, the building at Nieder-Weisel, near Butzbach (north of Frankfurt), has preserved the original structure of the early thirteenth century (before 1245) almost intact. This building, which today serves as the ecclesiastical centre of the Order of St John in Germany, again had the church on the ground floor and the hospital above, with three openings in the floor of the ward. A rare and late exception to this arrangement can be seen at Enns in Austria, built in about 1326: here, the Hospitallers had their hospital downstairs, a room of 24.6 by 8 metres below a small chapel of 7 by 6.8 metres.

As a rule, then, the church or chapel was downstairs, and the hospital or hospice was upstairs. Both floors were usually linked by an external staircase in wood or stone.[35] Some of them had extended single-storey porticoes, resembling longish halls. The thirteenth-century establishment at Sanginesio in the Italian Marche, for example, preserves such an entrance hall with arcades; but earlier still, preceding even the First Crusade, are the churches built by Cluniac architects in Burgundy.[36] The architectural history of these single-storey entrance halls is uncertain, but since most of the Knights who came to this part of conquered Judaea hailed from French-speaking Europe – 'Frankish' is a name used even in Israeli literature on the Crusades – the possibility of such an influence should not be discarded. Was this what we had found in the ruins above the first-century floor of Emmaus – was it perhaps the collapsed rest of the prototype, developed from Burgundian models and introduced in Europe after the return of the first Crusaders? It was high time for us to go to Aqua Bella.

Aqua Bella – the 'Beautiful Spring': a medieval Latin name which conjures up images of Arcadian delights. And indeed, the area, nine kilometres west of Jerusalem and just south of the A1 motorway, is a National Park and has become one of the most popular weekend destinations for today's Jerusalemites. Jewish weddings are celebrated within the Crusader compound – on my latest visit, I saw the table for the bridal pair set up in the 12th century Hospitallers' Chapel. They did not know that they were about to dine in a medieval place of Christian worship. Near the entrance to the site, there is a large parking lot, a snack bar, restrooms, and a 'picnic-recreation area' by the spring and the rivulets which meander through the gardens. Here, the valley of the Nahal Kesalon is anything but a dry watercourse. The river and the natural springs turn it into an evergreen pleasure ground, with oaks and terebinths, almond and carob trees a part of the natural woods at the site, and vineyards on the adjacent hill. What a delightful place to be for a twelve-century Knight Hospitaller, recuperating from illness and battle injuries. For this is what Aqua Bella was at that time: a resting place for sick and injured knights, and for retired knights living out their days in these gorgeous surroundings.

Aqua Bella is opposite Castellum Emmaus (Fontenoid), today's Abu Gosh, the Hospitallers' main hospice and church establishment, which was built c.1140. It served as an outpost, and even the injured and recovering knights were probably expected to help guard this southern side of the access road between the Mediterranean port of Jaffa and Jerusalem. Despite the fact that the castle of Belmont was only a couple of kilometres away, and on the same side of the road, the semi-fortified structure of the courtyard buildings at Aqua Bella still tells us that the Hospitallers were not prepared to run any risks. In any case, it is the largest and best-preserved courtyard manor house in the Crusader Kingdom of Jerusalem, measuring 27 metres east–west by 36 metres north–south.[37] At the centre of the establishment there is a square courtyard measuring 15 by 15 metres, with an east-facing entrance. A two-storey, barrel-vaulted building on the northern side may have been used for stabling and storage, but to us, it looked more like an agricultural-cum-culinary production site: from the top floor, goods would have been lowered down through a wide, square opening, to be processed 5.86 metres below (we measured it ourselves), in a room measuring 7 by 15.1 metres. Blackened walls and corresponding smoke-stained traces above betray the existence of fires probably used for frying and stewing. The stables would have been in the northern rooms opposite the entrance.

Fascinating as this may be for Crusader connoisseurs, it was not really what we were looking for. Facing south, the other double-storeyed structure excited our curiosity: for here we saw the parallels to our own site. Facing east, there was an arcade on the ground floor, and an exterior stone staircase led to the upper level. Upstairs, we measured a room 21.8 metres in length and 6.73 metres wide, with three bays of groin-vaults with moulded consoles. Three wide windows, some of them with clearly visible Hospitallers' builders' marks on the arched stones, would have lit the room. Was this the chapel? It certainly appeared to be a rather splendid room, and something resembling a small semi-circular apse was visible at the east end.[38] We hesitated. An upper-floor chapel would have been unusual. However, beautiful walls and windows would have been anything but inappropriate for a hospital ward – after all, the Hospitallers used to call the people they were caring for 'Our Lords the Sick' (*seignors malades* in medieval French), and treated them accordingly. If this deference was their attitude towards the impoverished local population, who we know from records was certainly their main target group at the central hospice in Jerusalem, how much more would they have lavished the beauties of interior architecture on their own veterans? We had to look on the ground floor again.

At an odd angle near the east side there is an olive press, which may have led some scholars to assume that this was a room used for food processing. However, the olive press is clearly secondary: it was probably brought here during the Mameluke period. On the other hand, this east-facing side of the room has a 5 metre wide, elevated area with a window, and niches which may have been used for liturgical implements. Soot-blackened spots above the elevated area, lighter than those caused by open fires in the building opposite, point to the use of candles and sconces. Similar traces can be seen at regular intervals on the walls and the ceiling throughout the room. It was a simple structure: no wall plaster has survived, but the remains of plaster on the vaults indicate that this loss may have been caused by later Mameluke use of the downstairs room as a shed for animals. As we saw in Chapter 2 at Abu Gosh/Fontenoid, their acidic emissions tend to damage or destroy wall plaster and elaborate frescoes.

We discovered two openings in the ceiling, now bricked up, which would have served the traditional purpose of enabling the bedridden to listen to the services. Moreover, the main entrance from the courtyard was anything but modest. Crusader voussoirs shape the vaulted doorway, various stonemasons' marks can be seen, and there are several Jerusalem Crosses and fleur-de-lys decorations, and stones marked with a 'B' (probably referring to the Crusader King Baldwin III, who had succeeded King Fulco, the first regional 'protector' of the Hospitallers and friend of Frà Raymond du Puy, the energetic Master of the Order from 1120 to 1160). Baldwin took a particular interest in the estates owned by the Hospitallers.[39] This entrance area is far more elaborate than the one on the other side of the courtyard (which led into the room used as temporary storage and for food processing). Anyone walking through this decorated door, with its 2.13-metre-deep walls and height of 2.35 metres, would have known that this was not just any ordinary building. On the other side of the room the south door, facing away from the protected inner courtyard into the open area, was no less impressive: 2.66 metres high, and with walls 2.80 metres deep. We concluded that the chapel would have been on the ground floor and the hospice upstairs, possibly with a small altar, as can be seen at San Giovanni di Prè in Genua.

We measured all the rooms again, to be absolutely certain, and what interested us most at this stage was their length and the height. Supposing Aqua Bella was a slightly later and solidly fortified successor to our own building site, could we assume any parallels between the dimensions of these buildings and the structure we had begun to excavate? Our Hospitallers' structure, fascinating as it suddenly had become, was, as far as we were concerned, still a 'hindrance' on our way to the first century. Any yardstick to help gauge its size would be welcome. The upper floor above the chapel, with its groin vaults, could not be measured exactly, as the roof was missing: but we took the measurement of the inner courtyard wall of the chapel from the beginning of the ceiling to the floor at the stone staircase. It was 5.31 metres high, about half a metre less than the height of the storage and kitchen room opposite (which we had measured through the hole in the ceiling). We now had the yardstick we needed to estimate when we might hope to reach the floor at our own site: but even more importantly for our plans, we measured the length in order to get an idea of where to open new squares in the future. Always assuming that our Crusader structure was a smaller, less well-fortified predecessor to Aqua

Bella, would we have to allow for 20 or 30 or even more metres, and in which directions? The storage and kitchen room is 15.10 by 7 metres, and the chapel 21.30 by 6.73 metres in total (or 18.30 by 6.73 metres without the elevated altar room).

Back at our site, we went straight to the well which marked the end of the open area behind an olive tree, where a pathway went past the so-called Old Synagogue. This well must have been outside the medieval building. From there to the beginning of the arcade in Area B is exactly 18.5 metres. Satisfied, we now had at least a working hypothesis: the arcade did indeed belong to the entrance area of a Hospitallers' chapel of the Burgundian and Italian type, and while the single-storey portico was not emulated by other Crusader architects in the Holy Land, the overall length of the building was neither markedly shorter nor longer than that of the Aqua Bella type. It was food for thought, and we invited Adrian Boas, Israel's leading Crusader historian, to visit us during the next season. We wanted to discuss with him why this establishment was not mentioned in any surviving source. All there is, in fact, is a reference to the Saltus Muratus, traditionally understood to mean a forest or a woodland estate surrounded by a wall, and usually identified with the tower enclosure 50 metres further east: around 1169, the Hospitallers (under Frà Gilbert d'Assailly, Master of the Order 1163–70) tried to lease it to Duke Bela of Hungary, for a sizeable amount of money and for as long as he should remain in the Holy Land, or until his death:[40] it seems the Hospitallers were temporarily interested in relinquishing their direct resposibility for the terra de Emmaus, the villages and lands of the Order in the wider region of Fontenoid. In the surviving document, Aqua Bella, Belveer (Castel) and Saltus Muratus are mentioned explicitly, 'with their culti-vated lands, vineyards, orchards and woods, with the wheat and the barley, wine and fruit, animals and everything that is found in them'. Nothing apparently came of this arrangement, but the record has sur-vived. Strikingly, chapels, hospitals and hospices are not mentioned, although they certainly did exist at Fontenoid and Aqua Bella by 1163. And thus, the nature of the area at Saltus Muratus remained unspecified. The name, as it was understood, did not help very much either: no-one would have expected to find a two-storey building with chapel and infirmary just outside the walled-up structure of a Crusader tower.

Having concluded our second season, we decided to focus on the Jewish first-century evidence again in our evaluation of the finds: such evaluation and analysis is a part of the time-consuming work which all archaeologists have to do for months after every digging campaign. There was one nagging question which we knew could be answered by a bit of proper research: did Saltus Muratus really mean a forest or woodland estate surrounded by a wall? The Crusader tower or citadel near our site measured merely 15 by 30 metres, with walls up to 5 metres thick. There was no evidence of an estate with a wall around it, nor of walled-up woodland anywhere in the immediate vicinity. The solution came when I looked into glossaries and handbooks of medieval Latin – the Latin written and spoken by the Crusaders. In those days, Saltus meant 'attack' or 'assault'.[41] This insight changed the whole scenario. Not only did our excavated strata appear to be older than Aqua Bella, Fontenoid, and other Hospitaller buildings in Judaea, but we were now beginning to look at a fortified stronghold which may have been a part of the very first phase of Crusader architecture, when the Knights were still fighting and attacking, not least in the valleys and along the roads. But even so: first of all, we had to return to the Emmaus of Luke and Josephus.

An earthquake and a Roman number

During the winter and spring of 2002/03, we looked into ancient, medieval and modern earthquakes. We were not the first to ponder on this natural phenomenon. In their mythical mood, the ancient Greeks made the god Poseidon responsible for earthquakes. With his trident, 'the one who shakes the earth' split rocks and churned up the seas. Thales of Milet, the Ionic philosopher and astronomer of c.585 BCE, thought the earth was floating on primeval water and lost its balance during storms. Later thinkers developed somewhat more scientific theories, but to all of them, earthquakes were an observable reality. The eastern Mediterranean basin was and is prone to them, and Israel is no exception. In the Holy Land, they have not been very frequent – statistically, about one per century: but when they occur, they shape history. The prophet Amos, for example, dates his own period by a reference to an earthquake in c.760 BCE (Amos 1.1). Other books of the Old Testament mention earthquakes as

signs of God's wrath (Ps. 18.7; Isa. 13.13, etc.). In 31 BCE, an earthquake hit
Judaea, 30,000 lives were lost, and some of the traces can still be seen in
the excavated area of Qumran.[42] When Jesus died, an earthquake occurred
in Jerusalem (Mat. 27.51–54), and a split in the rock of Gologotha caused
by this earthquake on the 7 April AD 30 can still be seen in the rockface at
the Greek-Orthodox Chapel in the Church of the Holy Sepulchre. The
apostle Paul and his companion Silvanus/Silas were rescued during an
earthquake in Philippi (Acts 16.26).

There are lists of ancient earthquakes, and detailed seismological
studies. When we turned to those published about the Roman province of
Palestine in the Byzantine, Crusader and Muslim periods, we found that
the area of Emmaus-Colonia had been shattered by earthquakes several
times during the pre-Christian period, but that there was a lull until the
eighteenth century, when two earthquakes were recorded, in 1752 and
1759.[43] A drawing of 1586 by Giovanni Zuallardo shows an unidentified
building standing only to its second-storey roof.[44] Since the collapse of the
building occured at one stroke, with rows of stones jammed tightly into
the ground and a large area of plaster lying intact, face down, we concluded that a serious earthquake must have done that damage after 1685.
Thus, the first, the second or both of these earthquakes were likely to have
been responsible for the collapse we had found at our site. Conversely, no
evidence was forthcoming that either any of the Jewish buildings of
Emmaus before AD 70 or the Roman structures of Vespasian's veterans'
colony had been damaged or destroyed by an earthquake.

It was a result which gave us the much-anticipated latest possible date,
the *terminus ante quem*, for Ottoman occupation, including the squatters
who may have left that clay pipe and some pottery of the so-called Black
Gaza rim type on the floor. It also helped to explain why so much
evidence – Byzantine, Roman, and above all the Jewish finds of the
Emmaus period before AD 70 – turned up in debris which was higher than
the chronological strata where they should have been. Twentieth century
robbers may have dug trenches – we found evidence of one in Area D –
but their destructive work was limited. What really toppled, disturbed
and mixed the layers was the earthquake period between 1752 and 1759.
Our discoveries of the Sh'ma ostracon and the first of the purification
vessel fragments above the first-century floor were no longer enigmatic.

From then on, we knew we could expect to find almost anything in places where it did not 'belong'. Prepared for the third season, we began our field work on 25 August 2003 and made the discovery of the second Klal fragment mentioned above. Patiently waiting for the appearance of the Emmaus floor which we had learned to expect some five metres below the Hospitallers' arcade, we now had accumulated sufficient archaeological evidence for the Jewish village to remain optimistic.

Area B, the one of the two northern squares which was least affected by the earthquakes, with the outer wall and the first 60 centimetres of the vault still standing, looked most promising. Here we began to go deeper, carefully and centimetre by centimetre, to avoid damage or destruction of other evidence. And all of a sudden, we found a stone with the Roman number 56, in the southwest corner of the area. It was in a rough condition, and like so many Roman stones found elsewhere, it was probably modified and in secondary use, to serve an unnown purpose. We were immediately reminded of the Pontius Pilate inscription found in 1961, turned upside down and used in a step in the theatre of Caesarea. The inscription was clearly legible, though, encased by slanting lines which once separated it from other parts of a text now lost. It read \ LVI /. Since it was obviously in Latin, whereas the common language of pre- and post-Roman inhabitants was Greek (if not Aramaic or Arabic), this looked like evidence of the Roman *colonia*. One of the student volunteers suggested it may have been the house number of Cleopas' home after it had been taken over by the Romans. But he said it under the midday sun and we put it to him that there might just conceivably be a more likely explanation.

In a military context, the number LVI could simply be a reference to the fifty-sixth centuria: until Emperor Hadrian, a legion had 60 centurions, who were the commanding officers of a centuria, the smallest unit of a legion. Since this place became a veterans' colony after the destruction of Jerusalem and the Temple, the number could have been used to identify the house of a veteran *centurio*. On the other hand, the Romans had a system of land partition, the *centuriatrion*, which used units called *heredia*, little allotments, in blocks of 100 each. This was particularly widespread in the colonies. Thus, if this was the system employed by Vespasian at Emmaus-Colonia for his 800 veterans, the number 56 would have come up eight times, once in each of the separate allotments, and our stone could be the first to be found. In future seasons, we shall look for evidence of the chequerboard grid system of streets between the allotments which may lie outside our present areas. But we may have to be patient once again, for such evidence would be hidden either under the access road to the motorway and the Old Synagogue, or on arable land privately owned to the north of our excavation site. Should we find it one day, and should it turn out to be both pre- and post-AD 70, it would be a nice little addition to the growing list of evidence of a Jewish-Herodian village built under the influence of Roman architectural models before Vespasian even arrived. On the other hand, if such a grid system was only added to the lay-out of the village by the Romans after AD 70, we might be able to find out how much the Romans changed at Emmaus, and if they interfered with the infrastructure of the village, after all. In any case, there now is the distinct possibility of finding further traces which will contribute to our knowledge of both the Herodian period and the period under Roman occupation.

In terms of other finds, we had no reason to complain. A small, un-datable silver earring stimulated a lively debate – who wore it and when? Needless to say, speculation was rife: Cleopas' wife, perhaps? In a more serious vein, we thought of a wealthy Abbasid owner: but in the end we agreed that we may never know.[45] Small pottery fragments from the Herodian, pre-AD 70 period were found in Areas A, B and D – more of the same, as it were, and continuous proof of the existence of a Jewish village at this site. The beautiful Klal stone vessel was found close to a floor in Area B. A floor – the floor to what? And from what period? Herodian, Byzantine or early Muslim? The deeper we dug, the more intricate were the different layers of occupation. We found a plastered white surface in Area A: the floor of the Hospitallers' entrance arcade? There were two stone door hinges, further evidence of an entrance area. Tantalizing as it was to develop one hypothesis after another, we decided to record the evidence, continue to work downwards and wait for conclusive finds.

At the same time, we made a completely unexpected discovery in our southeast Area D: a well-preserved aqueduct. We took soil samples and found traces of sediment left by running water. Measuring the height and the direction, we were able to follow its presumed course outside our area. Going west, we arrived at a source, some 150 metres from our site, which had apparently been cultivated and enclosed since the Bronze Age and is currently being used as the *mikveh* or purifying bath of an ultra-orthodox Jewish movement. Turning east, we arrived at an underground cistern, 35 metres from our site, behind the Old Synagogue. This was near the area we had identified during the first survey of 2000, briefly described in the Introduction to this book. Now cleared of the illegally accumulated debris and rubbish, the area presented beautifully preserved walls, originally built in Roman times, and extended by Byzantine and Crusader architects. Vaults at the entrance to what may have been a courtyard conformed to the type discovered in our Area B, and the width of the floor between them was 7.5 metres – exactly the width of the area we were calling the portico of a Hospitallers' chapel. A small stone stair-case leads from the northeast corner towards the area of the fortified Crusader tower.

Vaulted rooms in the undercroft of the Old Synagogue had given rise to the suspicion that something might be found underneath the new concrete floor of the courtyard. During our first season, a hole had been opened, and there it was and still is: a huge cistern. Equipped with torch-lights, our team and Zvi Greenhut of the Israel Antiquities Authority climbed down on a rope ladder in 2001, and saw a rectangular room filled with soil to about half its height. On the west side arcaded openings were visible, built in the typical Hospitallers' fashion, with stonemasons' marks on some of them. The northern end of the room betrayed signs of an earlier structure used and extended by these Crusader Knights. We realized that this would be an ideal venue for further excavations, but back then, in 2001, we left it as it was. Now, two years later, we returned, having been led to the cistern by the course of the aqueduct.

The water had come via the aqueduct, which first reached the well at the eastern end of our site and then apparently continued underground, as a tunnelled channel, in a northeastern direction. Two openings in the ceiling, now closed but visible from inside the cistern, indicated that fresh rain water was also fed in. It was a remarkable structure, and although the stonemasons' marks told us that the Hospitallers had been here, they did not normally build their cisterns outside the protected area,[46] and this one here was clearly outside the fortified structure of the Saltus Muratus. Was it indeed an earlier reservoir, used by the Crusaders simply because it was already there when they arrived: and how old was it? Byzantine perhaps, or even older? We compared it with known settlement areas in Judaea and beyond which preceded the Crusaders' period. Before long, we found a striking parallel, on the road between Jerusalem and Jericho: a site called Qasr Ali. As a survey published in 1993 showed, this was a Byzantine establishment with earlier Roman traces.[47] A fortified tower stood at a distance from the cistern, the chapel, and the living quarters. The arrangement of these buildings was a mirror image of our site: the tower, in a bend of the Roman road, was at the western end of the complex; 30 metres to the right there was the reservoir, northeast of the tower; the church was discovered, with living quarters – of which we had not found any Byzantine or Crusader traces yet – immediately adjacent to the east. And what is more, the Byzantine tower, 15 by 10 metres, was oblong, exactly like Saltus Muratus with its 30 by 15 metres. The Hospitallers, on the other hand, used to build their towers on a square groundplan. More work had to be done, but it looked as though we were on the trail of an unusual building history: it seems the Knights Hospitaller had found the walls and ground structures of the Byzantine establishment, which had not been destroyed completely by the Omayyad and Abbasid conquerers, and rebuilt and extended them for their own purposes.

We had hardly assembled our data and measurements when Adrian Boas visited us, in the company of Zvi Greenhut. Adrian Boas is a gifted poet, but above all, he is an experienced archaeologist, Senior Lecturer in Medieval Archaeology at the University of Haifa and widely respected as the leading historian of the Crusader period in Israel. He studied our aqueduct and the surroundings, immediately agreed to the new translation of Saltus Muratus as a walled position of attack, saw the parallels with Qasr Ali and suggested that we should look at another structure with an oblong tower, the keep of Har Hozevim, today a northwestern suburb of Jerusalem. Unfortunately, the site was destroyed after its excavation in 1993–4, but two excavation reports have been published.[48] Har Hovezim was an early twelfth-century farmhouse, with an elongated two-storey building, measuring 12 by 19 metres. Thus, it was certainly oblong: but any evidence of a fortified, tower-like structure was missing. Another Crusader establishment turned up in our research, however:

Castrum Regis or Château du Roi, also called Castrum Novum and Mi'iliya, near Akko in Western Galilee. First mentioned in 1160, but probably a few decades older, it presented a number of similarities to our earlier site at Emmaus: just south of a stream and a road, it possessed a church, a tower or *castrum* and living quarters. The church was to the west of the tower, and both structures were separated by some forty metres, exactly as at Emmaus-Colonia. There was a difference, however: the fortified tower was definitely square, being nine by nine metres – small, but typical of a Crusader building complex. Earlier structures, Byzantine or Roman, had not been found.[49] Satisfied that our Saltus Muratus was a rare exception, we agreed to mull things over, left the twelfth century, and planned to return to the first.

Hummus, Tehina, and a fresh assault

A decent meal refreshes the mind: seasoned diners know the truth of this saying, and at Kibbutz Tzuba we have been treated to some delicious bites. On the evening of our Byzantine-Crusader 'tower studies', the staple diet of Israelis, the *hors d'oeuvre* without which a meal is not a meal, was particularly exquisite: the freshly ground hummus with extra helpings of chickpeas tasted better than ever, and the Tehina, a first-class sesame seed paste, melted on the tongue. A glass of Merlot from Galilee did not come amiss, and every one of us felt inspired to divulge our views. Why had there been this unspoken unease about the time-consuming Crusader business? Had we not come to excavate the Jewish village of Emmaus? Quite so, of course – but over our meal, with generous helpings of amnun (also known as St Peter's Fish) we realized that this very early Hospitallers' compound was more than a contribution to the history of the First Crusade. We were beginning to collect the archaeological evidence for a Judaeo-Christian site spanning the millennia from the Benjaminites in the Bronze Age to the earthquakes of the eighteenth century. Those Hospitallers who had built their tower, the cistern, the chapel and the hospice over Byzantine structures were practising Christians, far removed from the killer image usually associated with the Knights of the First Crusade. Their infirmaries were open to the local Jewish (and Arab) population: the Muristan quarter in

Jerusalem, which preceded the Saltus Muratus complex by only a few years, served anyone who had nowhere else to go – in fact, the hospitals of the Order of St John in and near Jerusalem honour this commitment to the present day. And as we had seen in the crucifixion fresco of the early twelfth-century church at Abu Gosh, the theology of these Hospitallers and their artists was pro-Jewish, decidedly countering the anti-semitic imagery prevalent in European churches of the time.

The Hospitallers had 'found' their Emmaus at Abu Gosh/Fontenoid, below the hillock of Qiryat Yearim, and had called it Castellum Emmaus. But by a quirk of history, they built their earliest compound outside Jerusalem precisely at the spot where the true Emmaus of Luke's Gospel must be located. As we now knew, their Byzantine Christian predecessors had established an extensive settlement, with a monastery invisibly hidden under the present motorway, and with further buildings extending northwards into the area between the later Saltus Muratus and our immediate excavation site, and with a lookout in the terraces of Moza. The Jewish villagers had been at Emmaus from the Benjaminite Bronze Age until AD 70. After the late second century, they returned to collect the branches for their tabernacles. In other words, the biblical history of Moza, the Christian history of Emmaus, and the Jewish history of the Mishnaic period met at this site.

And if this was not enough, there was the Canaanite evidence: there were the Muslim settlements between the mid seventh and the late eleventh centuries, and again after 1291 until the seventeenth-century earthquakes. And suddenly, we had an archaeological vision: centring on the village of Emmaus in the Late Second Temple Period, we saw the creation of a National Park, where visitors would walk through 4,000 years of human history, from the terraces of Moza to the Crusader chapel-cum-hospice which remained standing, happily used by Ottoman squatters with their clay pipes, until 1759. For the intrepid visitor, twentieth-centuries remains could be integrated, including the ruins of the villa once owned by the Hitler-loving Mufti of Jerusalem, destroyed in 1948, and a Jewish house a few metres north of the cistern, also damaged during that conflict but reconstructable, and still privately owned, which could become a museum. So close to the road, access from Jerusalem and Tel Aviv would be easy; in fact, it could be a stopover for people arriving from or leaving for the airport. But our vision had to give way to reality. The next day, we would launch a fresh assault on the seemingly intractable stratigraphy. It was all there. All we had to do was to persevere.

The next day, Zvi Greenhut, the most indefatigably supportive of friends, arrived with a few books and articles which I had asked him to look for in the library and archives of the Israel Antiquities Authority. Among them was a complicated-sounding collection of essays by the most prolific of British Crusader experts, Denys Pringle. When he wrote them, he had not investigated the site of Saltus Muratus, but he made an observation which could be the clue to the riddle of the post-Byzantine, post-Abbasid developments: having investigated the later Crusader 'manor houses' or rural administrative centres at El Qubeibe/Parva Mahomeria – which the Franciscans had turned into their very own Emmaus during the fifteenth century – al-Jib/Gibeon, Jifna/Jafemia, Burj Bardawil and Rama/ar-Ram, he concluded: 'In such complexes, the first building to be constructed was often a defensive tower, to which other structures were later added.'[50] Applied to our site, this made a great deal of sense. The tower, built in the valley near the road as a fortified position of attack – and by definition also of defence – during the decades between 1099 and 1140 before Judaea was finally 'pacified', soon became the focal point of an early centre for pastoral care and nursing. The regional population, Jews and Muslims, early pilgrims who had arrived under the protection of the Crusaders, and the Knights Hospitaller themselves were all treated as equals, and for the Christians among them, the chapel was a central feature of the establishment. Close enough to the fortified citadel, the Hospitallers who ran the chapel and the hospice knew they could always take refuge there if necessary, whereas the Knights who guarded the position in the tower kept an eye on strangers. A tell-tale indication of this arrangement was the thickness of the walls: 4–5 metres at the tower, but only 1.5 metres at the two-storey building nearby. The Hospitallers who were in charge of the hospital and the chapel did not want to frighten away the pilgrims and the sick with a display of military strength – 40 metres away, the tower was close enough as it was. Here, charitable accessibility was paramount. And the site was chosen in a considered way: just 8.5 kilometres west of Jerusalem, it was a place of refreshment and recuperation for people before they entered the holy city, and for those living outside Jerusalem, it was an attractive place anyway. Interestingly enough, no archaeological traces of a hospice or hospital have been found at Abu Gosh, a few kilometres further down the road towards the coast. Could it be that Emmaus-Saltus Muratus remained the Hospitallers' 'open' hospice even after 1140, when Fontenoid/Castellum Emmaus had been built? Aqua Bella certainly was no alternative, as it was exclusively the home of sick and retired Hospitallers.

Nile perch, eggshells and the first century

Close to the motorway, our Area D was the only square which lay partly outside the walls of the medieval and earlier periods. The aqueduct, built along the wall, determined the outer perimeter. Two things had to be done in the next season. First, we would have to excavate to the south of the aqueduct, and second, we would have to take down the baulk we had left between Areas A and B. In archaeology, a baulk is a strip of earth left between excavation trenches or squares for the study of the complete stratigraphy of the site. From above, and looking at the baulk itself from both sides, you gain a complete picture of the different layers. By August 2004, when we began our fourth season, we had seen and analysed enough and had a clear impression of the stratigraphy from the western end of these squares. We were now at the 5-metre level, which gave us the height of the Crusader building by the yardstick of Aqua Bella. The baulk was no help any longer: it was in the way if we wanted to establish the complete floor and anything underneath it. And besides, taking it down carefully, we might find further useful objects from the different periods. Two helpers from Jerusalem arrived, Chaim and Samuel Zini, father and son, and they had hardly begun sifting the soil when they saw a beautifully chased pipe, made from animal bone. It complemented the clay pipe we had found before. It seems that the Ottoman settlers – in view of the artistry invested in both pipes, we did not call them squatters any longer – had begun to take up the habit of smoking soon after the introduction of tobacco in Europe and the Middle East after 1560, and indulged their habit until their departure following the earthquakes.

We could not get these seventeenth-century earthquakes out of our heads. What if one of them, the one which did destroy the building, had struck so suddenly that people had been killed and buried under the debris, and human skeletons would turn up on the floor? As everyone excavating in Israel knows, skeletons are bad news these days: the ultra-orthodox movements would treat them as Jewish, regardless of their true identity, and insist on (re)burying them. It could mean the closure of our site. Instead of a Crusader chapel, remains of a Roman veterans' colony and the centre of a Jewish village, we would have a graveyard protected by Argus-eyed Haredim. And since some of them were passing by our site every day, on their way from the Bronze Age mikveh to the Old Synagogue, looking at our dig with genuine curiosity, we knew there was no chance of hiding any skeletons in our cupboard. But nothing of the sort was discovered.

Instead Egon Lass, who was beginning to love the beauty of the Crusader stones, assembled one voussoir after the other, admiring the finely chiselled traces produced by the stonemasons. We now had so many of these voussoirs that we knew there must have been a vault in the room, not just an arcade at its entrance. The lower parts of the northern wall were intact with surviving traces of plaster. To the south of the plastered wall, a deeper floor became visible, with a wall of its own, and which preceded the Crusader structure. It looked decidedly Herodian-Roman, rather than Byzantine. Was this 'it'? We found more Herodian pottery in the soil, eastern terra sigillata fragments among them, and, as in previous seasons, several tesserae, some of them still clustered and probably from a mosaic floor. And then, two things happened simultaneously: while one group of our team found a niche in the northern Hospitallers' wall and tentatively interpreted it as a niche for a stoup (used by Christian pilgrims to cross themselves with holy water before entering the church), a second group opened up another, deeper part of the soil and found a structure which looked suspiciously like a tomb. The dreaded moment seemed to have come, after all.

It was too deep for an Ottoman burial. It could just about be a Crusader burial, lowered deep into the ground, or even Byzantine, if not earlier. In the portico area of the chapel, a Crusader tomb or one belonging to an earlier Byzantine establishment would have made sense – priests or bishops were often buried in such places. Not quite with trembling hands, but very carefully and with bated breath, we dug deeper. And then, our sigh of relief when Egon Lass, who was the first to risk a closer look, pronounced the result: these stones were an accidental assemblage, they were floating on the lower floor, there was no tomb and certainly no skeleton. But the side effect of these investigations was a truly exciting conclusion: in Areas A and B, the inhabitants of the post-Jewish and post-Roman periods had not built into each other's houses, as the Romans had done with the Jewish building of the Emmaus mentioned by Luke and Josephus. They had built on top of each other, leaving us their floors. The reasons for this architectural development were apparent enough: for the Mamelukes, who conquered the site in c.1291, the Hospitallers' building, with its height of more than five metres, was simply far too lofty. Where we today, on moving into a house where the ceilings are too high for our tastes, would put in false ceilings, the Mamelukes put in a higher floor. The Crusaders in turn had preferred simple stamped floors on a stone surface, as we found them on the ground floors at Aqua Bella – no fancy Herodian or Byzantine mosaics for them – and here, they built their chapel floor above the earlier structure.[51] Our hopes were high: the first-century floor was within our grasp.

Meanwhile, over in Area D, we found a bronze chalice. Broken into several fragments, but with the base intact, it was a beautiful piece, and we joked that this was of course the Holy Grail, hidden by the Crusader Knights. Nearby, another discovery proved to be more conclusive: a stone decanter, almost complete – only the bottom and the endpiece of the handle were missing. The date was no mystery: it was a Roman type of decanter, belonging to the mid/late first century. It made our day, for not only was it a beautiful piece, it also was our first 'household appliance' from the Roman veterans' colony, used immediately after the takeover of AD 71/72. Not far from it, but slightly lower, we found rims of bowls and the base of a bowl in eastern terra sigillata from the early/mid first century: further corroborative evidence of a pre-Roman Jewish presence at this site, once again confirming the accuracy of Flavius Josephus in linking the Jewish village of Emmaus with the Roman *colonia*. We decided to take away the central part of the aqueduct, so that we could dig deeper along this stretch of the outer wall in Area D. And as archaeologists should always do when they take away later strata with building remains, we recorded every stone in its exact position on graph paper – precision work in which Egon Lass has no peer – and took photos from every conceivable angle. Should they feel inclined to do so, future generations of scholars will be able to produce a virtual-reality reconstruction of this section.

Back in the now baulkless double Area A/B, we found three connected stones from the ceiling. Remarkably, traces of soot from candles or candle-lit lamps which had apparently been hanging from the ceiling were clearly visible, and further underlined our assumption that this could have been the ante-room of a chapel. Four metres south of the wall with the niche, a stone-encased structure is exposed, just to the left of what once must have been the centre aisle of the portico leading into the church. At first sight, it looked like a baptismal font, deep enough for a person of average height in the Middle Ages to stand upright in and be baptised by a priest standing on the floor. An opening at the eastern end appeared to be leading into it: the baptismal candidate would have entered the water-filled basin, representing the River Jordan, from the east and, spiritually cleansed in the act of baptism, have turned round to leave, now looking in the traditional eastern direction, towards Jerusalem.[52] Courageously, in view of the potential consequences, Rafi Lewis suggested that it was a grave, with the eastern stone encasement simply lost, and Egon Lass hesitatingly agreed. So who was right? Measuring 0.48 by 1.7 metres, it was big enough for both purposes. We dug into it, but our pickaxes found nothing. If it was a tomb, it was empty, and there were no traces of a burial. There was no conclusive proof of a baptistry, either. We concluded that a baptistry remained possible. As so often in archaeology, there was no absolute certainty. Thus, we decided to publish both options, with our drawings and photographs, in our seasonal report for *Hadashot Arkheologiyot*, the official journal of the Israel Antiquities Authority.

We turned our attention to a couple of deep hollows we had dug near the east-facing end of Area B, reaching below the Crusader floor. Were the two pits left by the early Muslim occupiers, or did these holes which we had opened merely appear to be pits, and in reality provided access to the first-century floor? We had to widen and deepen the area, but before we risked the accidental destruction of evidence, Egon Lass took samples of the soil. And he knew what to do with them: in Israel, Egon is the unrivalled master of Flotation Analysis, a technique for finding and analysing tiniest remains of botanical and organic sediments from a living soil. Screened through a two-millimetre mesh, the remains will be cleaned in water, dried and finally studied through maximum-strength magnifying glasses, which Egon prefers to wear like spectacles.[53] The main aim of this kind of analysis at sites in Israel is the identification of food remains: what did the people eat during a given period, and what does this tell us about their living standards? Here, Egon found eggshells and the characteristic, unmistakable bones of Nile perch. Eggshells were anything but spectacular. Nile perch however, also known as *Lates niloticus*, is a large and carnivorous fish which is at home in the sweet-water rivers and lakes of north and central Africa. How did it get to Emmaus? Surely not via the Nahal Sorek. It was imported, and those who imported it had access to trade routes and, above all, to an income which enabled them to pay for this delicacy. At that stage, we did not know if the living soil from which Egon had taken his samples was the bottom of an Omayyad pit, a Byzantine floor or the first-century floor of the Judaeo-Roman period. But in any case, it was useful additional evidence of an earlier observation: the people who lived here throughout the ages chose Emmaus not least because of its privileged surroundings, its immediate access to the main trade route between the Mediterranean ports and Jerusalem – and because they could afford the standard of living which came with a house on this prime site. What had been true of the Jewish kings and their standard-bearers continued to be true of the Jews at Emmaus in the Late Second Temple Period, the Romans, and those who came after them. And if this should eventually turn out to have been an Omayyad or Abbasid pit after all, it would again be true to character – the wealth of these Muslim conquerers was legendary.

On the final day of the fourth season, we found Fatimid pottery fragments – the last missing link, as it were, in the continuous occupation of the site from the Bronze Age to the mid-seventeenth century, since the Fatimid Dynasty ruled from 909–1171. This was the type of pottery gladly used by the Crusaders, who did not produce their own household utensils if they could help it. It was 8 September 2004. Results of the analysis of the four coins we had found, of the bronze chalice, and other objects like a bronze ring and a very unusual object made of animal bone (which some of us thought was the bridge of a musical instrument, or perhaps the side of a bone-made box for jewellery), would arrive from the laboratories of the Israel Antiquities Authority at some stage between the autumn and the beginning of the next summer season in 2005. We left Emmaus-Colonia 'with one auspicious and one dropping eye'.[54] Our hopes and expectations had been surpassed. We had established the existence of a Jewish village in the Herodian or Late Second Temple Period, the Emmaus mentioned by Flavius Josephus, and by Luke. We had found evidence of continuous habitation, of wealth, of piety, of destruction and perseverance. And yet, so much remained to be done. We would have to come back, and there was no one on that last day of the 2004 season who did not feel that this site was worth many more years of digging.

Notes

1 For details, see E. Eisenberg, 'A Settlement from the Beginning of the Early Bronze Age I at Moza', *Atiqot* 22 (1993), 41–8.

2 'Nahal' is the Hebrew word for the Arabic 'Wadi' technically a water course which is dry except in the rainy season. In the valley of Moza-Emmaus, these are never quite dry, however, and irrigate the fertile area throughout the year. For the initial report on the first of these two digs see: A. De-Groot and Z. Greenhut, 'Moza', *Excavations and Surveys in Israel* 15 (1996), 83–4.

3 For a discussion of the evidence, see A. De-Groot and Z. Greenhut, 'A Sceptre Head from Moza', *Qadmoniot* 113 (1997), 44–5 (in Hebrew).

4 See Z. Greenhut and A. De-Groot, 'Moza', *Hadashot Arkheologiyot* 115 (2003), 55–7; cf. two publications in Hebrew by the same authors: Z. Greenhut and A. De-Groot, 'Moza – A Bronze and Iron Age Village west of Jerusalem', *Qadmoniot* 123 (2002), 12–17; and A. De-Grot (*sic*) and Z. Greenhut, 'Moza: A Judahite Administrative Center Near Jerusalem', in E. Baruch and A. Faust (eds), *New Studies on Jerusalem*, vol. 8, Jerusalem 2003, 6–14.

5 Cf. 2 Chronicles 34.1–36.21; 2 Kings 23.1–24.17; Jeremiah 22. 13–19.

6 I owe this information to a personal communication by Zvi Greenhut. An alternative vocalization for Nasas would be Noses.

7 Y. Leibovitz, in *Alon* 5–6 (1957), 25 (in Hebrew). The full official report has not been published yet; the files are accessible in the archives of the Israel Antiquities Authority. See also A. Ovadiah, *Corpus of the Byzantine Churches in the Holy Land*, Bonn 1970, 64–5; 139–40; *id.*, 'Supplementum to the Corpus of

the Byzantine Churches in the Holy Land' *Levant* 12 (1982), 97–8. Ovadiah also refers to the survey carried out by the young Dimitri C. Baramki in 1930.

8   *Vita Sabae* 67; in his Greek text, the spelling is Kolonia, confirming that the Latin name Colonia had survived outside the Aramaic tradition of the Talmud.

9   For a preliminary report, see G. Baki, 'Moza', *Hadashot Arkheologiyot* 13 (1965), 8–10 (in Hebrew), with drawings.

10 C. Schick, 'Newly Discovered Rock-Hewn Tomb at Kolonieh', *Palestine Exploration Fund, Quarterly Statement* (January) 1887, 51–5. In 1973, Emanuel Eisenberg found two Byzantine tombs, one of them with three skeletons, north of his Bronze Age discoveries ('Motsa', *Revue Biblique* 82 [1975], 587).

11 Coordinates 16550–13320, 16570–13330.

12 Matthias Amstutz, Christoph Bauernfeind, Christopher Hadisaputro, Dirk Heinze, Daniele Scarabel and Ralf Zimmer. In the following seasons, my students Eva Schwendimann and Andreas Wäsch joined our team, and eventually, further helpers volunteered from other universities in Germany, UK, USA, and Israel. Former students like Martin Gerber from Switzerland volunteered, realizing that age does not matter where there is fitness and a will. The 2004 season was the most international one so far, with Fabienne Betschon from Switzerland, Anke Merkel and Mareike Grosser from Germany, Chaim and Samuel Zini from Jerusalem, Tim Moore, the newly appointed research scholar at the British School of Archaeology (now called The Kenyon Institute) from the UK, and Avital Rabin from the USA joining the team. In 2002, Rafi Lewis, then a staff member of the Jerusalem Archaeological Field Unit and a student of archaeology at the Hebrew University of Jerusalem, offered his services; he has since become an inspector at the Israel Archaeological Authority and is an indispensable resource of knowledge, advice, fun and tireless pickaxe swinging.

13 A.M. Schwemer, 'Der Auferstandene und die Emmausjünger', in F. Avemarie/H- Lichtenberger (eds), *Auferstehung – Resurrection*, Tübingen 2001, 95–117, here at 100–1.

14 M. Hengel, *Between Jesus and Paul*, London 1983, 107–8. See also G. Schmitt, *Siedlungen Palästinas in griechisch-römischer Zeit. Ostjordantal, Negeb und (in Auswahl) Westjordanland*, Wiesbaden 1995, 53. Schmitt estimated a distance of 40 stadia between Jerusalem and Emmaus, and is quoted with this distance by Schwemer; as we saw above, in our reconstruction of the actual Roman road, the real distance would have been about 46, even closer to Luke's 60 stadia (see the discussion above). Obviously and rightly, neither Schmitt nor Schwemer see a problem is this variation, nor do they regard it as an argument against Luke's trustworthiness. Schwemer argue that Josephus, who

has merely 30 stadia, gave a slightly shorter distance on purpose in order to stress the closeness of Vespasian's veterans' colony to Jerusalem.

15 M. Fischer, B. Isaac and I. Roll, *Roman Roads in Judaea II. The Jaffa-Jerusalem Roads*, Jerusalem 1999, 224.

16 For example, P. Benoit, *The Passion and Resurrection of Jesus Christ*, London 1969, 271–4; J. Murphy-O'Connor, *The Holy Land. An Oxford Archaeological Guide*, Oxford/New York 1998, 320–1, and P. Walker, *The Weekend That Changed the World*, London 1999, 52, who are convinced that Moza-Qaloniyeh is the only viable option, but solve the apparent difference of 30 versus 60 stadia by suggesting that Luke's story describes the way there and back, so that his 60 are twice the 30 of Josephus. Ingenious as this sounds, the Greek of Luke 24.13 is precise enough: he really means a one-way distance. And as we have seen, such an attempt to 'harmonize' Luke and Josephus is not necessary, anyway. Another interesting observation was made by R.M. Mackowski in 'Where is Biblical Emmaus?', *Science et Esprit* 32 (1980), 93–103. He noticed something odd about the Madaba Map, the unique mosaic of the Holy Land of c.AD 560, which has been preserved as a damaged floor mosaic in the church of Madaba (modern Madeba), 30 kilometres south of Amman in Jordan. Mackowski suggested that 'Nicopolis', seemingly shown too close to Jerusalem, should actually be Moza. This is certainly wrong, since Nicopolis is shown on the Madaba Map as a proper city with more than one (early fifth-/early sixth-century) church. However, the Madaba Map has a habit of mentioning the traditional biblical name next to the 'modern' (i.e. sixth-century) name, if there is a difference. But here, we read only Nicopolis. Its alleged or presumed identity with Emmaus is not mentioned. This means that the artist and those who commissioned him either did not know or did not accept that Nicopolis was supposed to be the Emmaus of Luke's Gospel. Since they did not know, either, where the real Emmaus was located, they simply omitted the name altogether.

17 'Hellenistic' is a general term for the period between the death of Alexander the Great (323 BCE) and the defeat of Antonius and Cleopatra (30 BCE) which signalled the beginning of Augustus' unrivalled rule over the Roman Empire.

18 For a description of the site and its architectural history, see S. Gibson, *The Cave of John the Baptist*, London 2004, 101–7.

19 Cf. in the New Testament Hebrews 11.32, where Samson is singled out, together with Gideon, Barak, Jephtha, David and Samuel, as 'men who through their faith conquered kingdoms, did what was upright and earned the promises'. He was a controversial hero, one of the judges of Israel (read all about him in Judges 13–16), a brilliant but cruel fighter whose sexual peccadillos, ignominious defeat, imprisonment and final victory have inspired one of the best operas of late French romanticism, Camille Saint-Saëns' *Samson et Dalila*, as well as Handel's oratorio *Samson* and Milton's

Samson Agonistes. Apparently he became the patron saint of this fortfied monastery not least because of its own architectural show of strength; the ruins are well worth a detour, as are the magnificent Iron Age necropolis and other remains from different periods.

20   Christians are still called Nozrim in modern Hebrew, a name derived from the Greek description of Jesus as the Nazorean, Greek *Nazoraios*, which occurs more frequently than 'Nazarenos' in the New Testament, although both forms go back to the Hebrew root of the place name Nazareth, Nazara in Hebrew, from 'Nezer', 'shoot' (cf. the messianic prophecy in Isaiah 11.1 and Matthew 2.23, and see C.P. Thiede, *The Cosmopolitan World of Jesus*, London 2004, 17–18).

21   On Raymond du Puy, the Hospitallers and their history, see Chapter 2 above.

22   On the first Hospitallers' establishment in Jerusalem, see Chapter 2 above. The eight-pointed cross with equidistant beams was also known in the Byzantine, Armenian and Coptic Churches. Some Hospitallers' crosses resemble these forms quite closely, probably on purpose, so as to underline an ongoing Christian tradition. In case of doubt, the Hospitallers' design which eventually become the 'official' form can be distinguished from these earlier types by the 'indentation' in the outline between every pair of two points.

23   See below, Chapter 7.

24   The report was written by Gabriela Bijovsky, with references to Y. Meshorer, *The Coinage of Aelia Capitolina*, Jerusalem 1989, and W. Hahn, *Money of the Incipient Byzantine Empire (Anastasius I – Justinian I)*, Vienna 2000, 491–565.

25   Cf. Y. Meshorer, *Jewish Coins of the Second Temple Period*, Tel Aviv 1967, 30.

26   Cf. C.P. Thiede and G. Masuch, 'Confocal Laser Scanning and the Dead Sea Scrolls' in: L.H. Shiffman, E. Tov and J.C. VanderKam (eds), *The Dead Sea Scrolls Fifty Years After Their Discovery. Proceedings of the Jerusalem Congress, July 20–25, 1997*, Jerusalem 2000, 895–905, with seven plates.

27   Lifta, at the Nahal Sorek, northwest of Jerusalem and just 4.5 kilometres from Temple Mount, is another village which deserves further excavations. It is mentioned in Joshua 15.9 as 'The source of the waters of Neftoah' and appears to have been inhabited by Jews until AD 70.

28   For a list of ritual requirements, see also Mark 7.3–4. Cf. H. Strack and P. Billerbeck, *Kommentar zum Neuen Testament aus Talmud und Midrasch, I–IV*, Munich 1922–28, here at I, 327–31. See also R. Deines, *Jüdische Steingefässe und pharisäische Frömmigkeit. Ein archäologisch-historischer Beitrag zum Verständnis von Johannes 2,6 und der jüdischen Reinheitshalacha zur Zeit Jesu*, Tübingen 1993; and S. Gibson, 'Stone Vessels of the Early Roman Period from Jerusalem and Palestine. A Reassessment' in G.C. Bottini, L. Di Segni and L.D. Chrupcala (eds), *One Land – Many Cultures. Archaeological Studies in Honour of S. Loffreda*, Jerusalem 2003, 287–308.

29   The Mishna later records that pottery vessels that have become ritually unclean must be broken, whereas stone vessels, even if they should have become unclean by accident, retain their ritual purity and need not be discarded (Mishna Kelim 10.1; Parah 3.2–3).

30   For a general assessment, see among others, A.N. Sherwin-White, *Roman Law and Roman Society in the New Testament*, Oxford 1963, 186–93; more specifically B. Kollmann, *Jesus und die Christen als Wundertäter*, Göttingen 1996.

31   A different type of stone vessel, no longer lathe-turned, simpler and less valuable hand-carved jars, were occasionally produced after AD 70 and until the Bar Kochba Revolt – some stone jars were found in the caves of the revolutionaries. Our vessels belong to the pre-AD 70 type and could not have been made or deposited after AD 70 anyway, since the village was occupied by the Roman veterans until the late second century, when the production and use of any type of stone vessels had definitely ceased.

32   For the numbers of inhabitants and visitors, see the analysis in W. Reinhardt, 'The Population Size of Jerusalem and the Numerical Growth of the Jerusalem Church' in R. Bauckham (ed.), *The Book of Acts in its Palestinian Setting (The Book of Acts in its First Century Setting, Vol. 4)*, Grand Rapids/ Carlisle 1995, 237–65.

33   See also L. and K. Ritmeyer, *Jerusalem in the Year 30 AD*, Jerusalem 2004, 38–51.

34   Cf. P.H.R. Mackay, 'Torphichen preceptory: A Footnote to the Published Descriptions', *Proceedings of the Society of Antiquaries of Scotland*, Vol. XCIX (Session 1966–1967); see also G.Th. Beatson, *Knights Hospitallers in Scotland and their Priory at Torphichen*, Glasgow 1903.

35   On these architectural features, see E. Grunsky, 'Doppelgeschossige Johanniterkirchen und verwandte Bauten', doctoral dissertation, Tübingen 1970.

36   See, among others, C. Heitz, *Recherches sur les rapports entre architecture et liturgie à l'époque carolingienne*, Paris 1963. A Cluniac monastery may have been identified in the remnants of a complex at Palmarea near Haifa; see A.J. Boas, *Crusader Archeology. The Material Culture of the Latin East*, London/New York 1999, 139.

37   For a brief architectural portrayal of the site, with photograph, see A.J. Boas, *op. cit.*, 74–5, and cf. the earlier descriptions by D. Pringle, 'Aqua Bella: The Interpretation of a Crusader Courtyard Building', in B.Z. Kedar (ed.), *The Horns of Hattin*, Jerusalem/London 1992, 147–67; *id.*, *The Crusader Churches of the Crusader Latin Kingdom of Jerusalem*, vol. I, Cambridge 1993, 239–50; and above all, R.P. Harper and D. Pringle, *Belmont Castle. The Excavation of a Crusader Stronghold in the Kingdom of Jerusalem*, Oxford 2000, 205–8. Pringle also mentions the Arabic names of the site, Khirbet Iqbala (a bowdlerization of the original Latin), and Dair al-Banat, the house of 'the convent'. However,

anyone looking for the right motorway exit should follow the Hebrew/English indication to Ein Hemed.

38   Denys Pringle thinks that a stone base, 5.5 metres in front of the east wall, should be interpreted as the base for a chancel screen with a central door, and that this should be attributed to a second phase, when the room on the second floor was converted to ecclesiastical use, possibly as a monastic infirmary hall (in Harper and Pringle, *op. cit.*, 205).

39   In 1147, for example, he confirmed the lease of the Terra de Emmaus opposite Aqua Bella; see J. Delaville le Roulx (ed.), *Cartulaire général de l'Ordre des Hospitaliers de Saint-Jean de Jérusalem (1100–1310)*, 4 vols., Paris 1894–1906, here at vol. I, 135–136, no. 173.

40   See J. Delaville le Roulx, *op. cit.*, I, 222–3, no. 309; cf. D. Pringle, as in *op. cit.*, 217–18, where Pringle also discusses and dismisses alternative views.

41   E.g., J.F. Niermeyer and C. van de Kieft, *Mediae Latinitatis Lexicon Minus*, 2nd rev. edn by J.W.J. Burgers, vol. M–Z, Darmstadt 2002, 1218.

42   Josephus, *Jewish Antiquities* 15.121–3.

43   D.H.K. Amiran, 'A Revised Earthquake Catalogue of Palestine', *Israel Exploration Journal* vol. 1 (1950–1951), 223–46, here at 230; and *id.*, vol. 2 (1952), 48–65, here at 50.

44   Z. Vilnay, *The Holy Land in Old Prints and Maps*, 2nd edn, Jerusalem 1965, 126; see also note 50 below.

45   The earring is undergoing the usual methods of analysis used on silver and silver alloy, but the final results are still outstanding.

46   For evidence of cisterns below Crusader towers, see D. Pringle, 'Towers in Crusader Palestine', *Château Gaillard* 16 (1994), 335–50; repr. in *id.*, *Fortification and Settlement in Crusader Palestine*, Aldershot/Burlington 2000, VII. 1–28, here at 14.

47   I. Finkelstein and Y. Magen (eds), *Archaeological Survey of the Hill Country of Benjamin*, Jerusalem 1993, 387.

48   See A.J. Boas, *Crusader Archaeology. The Material Culture of the Latin East*, London/New York 1999, 70–1 etc. with further references. See also 139, for his reference to a monastery of Benedictine nuns founded at Bethany in 1138, with two churches, cloisters, a tower and a number of associated buildings.

49   Cf. Boas, *op. cit.*, 102–3; see also D. Pringle, *Secular Buildings in the Crusader Kingdom of Jerusalem*, Cambridge 1997, 71.

50   D. Pringle, 'Two Medieval Villages North of Jerusalem: Archaeological Investigations in Al-Jib and Ar-Ram' in: *id.*, *Fortification and Settlement in Crusader Palestine*, Aldershot/Burlington 2000, V. 141–77, here at 160. And he goes on to comment on one of the sites: 'At al-Jib, however, a solidly built early medieval structure already existed on the west side of the hill top. The strengthening of its walls and the insertion of narrow internally splayed windows may therefore represent part of the initial refurbishment of the

structure by its newly installed Crusader owner in the twelfth century.' It seems that Saltus Muratus with its additional buildings was a prototype copied and developed in later decades and centuries.

51 Without a wider context, the tesserae were not yet specific enough to be identified as Byzantine or Herodian, and we hesitated to ascribe them to the Jewish-Roman period of Emmaus, as we had seen a Byzantine mosaic floor in a room at Belmont Castle, on a hill in the compound of Kibbutz Tzuba, which apparently belonged to a fourth/fifth establishment, used by the Hospitallers who built their *castrum* to overlook and protect the roads from above soon after 1140. Even Jerusalem is visible on the horizon from up there. Apart from the sheer beauty of the view and the strategical position, offering the southern counterpoint to the terraces of Moza, the Byzantine Christians may also have liked a biblical connotation of Tzuba: they read the Greek translation of the Hebrew Bible, the Septuagint, and here, in Joshua 15.59a, it looks as though the first Jewish settlement on the hill had been equated with 'Zôbês', belonging to the towns and settlements of the tribe of Judah. There also was a rabbinical tradition which called the place 'Sebô'im', which the Byzantines would have heard about when they arrived, and this may have taken them back to Joshua 15.59a. But we cannot not know for certain. The Crusaders themselves had a different connection: for them, Tzuba, which they were to call Belmont, was identical with the hill of Mode'in (*mons Modin*), the home region of the Maccabees. (For a detailed analysis of the sources, see R.P. Harper and D. Pringle, *Belmont Castle. The Excavation of a Crusader Stronghold in the Kingdom of Jerusalem*, Oxford 2000, 13–24.) Down in the Sorek Valley, another onomastic shift took place in the late Middle Ages, long after the Crusader period: Jacob of Verona, writing in c.1335 – some 40 years after the last Crusader Knight had left the Holy Land – was the first pilgrim to record the belief that the fight between David and Goliath had taken place in this area, and that this was the Valley of the Terebinths (1 Sam. 17.1–12; see A. Milinier and C. Kohler, *Itinera Hierosolymitana et Descriptiones Terrae Sanctae bellis sacris anteriora et latina lingua escarata*, Geneva 1885, 223). A later pilgrim, Bonifatius of Ragusa, confirmed this new local tradition (in *De perenni cultu Terrae Sanctae*, Venice 1572). It was probably invented for the sake of convenience, since the topographically correct Valley of the Terebinths is several kilometres further south and could not be reached easily by travellers from and to Jerusalem. One is reminded of a reason which may have persuaded the Byzantine Church to choose Nicopolis as their new-testamental Emmaus in the mid-fourth century: well-equipped with all the amenities of a late Roman city, it was just so much more convenient, in spite of all the illogicalities associated with this choice, than the hard work involved in searching for the true place near Jerusalem would have been. In 1586, Giovanni Zuallardo made a series of drawings of buildings along the road between Jerusalem

and the Mediterranean (see Z. Vilnay, *op. cit.*), and one of them is entitled 'Vallis Therebinti'. It is a good sketch: a building is standing with a two-storey room adjacent to a single-storey arcaded entrance area. Above the building complex, Zuallardo wrote 'Calonia', and below, 'Hic occisus/fuit Goliath'. Also called Johan Schwallart and Jean Zuallart, he wrote '*Il devotissimo viaggio di Gerusalemme*' in Rome, in 1587; it has been published in various languages and editions. I am grateful to Shimon Gibson for the information and for copies of Zuallart's drawings. See also S. Gibson, *The Cave of John the Baptist*, London 2004, 107–8, and 342, note 4.54.

52   Such a setting, with the person to be baptised standing in water on a slightly lower level than the baptizer, occurs frequently in early Christian art, in the scene of the Baptism of Jesus by John. See, for example, the mosaic in the cupola of the Arian Baptistry in Ravenna, c.AD 500, or the Baptism of Christ in the illuminated Hitda Codex from Meschede, c.1020, or again in the Codex Egberti, Trier, from the tenth century. Another well-known example is the mosaic in the Ducal Chapel of the Norman Palace at Palermo, dated to the early/mid twelfth century. Emperor Frederick II, who led the Fifth Crusade (1228–9), had been brought up in this palace. Giotto's famous fresco in the Capella degli Scroveni in Padua, of c.1300, just postdates the time of the Crusades.

53   See, for example, E.H.E. Lass, 'Quantitative Studies in Flotation at Ashkelon, 1986–1988', *ASOR Bulletin* No. 294 (May 1994), 23–38; *id.*, 'Lost in the Maze: An Alternative Method of Designing Matrix Diagrams', *Bulletin of the Anglo-Israel Archaeological Society* Vol. 15 (1996–7), 41–49; *id.*, 'Chips and Shells: Flotation at Tel Yaqsh', in S.R. Wolff (ed.), *Studies in the Archaeology of Israel and Neighbouring Countries in Memory of Douglas L. Esse*, Studies in Ancient Oriental Civilization No. 59, 2001.

54   Shakespeare, *Hamlet*, I, 2.

Epilogue: Jewish and Christian History – Emmaus, a Site of the Risen Christ

'I believe with perfect faith that there will be a resurrection of the dead at the time when it will please the Creator, blessed be His name and exalted be His mention for ever and ever.'

Thirteen principles of the Jewish Faith, No. 13, from The Authorized Prayer Book of the United Hebrew Congregations of the Commonwealth, *Hebrew and English, St Ives 1998, 155–6.*

And the Lord shall do glorious things which have never been achieved, just as he promised. For He shall heal the pierced, He shall revive the dead, and bring good news to the poor.

Qumran scroll 4Q 521, fragment 2.

'Your dead shall live, their corpses shall rise.'

Isaiah 26.19.

Judaism and Christianity have been divided for almost 2000 years. Jesus and his first followers were Jews, the disciples and apostles were Jews, the texts collected in the New Testament were written by Jews: Christianity is Jewish. Yet the way Jesus and his most eminent followers (Peter and Paul above all) interpreted the ancient Law of the Torah alienated the majority of the Jewish faithful, and by the end of the first century, the breach between Jews and Jewish Christians appeared to be unbridgeable. The Jewish council at Jamnia condemned the followers of the man from Nazareth, the Nozrim, and expelled them from the synagogues; the Christians turned towards the gentile world, and by the mid second century not a single Jew could be found in a leading position or among the acknowledged writers of Christian literature. Christianity and Judaism had become rival religions in the Roman Empire.

An increasing anti-semitism shaped the Christian Church, beginning in the East and eventually infecting the West. Bishop Melito of Sardes condemned the Jews as murderers of God in his Easter Homily of c.AD 160 and opened the floodgates. Medieval pogroms, the expulsion of all Jews from England in 1290, from Spain in 1492 and from Portugal in 1497, were steps on the road towards the Holocaust in Nazi-ruled Europe. Courageous exceptions apart, Christians abandoned the Jews and helped to destroy one of the pillars of Western civilization.

The current state of Europe, hollowed out, agnostic to the bone, drifting in a godless wind, is a consequence of this demolition of Judaeo-Christian roots. In such a climate, it may appear to be a little quixotic to appeal for a return to the sources. But it must be done. Many avenues are conceivable, and many have been tested by Jews and Christians since 1945. Surprisingly, the Emmaus story told by Luke in his Gospel has not been among the sources quoted in these endeavours. The 13 principles of the Jewish faith, originally devised by the famous Rambam, Rabbi Moses ben Maimon – better known as Maimonides (1135–1204) – can be subscribed to by any believing Christian, and they end in a proclamation of every Jew's unflinching faith in the coming of the Messiah (here, Christians would want to add that he has already come but will come again, uniting Jews and Christians in the Last Days) and in a physical resurrection.[1] To put it differently, resurrection faith is one of the most pertinent links between Judaism and Christianity. When the Sadducees, the only Jewish movement who refused to believe in a resurrection, disappeared from the scene after the destruction of their only stronghold, the Temple, no one could then hinder the pious. The path was free for Jews who understood the Torah and the prophets from within, and it was left to liberal Protestant theologians of the so-called post-enlightenment era to re-invent the negativity of the Sadducees. Such illiterate attitudes should be of no concern to us. The historicity of the Emmaus episode does not depend on theological devices, and if we take it seriously, archaeology and the historical, literary sources will meet there.

As we saw above, even an intellectual, highly educated Jew, a Pharisaic priest and Roman historian like Johosaph Ben Mattityahu, alias Flavius Josephus, saw no reason to deny the possibility of a bodily resurrection, nor that Jesus had been raised and had appeared to his followers. The question which remained – and to which Josephus never found an answer – was not if and how it happened, but what it meant that one single Jew had been raised before all the others who trusted the prophetic promise of a resurrection of God's pious people. This of course was something the exclusively Jewish circle who had seen the crucifixion, the empty tomb and the risen Messiah Jesus had to come to terms with themselves. And somehow they did: they talked about it, convinced many of their fellow Jews and failed to convince many others.

The story of Emmaus is about two Jews who began and ended their walk as sceptics. They became believers not during their walk back from Jerusalem but at home, when Jesus broke the bread, in an instantly recognizable manner, and they finally put one and one together. Luke is at pains to avoid any resemblance to mythical story-telling. The one and a half hours they spend together on the way is not told like a theological road movie, where the experiences on a scenic route lead to a new awareness. On the contrary, much is left to the imagination in the mental cinema of the reader. As we saw in Chapter 3, Luke combines the prophetic message of Ezekiel 37.7–14 with an eschatological insight into the power of Jesus – they can recognize the changed resurrection body only when Jesus himself chooses the moment and the means – and links this with the brief note of an eyewitness who had told Luke that 'their eyes were held', an observation which made immediate sense to everyone who knew the road from Jerusalem to Emmaus and was aware of the fact that it would been a walk into the deep setting sun. It is the artistry of the great historian and author Luke which makes this account so sparse in the very areas where others might have wanted to speculate.

Luke does not even tell us what it was that Jesus explained to Cleopas and his companion when, 'beginning with Moses and all the prophets, he interpreted to them the things about himself in all the Scriptures'. He could have given us a list of references of course, and even if he had merely mentioned the resurrection passages, it would have been an impressive list: from the fifth book of Moses, Deuteronomy (32.39), via Psalm 68, Isaiah 26.19, Ezekiel 37 and Daniel 12.2 to Hosea 6.2, to name but a few. He could have explained what Jesus meant when he referred to 'the Scriptures' in the plural, which we find in the Greek text of Luke 24.27, and elsewhere in the New Testament, meaning a group of writings which included texts outside the core group of the Torah, the Psalms and the Prophets.[2] The Second Book of the Maccabees would have been an obvious candidate. Immensely popular among Jews since the late second century BCE, it contained several passages which expressed the certain expectation of a physical resurrection, including one in which even mutilated bodies would be restored (2 Macc. 7.9–14; 12.43–45; 14.46). Perhaps even more popular was Enoch, praised and quoted by Jude, the brother of Jesus, in his letter (Jude 14–15). In Enoch, the resurrection is discussed many times: 90.33 is central, but all chapters from 1 to 104 circle around the forms of the resurrection of the righteous, of Israel and the hope for a conversion of the gentiles before the end of times. Among the equally widely read Dead Sea Scrolls, at least two documents expressed the certainty of a resurrection: 4Q521 fr. 2, the so-called Resurrection Fragment, and 1QH 19:10:14, from the 'Thanksgiving Hymns'.

There are many more biblical and non-biblical texts which Jesus could have quoted and interpreted on the road to Emmaus: in short, referring to 'the Scriptures' in the search for a firm belief in the reality of a physical resurrection was by no means the minority pursuit of a few late Jewish scribes. But then again, there was much more about Jesus in the prophecies: there was the suffering of the Messiah in Psalm 22 and in Isaiah 53 – Jesus would indeed have needed those one and a half hours from Jerusalem to Emmaus to explain them to Cleopas and his companion.

In a way, Luke challenges his readers: 'Go and look for yourselves, read what Jewish prophets from Moses to Enoch have said, and realize that these prophecies were fulfilled in Jesus – and above all, do not be "foolish and slow of heart" like the two Emmaus disciples, who, as pious Jews, had read "the Scriptures" many times but had failed to understand them fully.' There is a sense of humour here, too. Jesus pretends that he does not know anything about recent events in Jerusalem. 'Are you the only stranger in Jerusalem who does not know the things that have taken place there in these days?' the two ask him, and he replies: 'What things?' The disciples duly give him their individual persepective of the crucifixion and the empty tomb, with a telling comment: 'But we had hoped that he was the one to redeem Israel.' So there had been hope, but a lack of understanding.

As we have seen a number of times in this book, this lack of under-standing of who Jesus really was occurred more than once during his earthly life. 'Their hearts were hardened', we read in Mark 6.52, after one such incident of mental and spiritual blockage. The two Emmaus disciples were no exception, but they were inquisitive enough to ask a leading question, and to listen to the answer for one and a half hours. After the moment of recognition, and Jesus' disappearance, one of them asks one of the most touching questions in the New Testament: 'Did not our hearts burn within us, as he talked to us on the road and explained the Scriptures to us?' Their return to Jerusalem, in a state of outer darkness after the sun had set, but with inner enlightenment, culminates in a joint Easter joy, when they reach the meeting place of the eleven disciples who had remained together after the suicide of Judas, and, before they can even open their mouths, hear that 'the Lord has risen indeed, and he has appeared to Simon' (24.34). It seems the circle around Peter and the Lord's relative Cleopas passed these stories on immediately, first orally, and then, thanks to Luke, in written form. There is no reason to doubt that the self-deprecating aside, about their lack of understanding, and their humility, expressed in the image of their hearts which were burning even before they had understood what was happening, were told frankly and faithfully by Cleopas and his companion themselves.

At one stroke, Luke assembles two resurrection stories – the one with Simon Peter (which is however not told in detail) and the Emmaus narrative. The importance Emmaus has for Luke is evident: the story of the three Jews on the road to Emmaus is a brilliant work of literary art, told in excellent Greek. It is, just as Luke had promised in his Prologue, a pivotal moment in a book composed of eyewitness accounts and thoroughly researched sources, structured in an orderly way and written 'so that you may know the truth concerning the things about which you have been instructed' (Lk. 1.1–4). And not only is it a story full of topographical and historical details, it is also the longest narrative in his whole Gospel.

At the end of this book, we may therefore be justified in asking why Luke tells this story. The rich fund of available eyewitness acounts which were used in the other gospels, and in Chapter 15 of Paul's first letter to the Corinthians (15.3–8) could have provided him with many an alternative. The answer may come from the excavation of Emmaus.

Again and again, we have seen that Emmaus was a village of the wealthy. If not before, then certainly since the Herodian Period and until

AD 70, the people who were living here belonged to the upper class. And the dedicatee of Luke's Gospel, 'His Excellency' Theophilus, was an upper-class representative too. As we saw in Chapter 3, his Greek title, *krátistos*, puts him on a par, in the Jewish Greek terminology of the time, with procurators and the eminent private secretary of Emperor Nero.[3] If Luke wanted him to understand the message of the Resurrection, what better narrative could he choose than the one where two wealthy Jerusalemite Jews return to their suburban villa and are honoured, as it were, by an appearance of the risen Christ? Luke does not tell us how Cleopas had acquired his wealth – in the years when his Gospel was published, it would have been known anyway. The popular myth of the poverty of Jesus and his wider family, which is not based on Gospel evidence, has been refuted more than once in recent times.[4] Theophilus, like his contemporaries, understood the message: Jesus was risen for the poor, the outcast, the lepers and all those who he had healed, he was risen for slaves, and for everyone who did not count in society of those days. But he was also risen for the wealthy and the influential, the movers and shakers. In fact, he was risen for everyone, as he had died for everyone. The wealthy village of Emmaus, known to people like Luke and Theophilus, was the cornerstone of this historical, sociological and theological edifice. All it took, for Theophilus and for anyone else, was to accept the message and live accordingly. Theophilus did, as we know – for Luke dedicated his second book, Acts, to him also, and he accepted the dedication.

Thus, Luke's strategy worked. We may even have an indirect confirmation of this in the so-called longer ending of Mark's Gospel, 16.9–20, written around AD 120: in verse 12, the Emmaus story is told without the name of the village and without the name of Cleopas, so that any connotations to social status are unrecognizable. All we read in 16.12 is this: 'Afterwards, he appeared in another form to two of them, as they were walking into the countryside.' It is the same story, but the elements which Luke knew and emphasized for Theophilus are missing. Whoever wrote the longer ending of Mark did not write it for a Judaeo-Roman 'Excellency'.

The Emmaus Mystery remains a challenge. It is a timeless story with a timeless message. Excavating the site where the Jew Jesus was recognized as the risen Messiah by two of his Jewish followers may be a step towards the penetration of this mystery. Archaeology can only reach so far: Christians proclaim that there is a 'Mystery of Faith', a *mysterium fidei*, while historians try to disentangle the mysterious and reach the facts. Both approaches are not mutually exclusive. The Jesus of History and the Christ of Faith belong together. Luke, who wrote the story down, and his dedicatee Theophilus, who accepted and believed it, may have shown us the way.

Notes

1   For tenet no. 13, see the first chapter epigraph above; no. 12 reads: 'I believe with perfect faith in the coming of the Messiah, and, though he may tarry, I wait daily for his coming.' Substitute 'return' for 'coming', and you have a perfectly 'orthodox' Christian statement of faith.
2   See C.P. Thiede, 'The Apostle Peter and the Jewish Scriptures in 1 & 2 Peter', *Analecta Bruxellensia* 7 (2002), 145–55, here at 150–5, and cf. p. 85 above, with note 9.
3   See p. 91, with note 15. For attempts to see Theophilus as an influential, high-ranking Roman, or a member of the Jewish elite, see, e.g. M. Hengel, *The Four Gospels and the One Gospel of Jesus Christ*, London 2000, 40, 272–3, note 423; R.H. Anderson, 'Theophilus: A proposal', *Evangelical Quarterly* 69 (1997), 196–215.
4   For details, see C.P. Thiede, *The Cosmopolitan World of Jesus*, London 2004, 13–20.